# The tomorrow of my yesterday

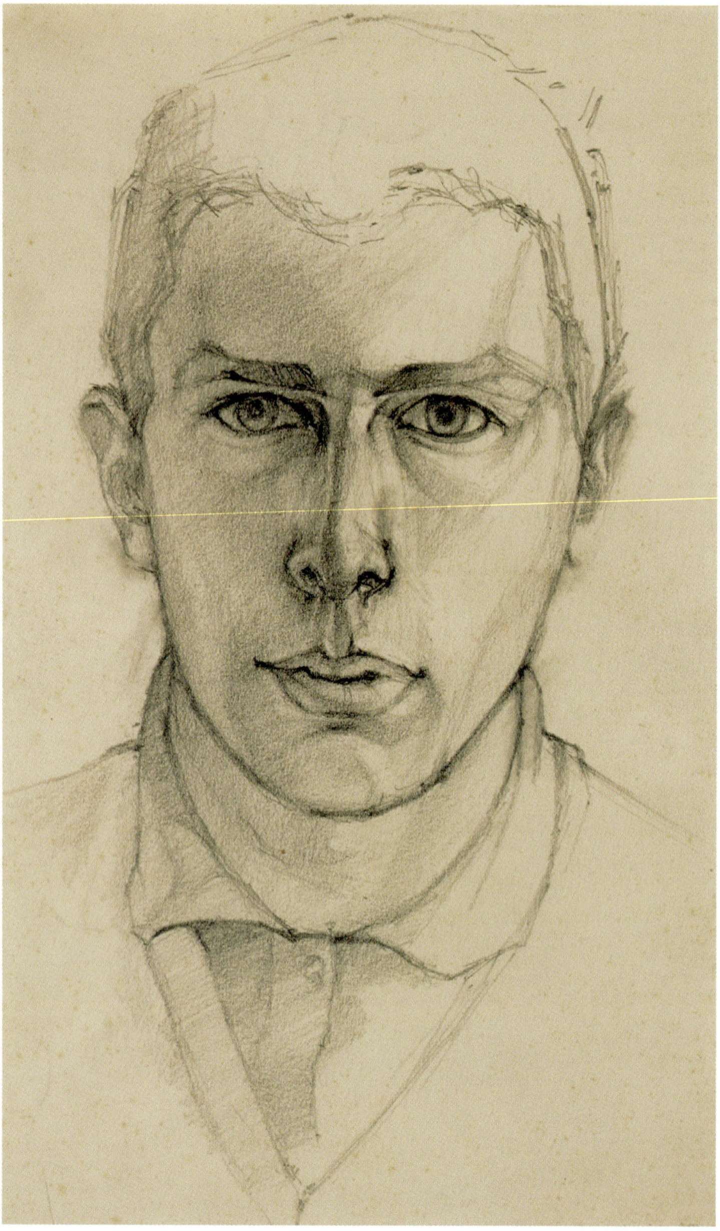

# The tomorrow of my yesterday

## The complete works of Barry Martin

by Julius Bryant

With essays by Adrian Glew, Richard Humphreys and Raymond Keene

Veenman Publishers

# Contents


6 Foreword by Richard Humphreys

10 Acknowledgements

13 1 Making an Artist

31 2 Metal Machines

59 3 Light Sculptures

73 4 Abstract Expressionism: a Crisis in Colour

99 5 Signs of Power: the Drawings

115 6 Surface Movements: Collages and Art Criticism

127 7 Word Art

139 8 The Artist as Chess Player by Raymond Keene

157 9 Sketchbooks and film in the Tate Archive, by Adrian Glew

171 10 Sculptures in Glass and Bronze

179 11 The Radian Series: mapping in watercolour

190 Appendices

# Foreword

Being curious about everything is not necessarily good for careers. Asking questions as soon as you have some answers is often bad for business. Barry Martin is an accomplished artist who is suspicious of accomplishment. He has great skills as a draughtsman, painter and sculptor and believes passionately in the traditional aesthetic virtues of great art museum art. When he talks his way round a painting by Titian or Mondrian you know you are in the presence of someone who understands how and why the work was made. And where it works and where it fails. On the other hand, he is still a mischievous and often iconoclastic product of the Sixties - performance, installation, film, video, words are part of his continuing armoury deployed in original ways to counteract any tendency towards comfortable conservatism, As soon as he catches himself drifting too far to the left or the right he swerves over, as it were, and thus keeps up the momentum of edgy enquiry and creativity.

Compared with many artists Barry Martin is fairly invisible in the contemporary scene, although he knows exactly what's going on. The way he works, both socially and artistically, doesn't lend itself to West, or East, End shows and he tends to say what's on his mind. In a world of diplomatic niceties that can be a disadvantage. But it is also a strength. He plays chess seriously and works in a studio on the edge of Chiswick House estate. He is fascinated by freemasonry and occult matters, without indulging the silly end of those things, and has a quietly religious sense of existence which means he can wait for the spirit to descend at unexpected times. These tendencles make him a little unusual and uncategorisable in the present artworld. And I'm not even sure how old he is - but he's looking well as those young at heart always do. The last forty years or so reveal a fantastic range of effort and inquiry.

I find I generally like what he's trying to do from whatever period I look at and can see those qualities of experiment, humour and seriousness which characterise his art from the beginning right up to today: Beautiful little paintings of oak trees done at school and strenuous figure drawings and oils done at art school give me that pleasing reassurance that he can do the orthodox stuff with ease and thus claim the full artistic licence which for many others really shouldn't be awarded. His abstract paintings and related kinetic sculptures from the early and mid-Sixtes onwards were pioneering efforts which still exercise their subtle effects and deserve to be better known. These are almost obsessively about movement whether it be optical, physical or conceptual. Often it's all three. The motorised steel sculptures are made with great skill and work slowly in drawing you into their clever rhythms. In fact they do still work mechanically too!

And of course he really was there being strange, disturbing and daring at St. Martin's in 1966 along with McLean, Long, Gilbert and George et al. His performance piece 'You Will, You Are, You Have' in the sculpture department basement that year not only featured these luminaries but had them in swimming trunks and blindfolded moving around various materials and forms to the sound of whale noises, trains and space babble. The event, which was filmed, was halted after 40 minutes and the effects were quite shattering - many participants were crying, fighting and so on. They were asked to return to the space a week later and saw it for the first time. In the discussion which followed the 'spacemen' could see the film, the actual space and compare both with their memories of the unsettling experience. It was conceptual art of the most intriguing and scientifically motivated sort which nevertheless left open the investigation of those dark, deep areas art is finally all about. In many ways this extraordinary event got a whole tendency going in Britain. And it is a sort of emblem of Barry's way of working. Not Cocteau's 'Orpheus' exactly but in the same spirit. His role is often that of a gentle Virgil leading his tyro Dantes down into the underworld. Such work was done in the interests of discovery and not of the controlling urge which similar projects often seemed to be.

Barry is a very intelligent artist but not conventionally a 'theorist'. This makes him very English in his love of actual experiment and his let's -try-it -and -see approach and meant the growing tendency in the academy in the Sixties and Seventies towards circumscribed paradigms, political, aesthetic or whatever, were not his bag. He debates, with himself and others, and allows things to emerge rather than staying with one set of ideas endlessly refined for reasons of security. His most extended painterly efforts in the 1970s, for instance, were followed by a complete change of gear in the 1980s as if he distrusted how good he was getting at doing them so the large collages of 1975-76 , which came out of highly deliberated work on tiny
sheets of corrugated paper, have a sort of Bauhaus quality in their orderly progression through musical permutations. And they clearly are about movement, following Martin's long romance with that fundamental theme. But you realise they are moving into an architectural, symbolic and metaphysical space, the space his art was probably always moving towards but which he hadn't anticipated.

And that brings us to chess, Chiswick and freemasonry. Martin's studio is small and has the quality of an alchemist's laboratory stuffed with ongoing efforts to find something new and living. Being in the grounds of an eighteenth century Palladian house it lies between the noise of the twenty-first century traffic and the ordered calm of a classical past which nonetheless has its resonant secrets and darknesses. It also lies very close to the houses of those two arch rivals of British art, Hogarth and Burlington. One the animated master of rococo pop art, the other a classical monumentalist, but both freemasons fascinated by the Craft's speculative geometry and search for the heart of things. Martin has conducted fascinating research into the history and meanings of the grounds and buildings and the deeper significances of Burlington's project at Chiswick. This seems important in understanding how Martin works. Place is important to him - architecture and landscape are both about now and the past. With an almost Iain Sinclairian sense of time's fateful threads he is looking for forms which will tap into the currents of time and history. The 1980s for many were a rediscovery of the past and Barry took an entirely independent path backwards in order to find a new position in the present. He seemed fated to find himself in his little time machine of a studio in a secret garden.

Chess seems to play a crucial role here. Barry is actually a fine player and reveals the nature of his intelligence through it. He organised a big chess event at the Tate a few years ago at which Duchamp's widow, John Cage and Richard Hamilton were present. He has made works based on Staunton's famous pieces and designed the British Grandmaster's magnificent tomb at Kensal Green Cemetery. Pieces moving through space to some higher order of direction is perhaps what it's all about, I'm not sure how best to put it. But the sculptural Word pieces which have Finlay's sense of craftsmanship and the beauty of carved typography mixed with a Heath Robinson feel for the inspired and absurd gentle machine are somehow to do with the aesthetics of chess. In their reversals of meaning through mirroring and eccentric movement they expose meanings under the surface of things in a way that chess does. Barry is close to something very powerful here in his witty reflexion on the 'deep thought' which artists are here to rediscover endlessly. We are back in the St. Martin's basement. The movement from then to now has been hidden but purposeful.

Richard Humphreys

# Acknowledgements

This book has grown as a collaborative project with the artist. Our aim has been to produce not a definitive art historical monograph but rather a biographically-based appreciation of the art, one that may encourage patient observation of the works themselves.

The proposal to produce a full-size study was put to the artist by his patron, Jan Mol, the art collector, sponsor of international chess tournaments, of a Formula One racing team and the founder of the Serious Fun Club. As well as making this publication possible Jan generously opened his London home to the public for a launching exhibition at 'Mol's Place', the former props warehouse of the Royal Opera House, in Covent Garden.

At Veenman Publishers in Rotterdam Gijs Stork managed the production with great sensitivity and understanding. Susie Clark liased over the publication and curated the accompanying exhibition with perseverance. The contributing authors Adrian Glew, Richard Humphreys and Raymond Keene all rose to the challenge and provided fresh perspectives from their fields of expertise. Among the private collectors who welcomed the artist and writer into their homes to see works of art Peter Egan and Myra Francis were most hospitable. Yvonne Crossley, founding proprietor of The Drawing Gallery in Duke Street St. James's, has the artist's special thanks. At the

V&A I would like to thank Nazek Ghaddar for her research into the artist's own publications record, Gill Saunders and Elizabeth James for their interest in Martin's work. On the domestic fronts, I would like to thank for their support over the years Barbara and Max.

Most of all, I would like to thank Barry Martin himself for inviting me to work with him on this book. We first met in 1989 when we both arrived at Chiswick House, he as William Kent's heir as artist-in-residence (via his leasing the gate lodge as his studio) and I as curator of the house museum. Totally unaware of his fame, but immediately impressed by the new work in his studio, I gradually came to discover his career and oeuvre in reverse. Over many well-lubricated lunches he withstood my patient probing, as the expert chess player that he is, but gradually unfolded his life at the centre of the London art scene since the 1960s. Unfortunately some of the most revealing and amusing recollections of his illustrious contemporaries were, and remain, 'not for publication'. Throughout, the ultimate goal of reviewing his career, work-by-work, has not been this book, but rather the next and best chapter in his art, the one that he is now painting.

Julius Bryant

The artist would like to thank all those who have magnanimously supported the production of this volume including the contributors, Adrian Glew, Richard Humphreys and Raymond Keene and the designers Ronald Meekel and Maaike de Jong. Particular thanks to Jan Mol and Julius Bryant without whose enthusiasm this publication could not have happened. Thanks also to my wife and family and many dear friends who, as always, have supported me in this venture.

Barry Martin

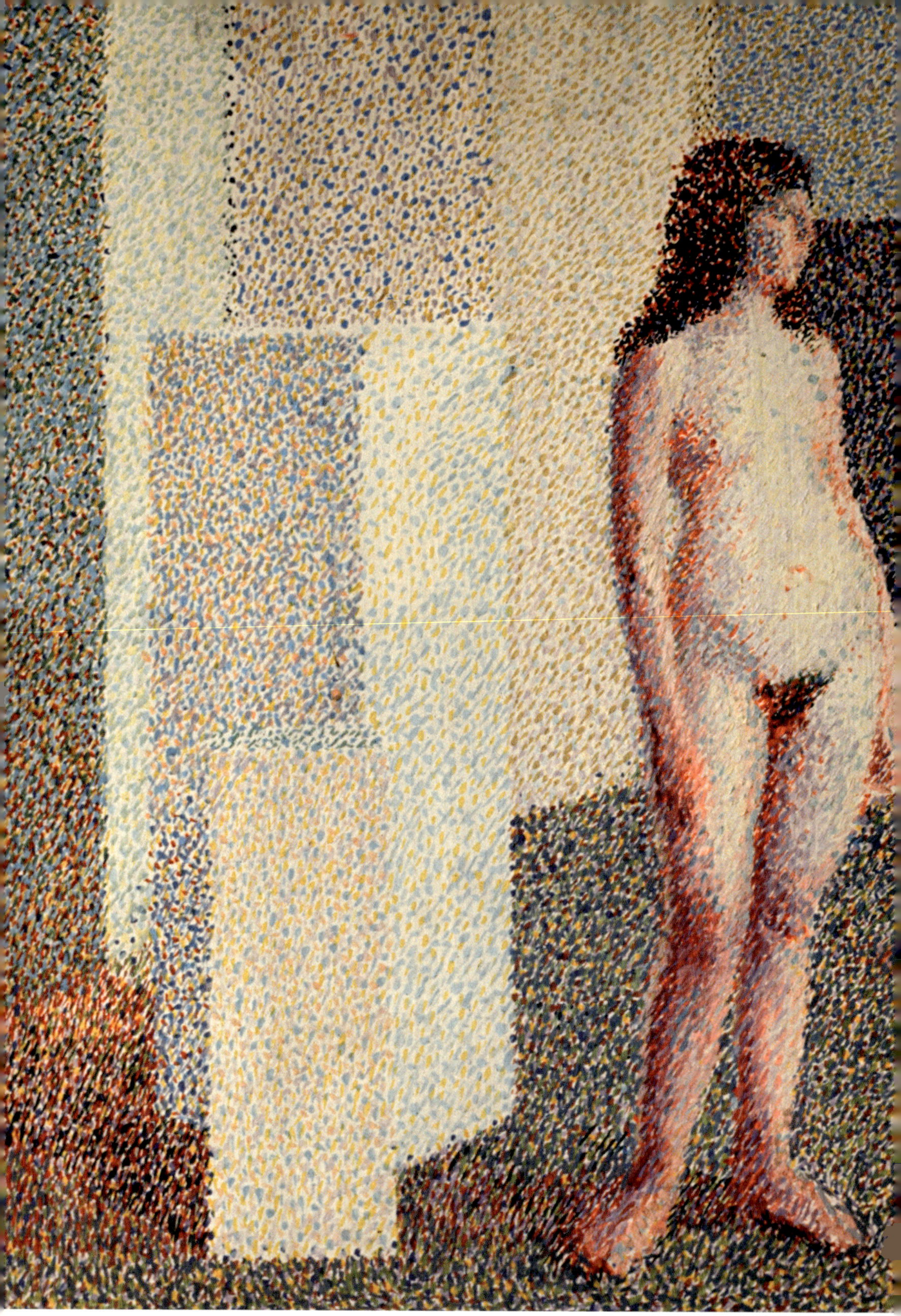

# 1 Making an Artist



An explosion rocks the cradle. It startles the two-year old boy awake. His opening eyes see a web of tiny lines spreading swiftly across the ceiling, turning into a giant jig-saw puzzle.
He stares up from his bed, fascinated. As if in slow motion his world gently fractures, splits, cracks and starts to rain down all around, covering him in white plaster dust. As he begins to cry out in fear unseen hands scoop the infant up into an uncle's embrace, wipe the dust and debris away and carry him downstairs, into the dark street. In the final weeks of the Second World War a V2 rocket has just reached Bromley in Kent and eighteen neighbours are dead in their beds. This is the earliest memory of Barry Martin. The earliest impression of life that he will remember, that will haunt him, is this moment of shock and sudden movement, of the unknown dynamic between life and death.

1963

*Pointillist Life Painting No. 1*

Oil on board

63 x 45 cm

Twenty-five years later at a Private View at the Serpentine Gallery in London's Hyde Park the young man is representing England as one of four young artists, each with their own gallery room, in an Arts Council exhibition on modern art in Britain. Now a graduate of Goldsmiths' College and of St. Martin's School of Art, he has been teaching at Goldsmiths' for three years. In 1970 his work is also on view in group shows in Berlin and at London's Hayward Gallery in the international survey exhibition on Kinetic Art. In *The Times* a review of the Hayward's show surrounds an illustration of Martin's *Moving Sculpture* on the gallery's terrace, where it is visible from across Waterloo Bridge and The Thames. Martin has developed a reputation for his home-engineered moving metallic ensembles and light-projection pieces. He is patenting his invention for generating programmed revolving lights- a new medium that will become synonymous with the psychedelic 'sixties and 'seventies through the discotheque light show. By 1970 Martin has found his medium as a master of Kinetic Art installations.



**Over the following decades, he will resist the temptation to consolidate his reputation by keeping to the field he has made his own**



Over the following decades, he will resist the temptation to consolidate his reputation by keeping to the field he has made his own. He turns polymath, regularly changing his materials but always exploring the same fundamental issue, of movement, as his life theme. Today, Martin's entry in *Who's Who in Art* describes him as a 'painter, sculptor, draughtsman, printmaker' and as an artist working in the media of stainless steel, bronze, glass, acrylic, charcoal and electricity. A well-read intellectual among his generation of artists, he has published in journals such as *Studio International* and contributed to books on chess. His entry in *Who's Who in Art* ends with a surprise, with the single word that signifies membership of the nation's elite of professors, bishops and museum directors, for this artist has been elected to that most venerable gentlemen's club, The Athenaeum. Martin was probably the only member present in the group photograph of British artists illustrated in *The Times*, March 2000, standing on the steps of the Tate Gallery to mark its relaunch as Tate Britain. Alongside Martin the group portrait of modern masters includes Maggi Hambling, Howard Hodgkin, Philip King, Michael Craig-Martin, Antony Gormley, Anish Kapoor, Richard Deacon, Mona Hartoum, Tracey Emin and many more. In 2007 he could be spotted in a similar group photograph of artists and designers in the London newspaper, the *Evening Standard*, taken to mark the 150th anniversary of the Victoria & Albert Museum. What inspires, drives and sustains an artist's working career over forty years in almost every creative medium, into media of his own creation? What are the issues he feels he needs to tackle, that unify his output? Martin feels sorry for today's celebrity artists whom he sees as a television-oriented generation chasing gallery contracts and Oscar-style art prizes. To Martin, the London art scene has become a reality game show with less of the conviction that he recalls in the 1970s and more of the cult of personality and fascination with consumerism that produced Andy Warhol and Pop Art in the 1960s. To Martin, art is not the product of ambitions for wealth and fame but rather a succession of experiments, of attempts to find ways of dealing with the big questions we all choose to set aside in order to get on with our daily lives. He has a Romantic notion of the role of the artist in society, as the one who takes on the burden of wider awareness of the universe, and of finding ways to connect the sense of self to everything else out there. Art objects can be made as poignant reminders of the gap, and can offer bridges. He sees his world as one large open laboratory in which he is both scientist and guinea pig, experimenter and test-case, trying to find not the universal answers but a language with which to convey them, what he describes as 'new hieroglyphs, new shapes of meaning'.

Martin never knew his American father. The son of Italian émigrés who arrived in the U.S.A. in the 1920s during the Depression, John Bonnell (born Bonnelli) worked as the accountant for his parents' farm in Virginia. With the outbreak of war he joined the U. S. Army's chemical engineering corps. With his fluency in Italian he soon saw action in Europe. In London he met Rosemary, an English girl of Scottish descent. In the early hours of the morning of 22 January, 1944, John Bonnell landed on a beach on the west coast of Italy, a few miles south of Rome, at a fishing town named Anzio. Part of a small British-American advance force, consisting of just one division each, he was welcomed by the locals and then headed on up the Albano road, towards the Alban Hills. The road seemed undefended, except by mines, which they were there to clear. But one found him first.

After the war Martin's mother married an English merchant seaman, who proved to be the source of a succession of exotic gifts. Objects of wonder from around the world brought a surreal ingredient to suburban life in Kent. A small boy's eyes widened every time the sailor returned home and opened his luggage. First there came from South America 'a poison bow and arrow!'.

From Brazil his stepfather brought Leonardo's *Last Supper*, made entirely from brilliant luminous butterflies, an object the boy guarded jealously from admiring neighbours. The iridescent blue still shines brightly in his mind's eye. His step-father may have felt this only child needed company for, when he was five, young Barry was presented with a fruit-eating monkey. And then came the bush-baby, who lived under his bed and in the bathroom of the family's flat. The boy's unlikely playfellow was promised to London Zoo but one day a startled plumber left the front door open and away it went, scampering off to seek its fortune in Bromley. Young Barry never saw his bush-baby again. If a psychiatrist were asked to speculate on the significance of this upbringing, one might see the loss of his actual father in the Anzio Landings as having left Barry Martin with a life-long need to find himself intellectually; his step-father may have been no war hero but he provided a strange role model, as an adventurous bearer of bizarre gifts with which to shake a mundane life awake. This is a role Martin seems to have played for the last forty years.

Another formative image from childhood is the day his grandparents brought to the home their first television. Around 1948, as he recalls, when he was five, a strange box arrived with a nine-inch square screen, emitting flickering images and sounds. The boy sat cross-legged on the floor before it, transfixed but bewildered, for the black and white face of a man had moving lips and a voice, 'but somehow the sound and the image seemed unconnected'. The small boy knew the man was meant to be saying the words but it did not make sense to him. Such was the excitement at the new arrival to the family that he felt he could not tell anyone. For a while, he

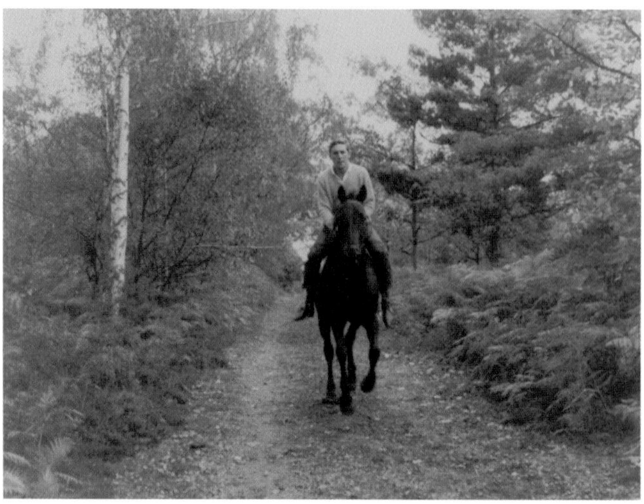

1962

The artist horseriding in the Berkshire countryside

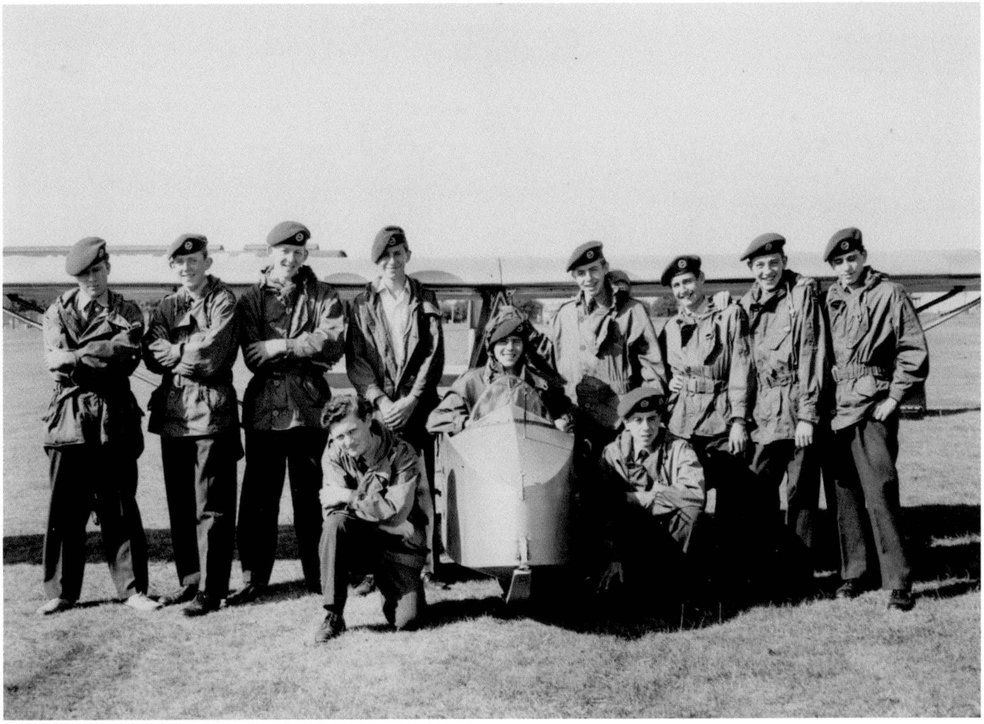

1960

*The artist with wings*: Martin on receiving his glider pilot's licence, standing 4th from left, R.A.F. Hawkinge, Kent



recalls, his curiosity grew along with his inability to accept the automatic association between visual movement and meaningful sound. Finally he revealed to his parents his dilemma, they scolded him, 'and it just clicked'.

Fishing for trout on the River Darent near Shoreham with three or four other boys remains vivid in Martin's stock of formative visual memories. He knew nothing of Samuel Palmer's 'valley of vision' at the time but would enjoy hooking a wriggling worm, catching and pulling a splashing trout out of the river, and then cooking and eating the fish over an open fire. The English rural landscape came home to him in its own right, in greater splendour, through flying over the South Downs of Kent. Martin trained, and qualified at seventeen, as a glider pilot. Few teenagers get to ride the updraft of the Channel winds, soaring in silence through clouds and blue skies above the rolling green hills behind Folkestalone. At the time he hoped to continue his training by joining the Fleet Air Arm, and then become an astronaut.

These were the sparks that penetrated an otherwise typical suburban childhood in the austerity of post-war Britain (where Government rationing of meat continued until he was eleven). Martin had the kind of upbringing that produced the backbone of society, the middle-management commuters of the first post-war 'Baby-Boomer' generation. From Little Firs Primary School in Bushey, Hertfordshire, Martin was sent to Bushey Grammar School and then to Brockley County Grammar School, near Bromley in Kent. A hearty lad, he excelled at all sports and succeeded academically, studying for 'A' levels in mathematics, economics, geography and art. He recalls being 'intensely inquisitive in the sciences, particularly physics and biology' and being fascinated by a post-Darwinian study that had become a school textbook. Sir D'Arcy Thompson's *On Growth and Form* (1917) is a well-illustrated treatise on the significance of energy in nature, as a greater determinant than natural selection, that Martin would return to over the years for inspiration. As Thompson explained in his chapter 'On Form and Mechanical Efficiency', a skeleton is like a steel bridge: 'the whole skeleton and every part thereof, down to the minute intrinsic structure of the bones themselves, is related in form and in position to the lines of force, to the resistances it has to encounter'.

Before the afternoons of school sports matches, Martin spent his Saturday mornings making art at Goldsmiths' College near Greenwich. Here he was first introduced to abstraction, movement and the qualities of sequence,

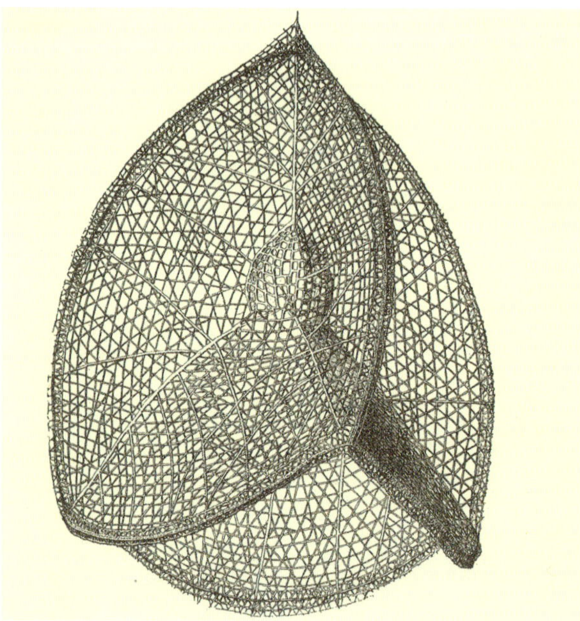

*A Nassellarian Skeleton* from *On Growth and Form* by D'Arcy Thompson 1917 (diam. 015mm)

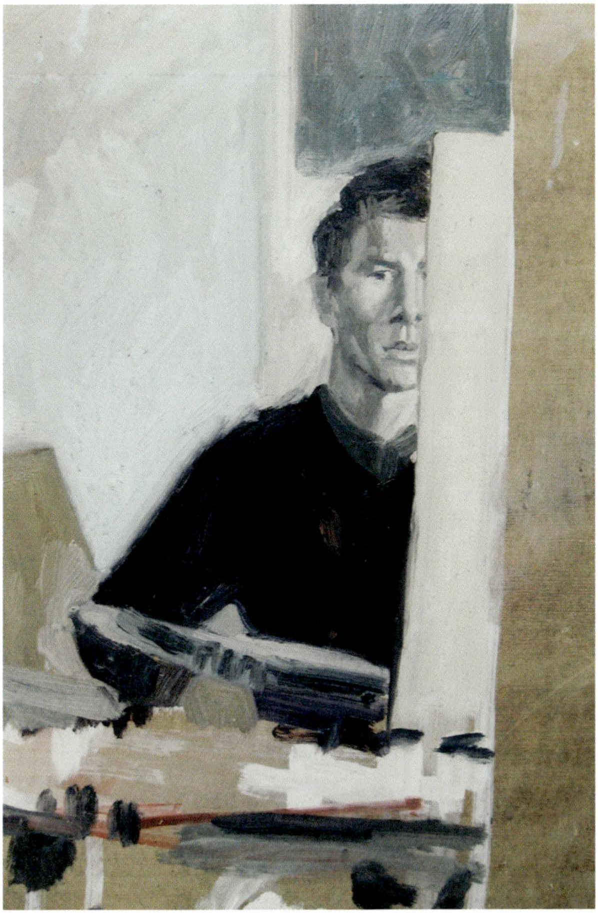

1960

*Self Portrait aged seventien*

Oil on board

74 x 61 cm



variation and repetition through making animations. From the Canadian Film Company's government-backed programme he learned to make elementary movies by scratching away the surface of the film itself. On alternative Saturday mornings he attended life-drawing classes at Camberwell School of Art where, while others struggled, he found his dexterity at recording human proportions on paper came naturally. Eyebrows were raised at his all-boys school on prize-giving day when, as guest of the headmaster, the athlete Roger Bannister (famed for having run the first mile in under four minutes, in 1954) found young Martin had chosen to be presented with a book entitled *The Nude*. Martin read Kenneth Clark's classic work from cover to cover and so gained his first grounding in the history of art.

Rather than join the Fleet Air Arm, or study economics at university as his parents had hoped, Martin opted for Fine Art at Goldsmiths' College, in the University of London. In his first year he was taught by Paul Drury, the true heir to the English Romantic landscape tradition of Samuel Palmer and Graham Sutherland. Despite his glass eye and eccentricities, Drury recognised how Martin's views of the Thames at Greenwich were 'full of movement and rhythm'. So many city-dwellers' paintings of natural landscapes are escapist in mood, but Martin found beauty within industrial life. His paintings of barges jostling in the harbour near Greenwich while being loaded with scrap metal from the breaker's yard reveal Martin's more urban orientation towards the English landscape. The views capture his absorbed observation of the series of processes: the destruction of spent machines, the cranes lifting metallic chaos into the air, releasing the mess as it drops, splaying out into myriad forms, only to be contained and shipped away to serve the new cycle of creation, use, waste, decay.

Martin's urban pastoral vision of London as a city of ephemeral kinetic sculptures also found expression in poetry. For example, in 1969 he composed a paean to Bankside Power Station as it faced redundancy, decades before the building's sublime beauty and potential for generating creative power was recognised by the founders of Tate Modern.





1961

*Greenwich Harbour*

Etching and Aquatint

15 x 22 cm

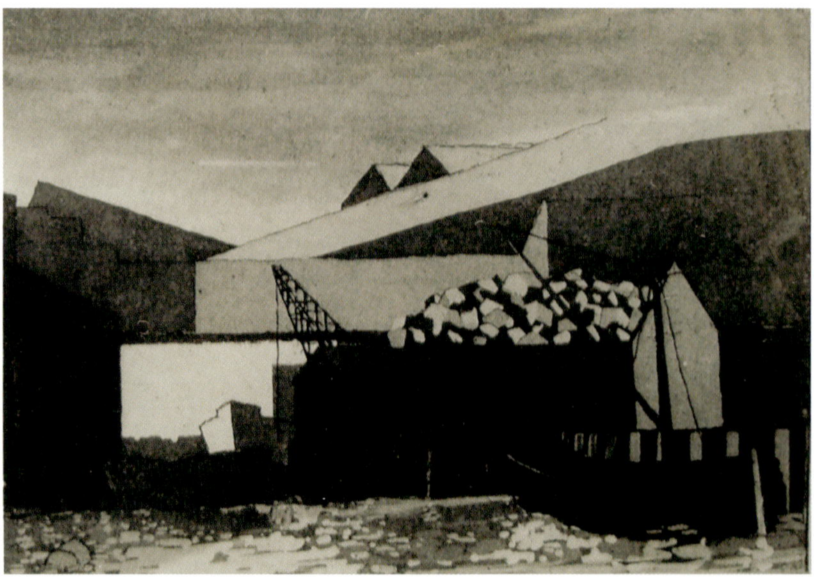

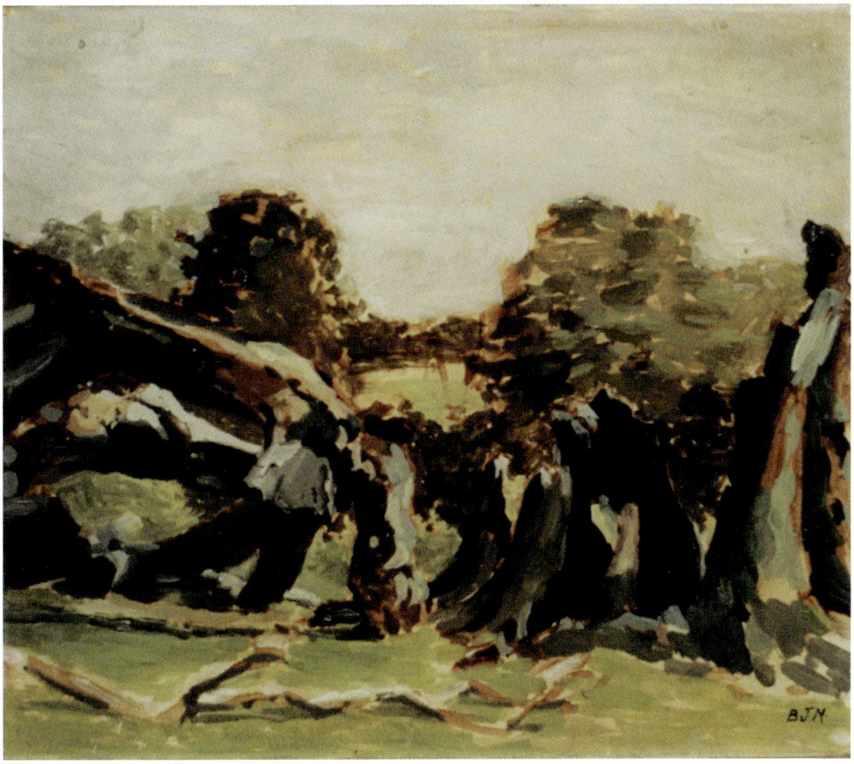

1960

*Trees struck by Lightning, North Kent*

Oil on board

12 x 32 cm

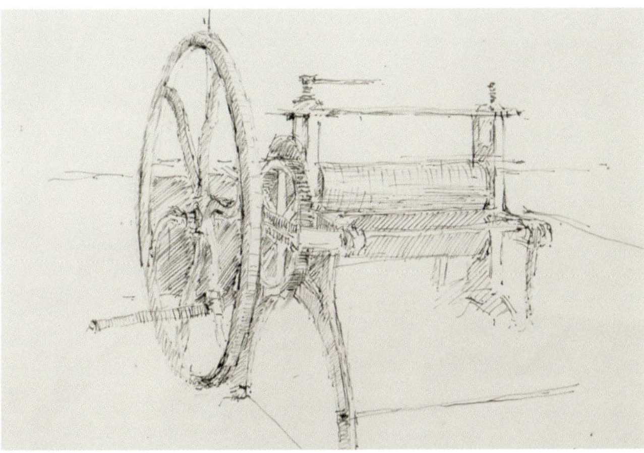

1962

*Paul Drury's etching press*

Brown ink on paper

20 x 28 cm

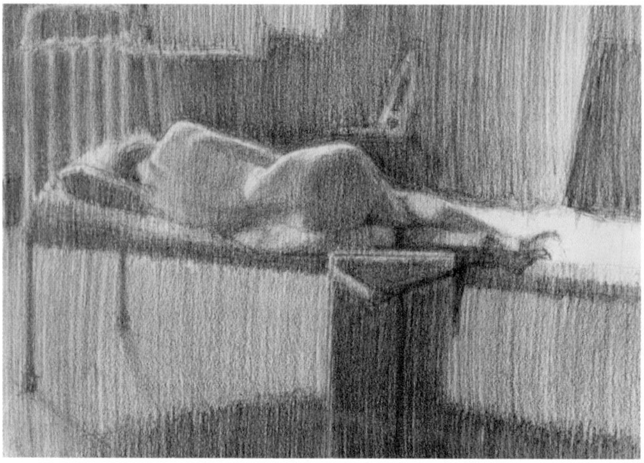

1961
*Nude Study No. 1*
Pencil on paper
28 x 39 cm

His poem is entitled *The Collector of the Sun's Rays at Two Hundred Feet*

*Beautiful pounding smoke, bellowing*
*Into the morning air, but slowly climbs*
*And pales, dissipated, spread-clear, lustrous,*
*Magnificent curling over a brick tipped top*
*And hides in friendly clouds*
*Double rivulets of coiling matter,*
*White as snow at source*

*But, on the return journey,*
*A brick tipped top had its lead severed, mortified;*
*Calmly standing bereft, deserted,*
*Smoke had ceased to pour,*
*Its glory locks were sheared away*
*And stark it stood unattended.*

While a student at Goldsmiths' Martin spent extra evenings in the life class where Sam Rabin ruled. He recalls him as 'the last person you would expect to see there- a huge retired professional wrestler with a shaven head, cauliflower ears and great pork-sausage fingers'. This was no understatement, for Rabin won a bronze medal for England in the 1928

Amsterdam Olympic Games as a weight lifter. Rabin's work at that time was familiar to Martin from his prints of boxers that hung in Lyon's coffee houses. He ran a tight ship. Anyone arriving five minutes late 'was chucked out'; but 'he drew like an angel', adding deft corrections into the corners of Martin's drawings. Rabin taught a purity of looking and 'mark-making' without any egotistical panache getting in the way.

Given his gift for drawing, Martin was able to let his mind wander. During the life classes he went beyond developing a personal style as a draughtsman to consider the space in which the model sat and its relative reality to the sitter and the artist. From life drawing he began to question

1962-3
*Life Painting*
Oil on canvas
128 x 128 cm

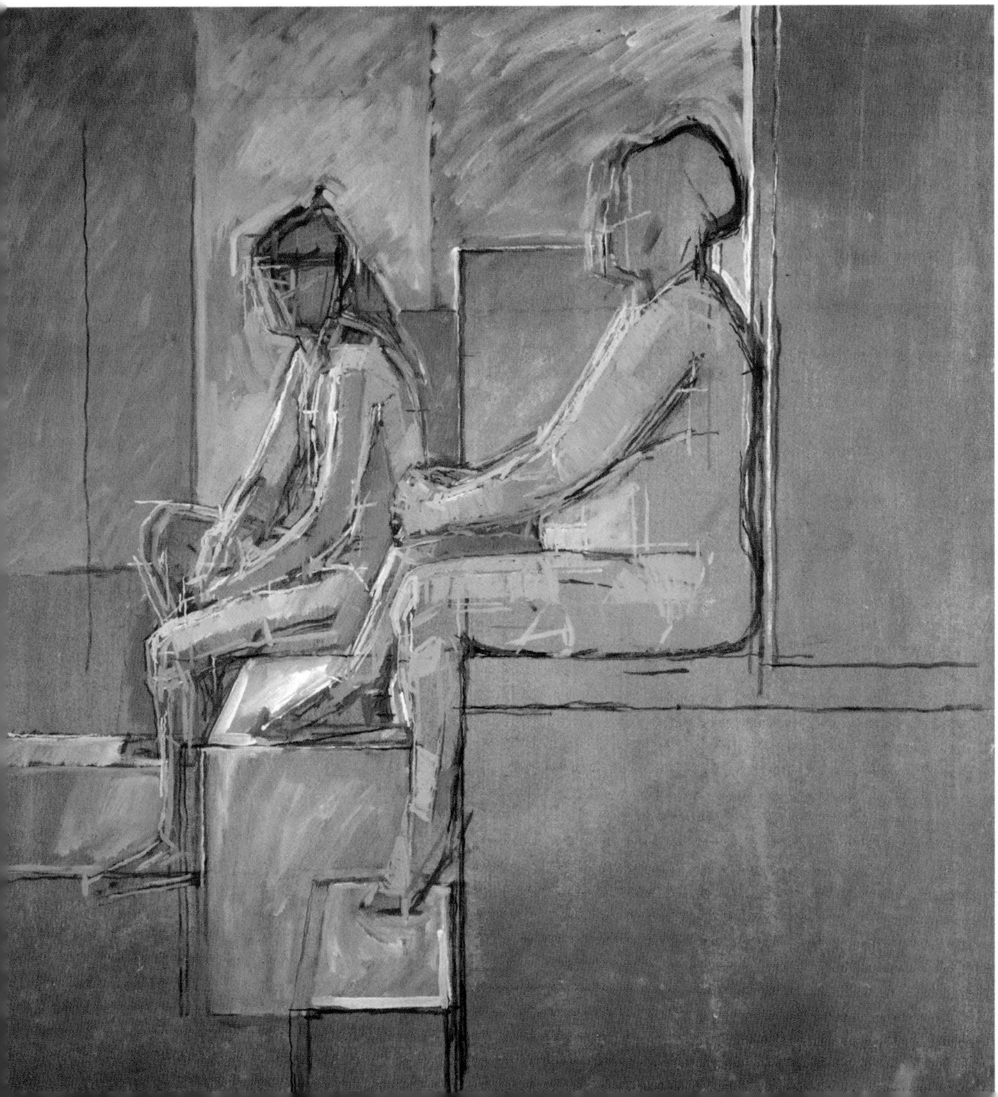

cognitive processes and read the philosophical writings of George Berkeley, David Hume and Immanuel Kant. He remains fascinated by the eighteenth century philosophers who asserted that space, time and the material world do not exist independent of man's consciousness, that ideas are not innate but derive from sight and touch, and who explored the ways in which words signify speech. Martin's interest in perceptual psychology developed to the point of being interviewed for postgraduate study in this field at Birkbeck College, University of London.

Saturdays need no longer be spent at Goldsmiths' so Martin used his time to explore his three favourite museums: the Science Museum, the Geological Museum and the Victoria and Albert Museum, all facing each other on Exhibition Road, South Kensington. He recalls most vividly not masterpieces of art but the vast Watt working beam engine in the Science Museum. So powerful but now functionless, it seemed like a caged beast in a zoo; the contrast between the sheer energy and the loss of factory context gives it an enigmatic presence that few sculptures can equal. The sublime sense of movement and the smooth perfection with which the parts interrelate still fascinate. He recalls also at the Science Museum

1974

The Victiria & Albert Museum:

The Victorian Cast Court

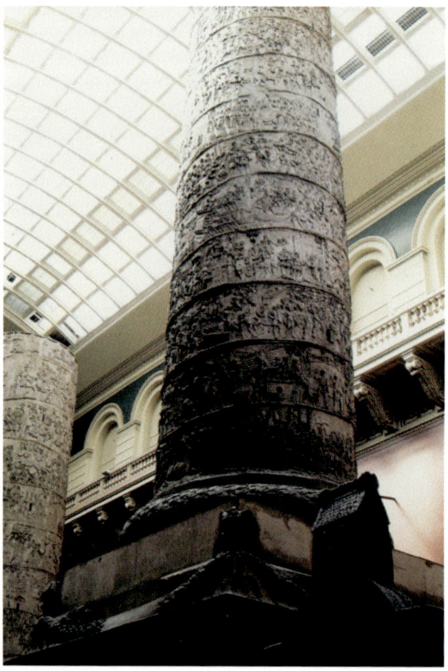

2007

Barry Martin revisits The Victorian Cast Court

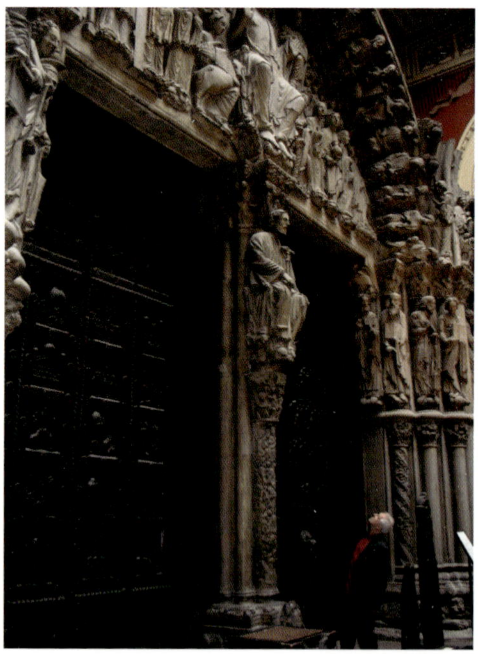

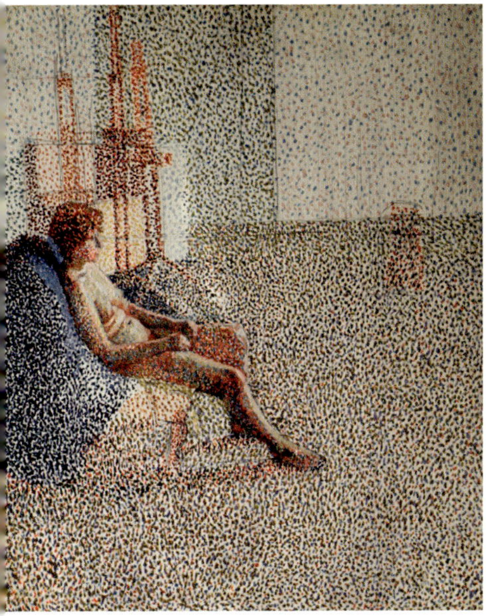

1963

*Pointillist Life Painting No. 2*

*Oil on board*

63 x 46 cm

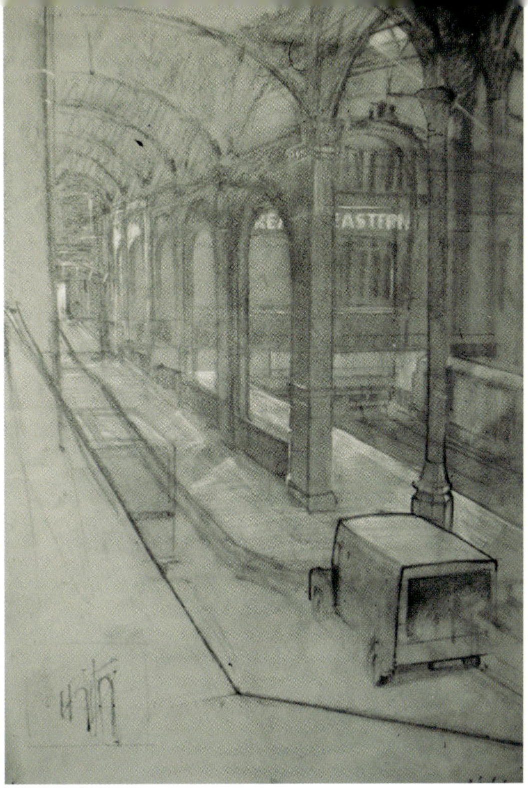

1961

*St Pancras station*

Charcoal, red crayons, white chalk on grey paper

60 x 43 cm



dwelling over a display of mathematical constructions, the Platonic solids, and other models illustrative of the calculations of Archimedes. And then there was the Science Museum's greatest draw, the aeronautical section which, at the start of the Space Age, seemed like the frontier to new worlds and knowledge. From the Industrial Revolution to a sense of the worlds to come, all lay at his finger tips, just out of reach beyond the rope barriers.

Across Exhibition Road the world of fine art presented by the V&A came as a shock. Martin still feels stunned by the cast of Trajan's Column from Imperial Rome, standing side-by-side in two halves stretching to the ceiling of the vast Victorian Cast Courts. As a student from working-class suburbia, who had grown up in a rented council house, who as a boy had known his social position from the shame of having cardboard patches tucked behind the holes inside his shoes, who had never been abroad, whose only window on the world was a nine-inch black and white television screen, the museums of South Kensington seemed like a wonderland. He recalls standing in astonishment in the Cast Courts on the steps of the cast

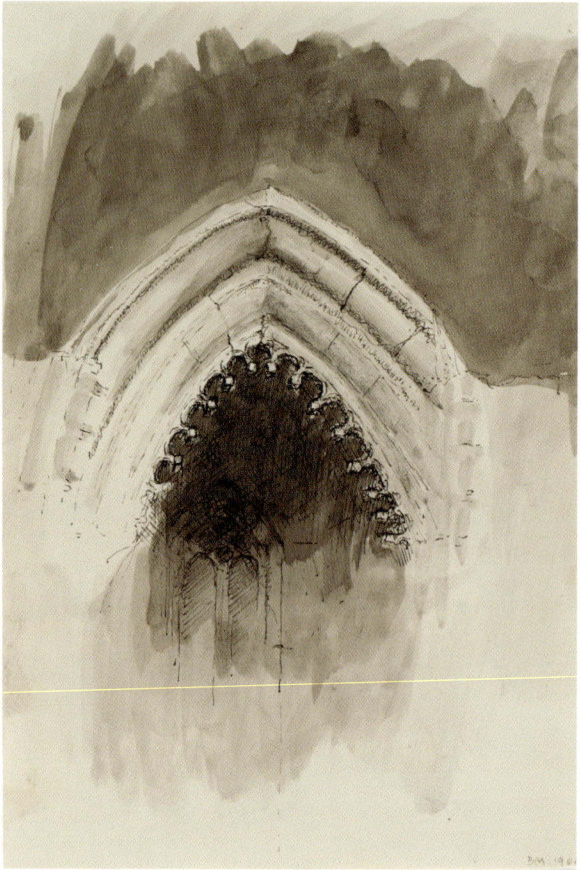

1960
*Study in the V & A Cast Court: Gothic Arch from Rosslyn Chapel, Scotland (coll. V ictoria & Albert Museum)*
Indian ink and wash on paper
24 x 21 cm

1960
*Study in the V & A Cast Court: Bust of St Jerome*
Pen and ink on paper
56 x 38 cm

1961
*Constucted drawing for Sculpted Head*
Pencil on paper
60 x 41 cm





of the entrance porch, the Portico de la Gloria, from the Spanish Cathedral of Santiago de Compostela, and thinking 'Christ! And this is only the front door!'

Martin was fortunate enough to spend six years in full-time training at art schools; there he followed in the main a self-planned course, pursuing both an artistic and intellectual programme. The underlying ethos of Goldsmiths' was of self-discovery through asking questions. In retrospect, Martin sees this approach to education as coming from the tradition of the nineteenth century amateur naturalist and empirical scientist, modestly seeking truth through enquiry for no commercial gain. At Goldsmiths' he was taught by traditional painters, such as Adrian Ryan with John Mansbridge teaching the history of art. The staff at Goldsmiths' also included Kenneth and Mary Martin (no relation), Basil Beattie, Dorothy Mead and Albert Irvin. At the end of his second year, to remain at college and go on to study for the National Diploma of Design, Martin had to submit for the Intermediate Exam in Arts and Crafts a life-drawing, a subject painting with not less than three

**St. Martin's provided a total contrast: 'it was egotistical, competitive, commercial, seeking the biggest and brashest for the international art scene' as he recalls, 'Goldsmiths' seemed monastic by comparison'**

figures in composition, a sculpture and a print. The actual N. D. D. required a life painting in oil, a print and a dissertation. This was a national system of art examinations that dated back to the nineteenth century and was ripe for reform. But Martin benefited from the discipline and diversity.

When Andrew Forge took over as Head of Painting in Martin's second year he brought his personal familiarity with the work of current New York artists, including Jasper Johns and Robert Rauschenberg. Forge introduced to Goldsmiths' the sculptor William Tucker whom Martin admired as 'very knowledgeable, and rational'. It was Tucker who encouraged Martin to pursue postgraduate study at St. Martin's. Martin had been an exceptionally productive artist at Goldsmiths', able to complete and move on to new work in both sculpture and painting. Tucker recommended him to St. Martin's, saying 'I think you'd do a great deal *for them*'.

St. Martin's provided a total contrast: 'it was egotistical, competitive, commercial, seeking the biggest and brashest for the international art scene' as he recalls, 'Goldsmiths' seemed monastic by comparison'. The social focus at St. Martin's was not the studio so much as the commercial gallery exhibition opening where student artists might secure contracts. At Goldsmiths' he had come to believe that the role of the artist was of



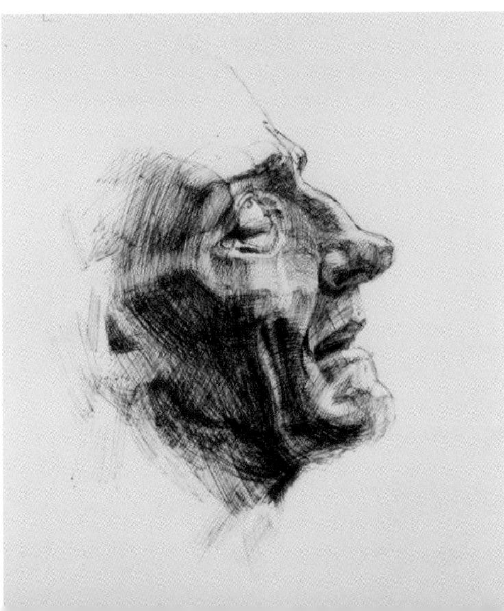

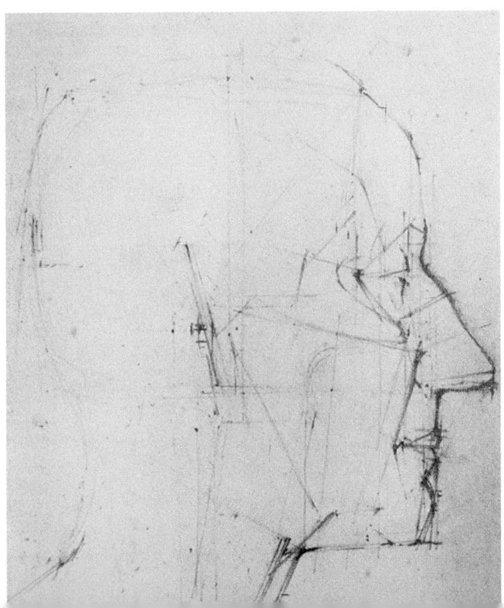

a social observer or humanist prophet, challenging the bourgeoisie by asking awkward questions, 'to help them really see the physical world, to mediate the inner and outer worlds through art, to co-ordinate the totality, to connect the self with the universe'. At St Martin's, as he recalls, many artists felt their job was simply to come up with something new and different within the Modernist canon of the autonomous art object that invites viewing 'on art's own terms' as formal compositions using the current set of materials.

The Sculpture Department was then the best known in the world. Under Frank Martin (no relation) it encouraged 'conceptual-style activities'. The greater commitment was to 'object-type sculpture' in the post-war idiom of Surrealist bio-morphic forms that Herbert Read had dubbed 'the geometry of fear' in his catalogue to the British Pavilion group show at the Venice Biennale of 1952. The strong attitude to sculpture made St. Martin's 'the Mecca for sculptors', attracting artists from as far afield as Romania and Israel. As Martin recalls, Anthony Caro was not yet fully committed to the department, for in the academic year 1966-67 he came into the studios 'about twice'. In Martin's view Caro did not subscribe to Frank Martin's approach that encouraged diversity in materials and goals. Despite Caro's influential retrospective at the Whitechapel in 1963 and inclusion in the Gallery's *New Generation* exhibitions in 1964 and 1965, he was not yet the prevailing influence at St Martin's. For Barry Martin, much of the new developments between 1966 and 1967 came from talking with a fellow student, Richard Long, who shared the need to find an alternative path to the metal sculptures that would become the St. Martin's house-style.

Having made kinetic sculptures at Goldsmiths', at St. Martin's Martin moved upscale. He felt he could make 'great big sculptures, like rooms that moved, and be among the sculpture ethos of making metally things'. He made large coloured metal and wood constructions (discussed in chapter 4). At the end of his postgraduate year at St. Martin's he was offered a full-time teaching position at Leicester Polytechnic but instead chose to accept the rival offer from Andrew Forge to join the staff at Goldsmiths' as a part-time tutor in painting. The immediate step, from student to teacher, was unprecedented at Goldsmiths'. He went on to teach on the Foundation and degree courses at Goldsmiths' and St. Martin's, and at other colleges, and served as an external examiner for the sculpture degree course at St. Martin's. In this way, the orphaned son of a Virginia farm accountant had grown up to find himself at the very centre of the London art scene at a key moment in its history.

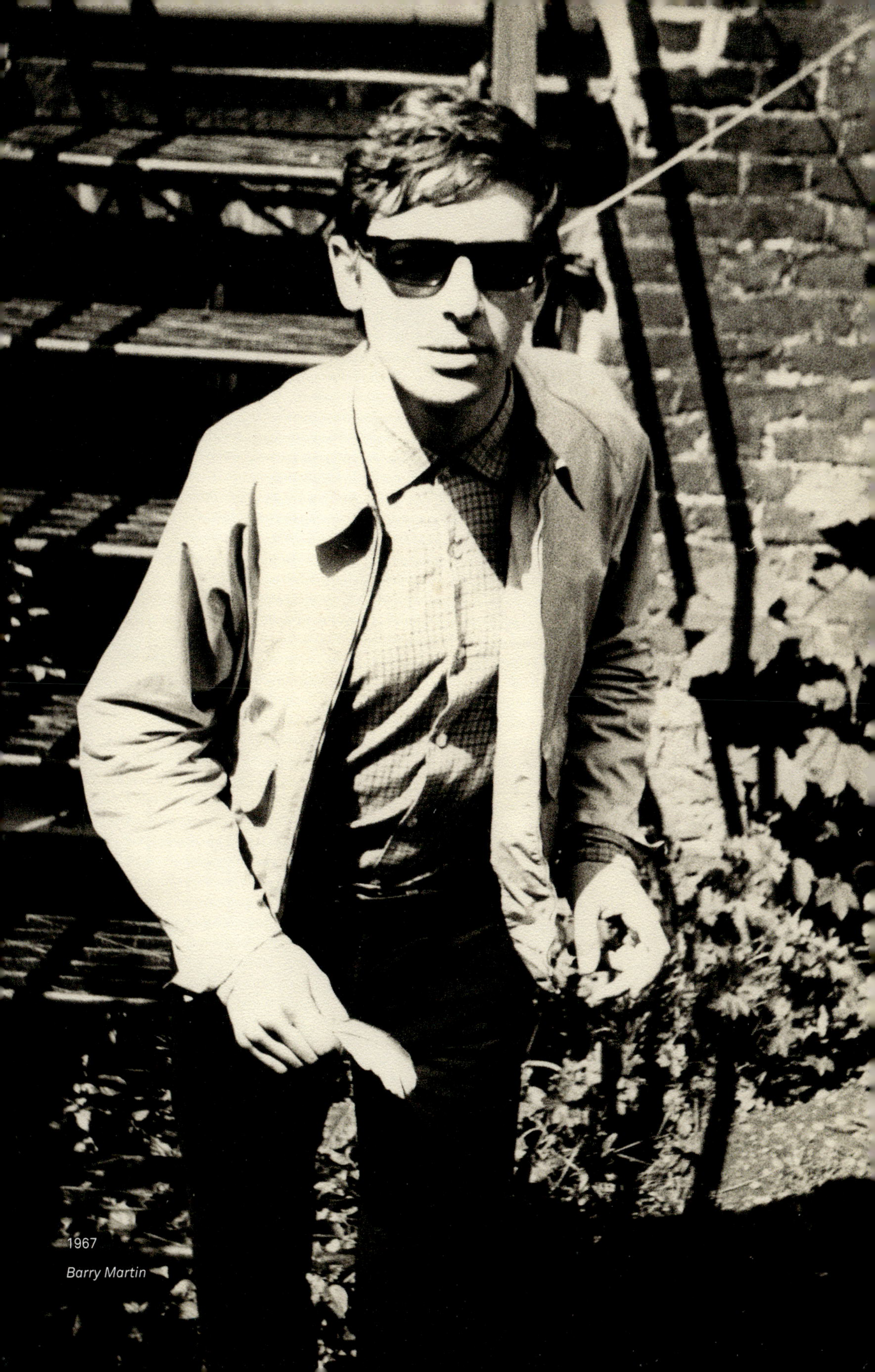

1967

*Barry Martin*

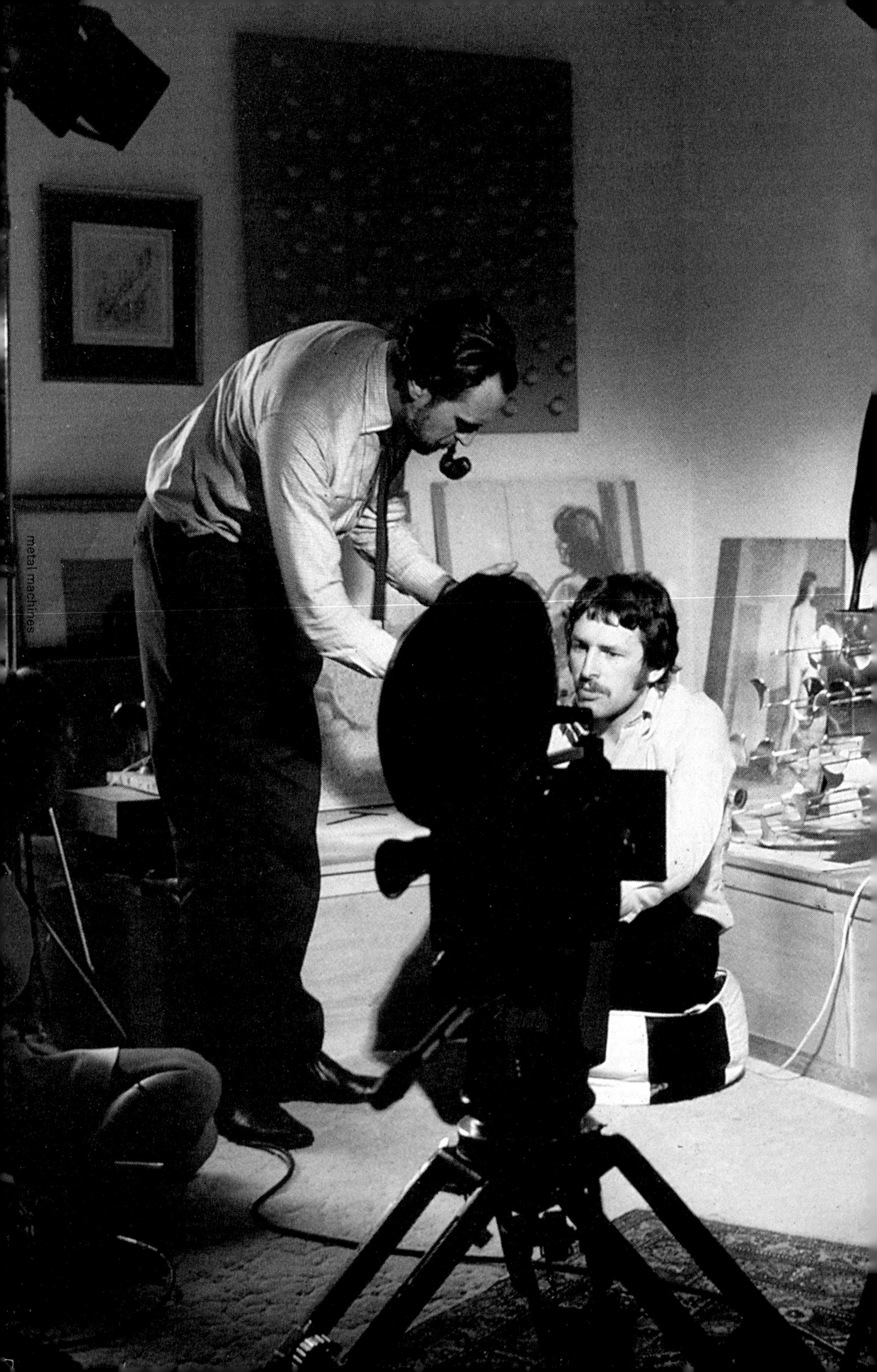

# 2 Metal machines



Another 'Summer of Love' is heating up. It's a sunny Saturday morning in 1968 and Barry Martin is taking a stroll down the King's Road in Chelsea. It's a good time and place to be an artist, especially if you're working part-time teaching art at Goldsmiths' College, earning enough to live and have time to do your own thing. Chelsea in 1968 is an even better time and place to be an artist if you're twenty-four, have a secure rented flat only yards from the Thames, and you're single. As if that wasn't enough to drive a young artist to the very brink of complacency, his first one-man show has opened in Chelsea's Oakley Street, next to Cheyne Walk, in a temporary structure on a building site, part of a new nation-wide scheme called 'Pavilions in the Parks'. It's been well reviewed by *The Times, The Guardian, Studio International* and others. Barry Martin is strolling down the centre of the universe, and it feels good.

1970

The artist interviewed for Central Office of Information film

In his first year as a teacher Barry Martin has done his best to change the world. A tutor told him that all you could really teach at art school is love, and believed that if all the students left loving one another he and The System would have scored. But to Barry, a tutor has a duty to help students recognise how much their response to their environment is preconditioned, to challenge them to find new ways to relate to people, society, religion, politics, locally, nationally, globally. Before he started teaching he only had his own problems to deal with. Now he has all theirs too. It's 1968 and he really believes 'the individual could start to reorganise society if he's educated to understand himself'.

It all comes down to categorisation. He's nearly home now, at 50, Christchurch Street, where an elderly widow, Mrs Howley, rents him the top floor and part of the first floor for £2 2 shillings and nine pence each week. It used to be his girlfriend's flat, but she left; something to do with....Unlike some fellow students, he hasn't married and settled into an art partnership. And right now he's looking for some kind of structure, something more solid in his life and in his art, something he can rely and build upon.





Back in his kitchen, the row of appliances, lined up like patient silent servants, seems to sum it all up. Each one has its job to do, like people in their categories. How do you see the whole space afresh for what it is when the act of seeing is not objective, but has been trained to classify,

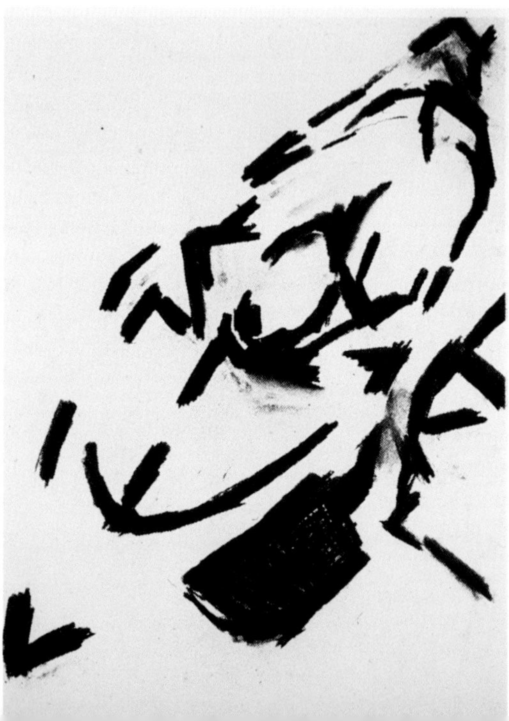

1963

*Machine Drawing No .3*

Charcoal on paper

76 x 56 cm

1963

*Machine Drawing No .2*

Charcoal on paper

22 x 30 cm

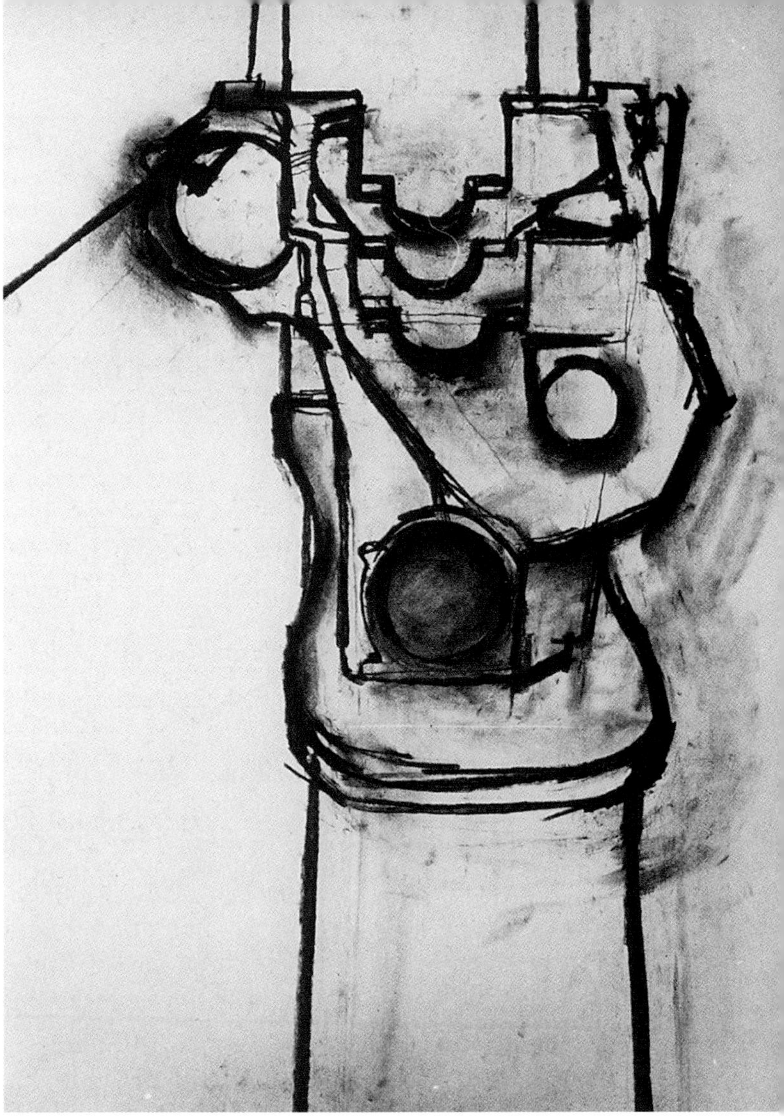

according to someone else's definitions? Category definitions run through society and seem inflexible. His current reading, *News from Nowhere* (1891) by William Morris, lies open where he left it on the kitchen table, offering a dream of a shared society, united in creativity. The role of the art college tutor, and of the artist in society, is about far more than spreading universal love. At twenty-four, Martin is in the process of building what he calls his 'presentation platform', his personal viewpoint from which to relate to society and he's building it in 'a very solid, unpretentious and serious way'. To him, the artist is not 'somebody who selects from the totality a particular position for himself', for 'in the 1960s there's a very strong feeling of art not being a centralising and selective activity, but rather a broadening and all-engulfing situation…categories are being extended…functions no longer exist in such a tight and defined way'.

These are the phrases he recalls from the television interview filmed here by the Central Office of Information last week. A press photograph underlines the seriousness of his intent, for it shows him between two new sculptures, eyes averted from the camera, not smiling, not trying to sell himself to anyone. Friends say it shows him stoned, but the drug culture just seems like escapism and has never tempted him. In fact, the press photograph shows him totally drained and exhausted by making art.

The need for structures runs deep. It had first led Martin to make machines in 1964 while training as a painter. He became increasingly drawn to the physical qualities of his materials, not only to the paint on his brush but to the canvas, its sides, the stretchers, like an actor losing his lines to wander off stage, fascinated by the way the scenery operated. Kinetic Art has its own story, with historical roots in the early 20th century, in Russian Constructivism, the Italian Futurists, and the British Vorticists, the Dadaists, Surrealists and members of the Bauhaus. Precedents go right back to the hydraulic features of the Renaissance garden and the clock-work automata beloved by eighteenth century aristocratic society. But Martin came to it his own way, from personal need.



In the library at Goldsmiths' the history of art reinforced his thinking. Martin recalls being particularly absorbed by *The Thinking Eye*, a collection of the writings of Paul Klee (London, 1961) and Robert Motherwell's *The Dada Painters and Poets* (New York, 1951). He read how Kinetic Art first



## Today, the art form can appear dated, symptomatic of its age

emerged between 1913 and 1920 in the work of Vladimir Tatlin, Naum Gabo and Marcel Duchamp, and was developed in the 1920s and 1930s by Laszlo Moholy-Nagy. Most definitions of Kinetic Art begin with art that moves, usually citing the clanking motorised machines by Jean Tinguely and the elegant air-turned mobiles of Alexander Calder. Art historians have classified Kinetic Art according to three main media: machines; mobiles (operating without motors) and moving light. Optical Art generates the illusion of movement, as in the paintings of Bridget Riley and Victor Vasarely. Some rely on the movement of the spectator to create the illusion of movement within the work or to interact with the work directly rather than leaving it autonomous. The first defining monograph, *Origins and*

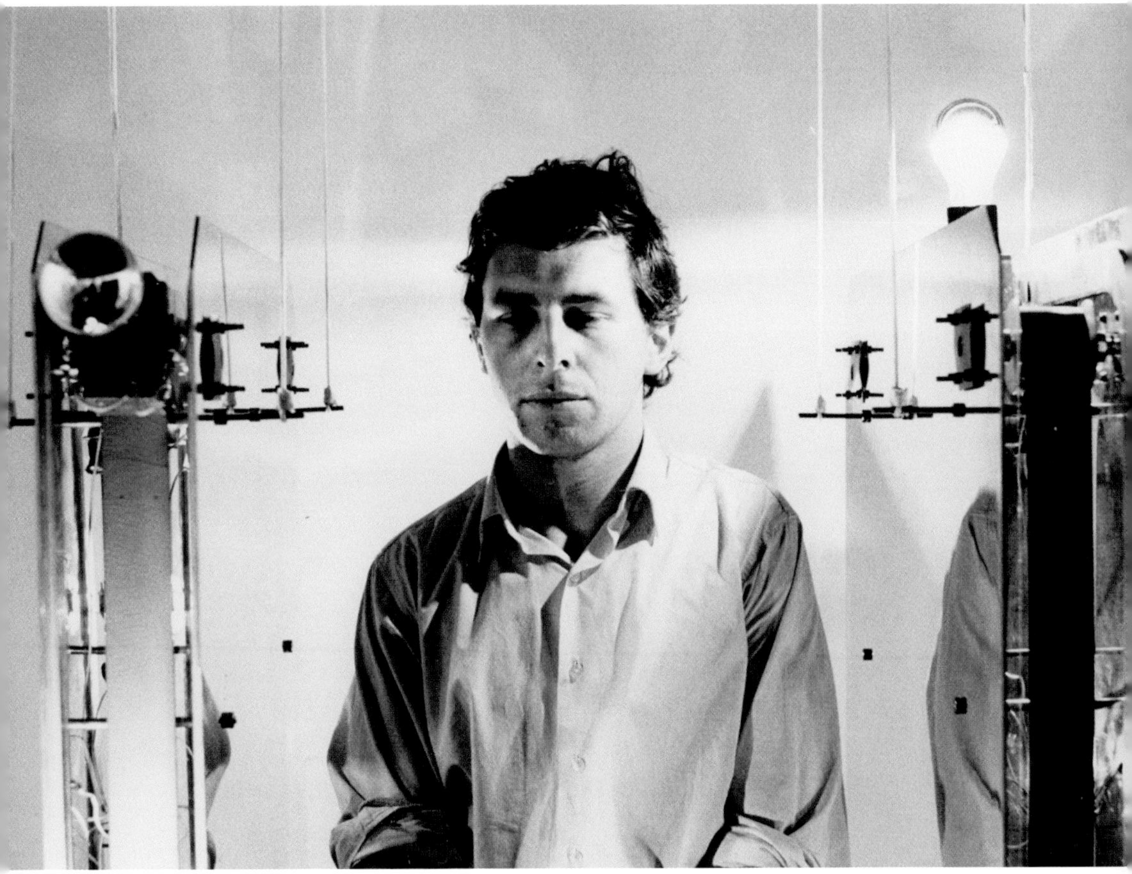

1968

The artist standing between components of *'Inter'*

two 137 cm squares Aluminium, steel, leather, 2 electric

motors 6 back reflector lights and programme

suspended 191 cms above ground

*Development of Kinetic Art* by the movement's champion, the French critic and exhibition curator Frank Popper (London, 1968, translated from French by Stephen Bann) embraced the whole sweep of 20th century painting and sculpture, from Impressionism via Futurism and Abstract Expressionism as a succession of approaches to the theme of representing physical movement in art. The same year Guy Brett concluded his book *Kinetic Art: the Language of Movement* (London and New York, 1968): 'It is impossible to be definitive because we are in the midst of the breakdown of traditional patterns'

Kinetic Art became most widespread in the 1960s. Today, the art form can appear dated, symptomatic of its age, when the race to the Moon seemed to be a sincere ambition, rather than simply the Cold War alternative to global destruction by the two superpowers. In focussing on Kinetic Art's use of movement, some historians risk losing touch with its central concern with Space and Time. Actual movement is not the end but rather the means through which Kinetic Art works incorporate and exist in Space and Time. Naum Gabo and Antoine Pevsner wrote in the *Realistic Manifesto* (Moscow, 1920) that 'Space and time are the only forms on which life is built, and hence art must be *constructed*'. They recognised '*kinetic rhythms* as the basic forms of our perception of real time'. In the 1960s, the decade of living Science Fiction, television could explain to hungry viewers how Space and Time are one and the same, how the Space-Time continuum makes them interwoven and interdependent, how at the micro-level everything is in a constant state of motion and that the universe has no physical frontier but is in a constant state of expansion. The isolated experimenters of pre-war Europe could now be claimed as the intellectual ancestry of a tradition now finding its time. In the spirit of exploration and progress of its age, Kinetic Art promised the discovery of new forms of perception, communication and new levels of aesthetic meaning.

Kenneth Martin (1905-84) taught at Goldsmiths'. His sophisticated, mathematically- precise constructions, first made in 1951, operated by air, heat or touch. Through repetitive movement his mobiles concentrate the viewer's gaze on proportional systems that seem to define logic within the universe, as if infinity is rational, not random chaos. To art students in London in the early 1960s such sculptural constructions offered an alternative to the medium still overshadowed by Henry Moore (1898-1986). The post-war generation of British sculptors had come to prominence in 1952 with their prize-winning show in the British Pavilion at the Venice Biennale. But Reg Butler (1913-81), Lynn Chadwick (1914-2003), Kenneth

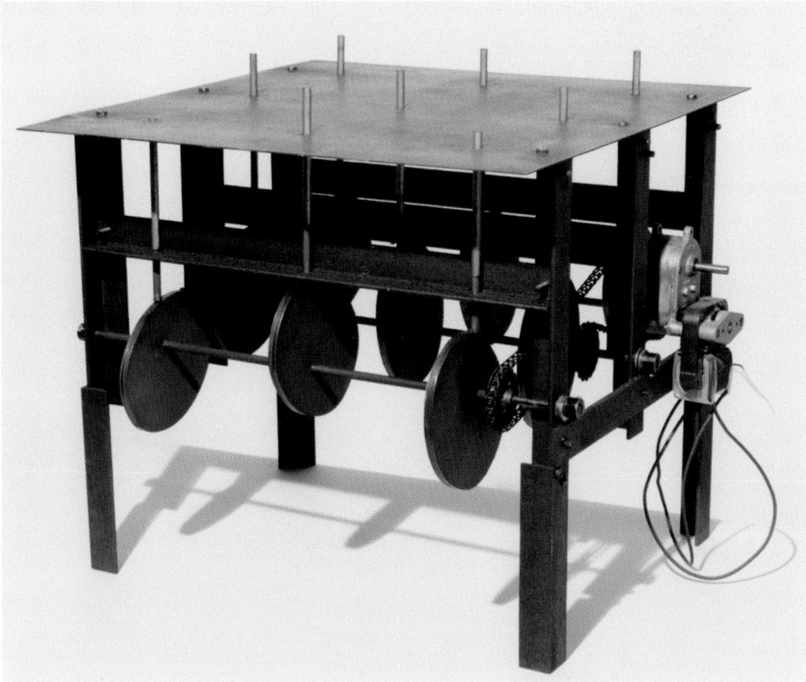

1964-5

*Metal Surface*

Brass, steel, wood, motor.

42 x 42 x 42 cm

(Tate Collection)

The steel rods at the top rose and fell in proportion and relationship to each other driven by the cams below.

Armitage (1916-2002), Eduardo Paolozzi (1914-2005) and William Turnbull (b. 1922) still upheld the tradition of sculpture as free-standing semi-abstract objects in the tradition of Moore's semi-figurative Surrealism. British sculpture had led its field in the post-war art world, despite the dominant tide of painting moving from Paris to New York. Martin had visited Paris in 1965 and seen the European contemporary scene of *Nouveau Realisme*, and became aware of developments in the Kinetic medium by artists such as Pol Bury (1922-2005), Jesus Soto (b. 1923), Takis (b. 1925) and Jean Tinguely (1925-91).

By 1968 Kinetic Art was not the only alternative on offer, for British sculpture had already come under a rival influence, from the American David Smith (1906-65) and his champion, Clement Greenburg

(1909-94). The critic had first visited Anthony Caro in his studio in 1959, and in 1968 would dub him the best 'since David Smith' and 'the Moses of English sculpture'. The combined influence of Greenberg and Caro soon proved decisive but was rivalled initially by the Kinetic school. Barry Martin's machines emerged in the same London as Caro's pioneering constructions but had arrived along an alternative, more European, path. This is the period of confluence, when European and transatlantic traditions met in London art schools and galleries, in a decade of confidence and ambition, when Barry Martin went to work on his metal machines.

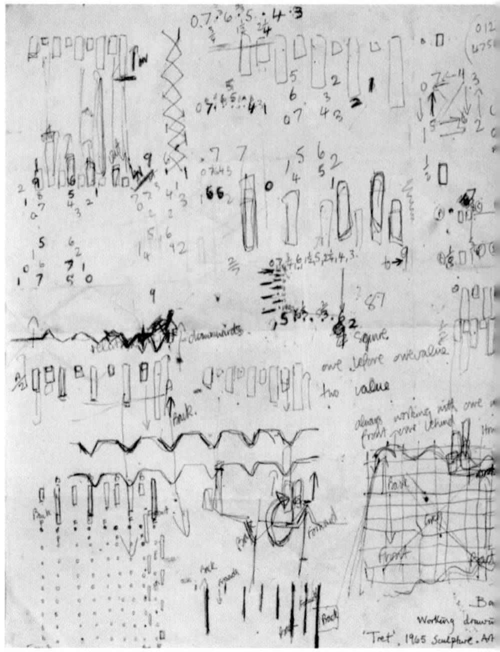

1968

*Tret*, sketch

(Collection: The Arts Council of England)

Ink on paper

*Metal Surface*, made in 1963, is his earliest Kinetic sculpture in the Tate's collections and his first free-standing piece. Made when Martin was aged twenty, it consists of a table-like structure assembled from coarse-cut raw steel. But this is not the whole sculpture, for *Metal Surface* only exists in time, as a continuous movement generated by the metal components. When in motion the horizontal square surface is penetrated by nine vertical rods that rise and fall at a slow, almost imperceptible, pace. Each rod is varied in length, proportionate to each other. Below the surface the open structure reveals nine ovoid cams with watch-springs and axles, each revolving horizontally to give a cylindrical movement, driven by an electric motor. Each ovoid differs in shape in proportion to each other, according to a geometric radial sequence. This causes the rods to move at different speeds and intervals. When the rods reach the top and bottom of each cam movement they appear to rest, flush with the metal surface, despite the fact that the cams are still rotating, giving an occasional twisting motion.

The main theme the piece invites the viewer to consider is the process of resistance, as the coarse, obdurate metal surface is only penetrated in precise, planned and measured ways. The slowness of the movement implies the presence of a relentless force and adds to the sense that the object has an existence in its own right, without function or reason. The open structure was intended to challenge the traditional idea of sculpture as a self-contained entity. From the 21st century, the artist can recognise that the piece also generates a sinister, enigmatic undercurrent. It reminds him of a favourite science fiction novel from childhood, *The Time Machine* by H. G. Wells (1895) in which the time traveller in his machine visits the year 802,701 where aesthetes and intellectuals inhabit the Earth's surface in a seemingly idyllic existence. To his horror, he soon discovers that they have grown dependent upon a subterranean race that have turned cannibal and feed on them. Wells's attack on the class system of Victorian Britain must have seemed timely to others for it was made into a movie in 1960.

In 2004 Martin explored the possibility of having *Metal Surface* built on a colossal scale, so that viewers could stand beneath it, almost as if in an underworld looking up at wheels slicing space; he got as far as having the wheels made in stainless steel but the cost proved prohibitive. He describes *Metal Surface*, when operating, as 'magical, rather like a brass orrery, only its elegance of movement is heightened by the brutality of its raw engineering'.

*Tret* (1965) was purchased by the Arts Council of England from Martin's first one-man show, in Chelsea in 1967. It was also shown at the Hayward Gallery exhibition *Kinetics-International Survey* in 1970. There (as



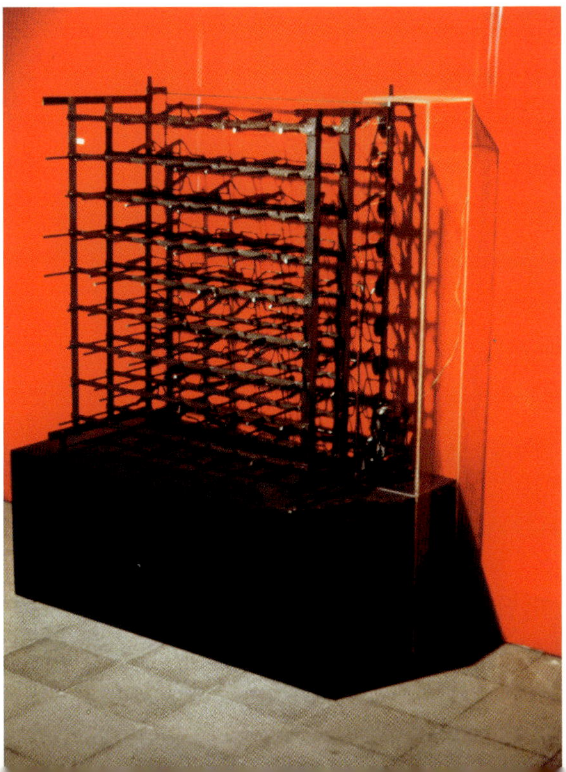

1968
*Tret*
127 x 122 x 33 cm
Steel, electric motor

81 steel rods move very slowly in and out of the structure. Each is related to the next rod and to the overall proportion of extension of all the rods.
(Collection: The Arts Council of England)

illustrated here) it was installed on a pedestal, set against a wall with a Perspex box to conceal the driving mechanism, but this was only for reasons of public safety. Like *Metal Surface*, it was made to be seen in its entirety. Ideally, it would be raised to eye-level and viewed in-the-round, suspended from above. The number nine recurs (a figure with mystical significance to Martin) as a grid arrangement of eighty-one steel rods, all in continuous lateral movement. The material is mild steel, as supplied direct from the manufacturer, its mid-tone grey enriched by the coating of working oil (Martin relishes the fact that 'this is a really oily piece'). Unlike *Metal Surface*, there is nothing to divide the parts, as every component relates to the occupied space, and there is never a moment of apparent stasis. The rods move in and out without rest or defining moment of climax, making the whole work unintelligible if viewed as sculpture.

Continually constructing and deconstructing itself, *Tret* defies the conventions of completeness. Through extension and containment, regular yet irregular, symmetry and asymmetry, the work continually eludes any conclusion and so creates a state of uncertainty. According to the artist 'this enigma of knowing yet unknowing pushes the viewer to the margins of perception, breaking down the old categories and barriers within which we normally think. It teases and taunts us beyond the comfort we demand from 'other' things, setting out a new order of understanding'. This 'otherness' is characteristic of an artist who challenges the viewer's routine systems of evaluation and invites us to create our own. He recalls 'this was in complete opposition to the libido-seeking freedoms of the `Sixties where the common reaction to the conventional habits of the time was to drop out. Nor was it simply about doing something novel as a sculptor'. Martin held, and still holds, the passionate conviction that the role of the artist is to make tools to help people think differently, to make a complete break with the past. In the new universe of Relativity Martin's machines offered paradigms for a new age of understanding 'in which space curves and parallel lines do meet in infinity'.

The sculptures also work on other levels, stirring sub-conscious associations. The slowness of movement in Tret gives the piece a strange sense of menace. During the six months of its construction Martin's girlfriend told him to read In *The Penal Settlement* (1919) by Franz Kafka, a short story in which condemned prisoners are strapped beneath a glass machine of moralising torture. Through its needles 'The Harrow' slowly etches into each prisoner's body the name of their crime, taking twelve hours to write the words deeper and deeper. *Tret*, by contrast, has no function other than to continue in unrelenting motion, perhaps offering some paradigm for the typical working life. *The Oxford English Dictionary* defines a 'tret' as an 'allowance of extra weight formerly made to purchasers of some goods for waste in transportation'.

Martin's own reading material while creating *Tret* raised issues that became fundamental to his career. At the Institute of Contemporary Art in October 1966 Martin exhibited as one of '4 Young Artists'. For his 'Artist's Statement' in the catalogue he expressed his conviction that he was on the brink of a new age, ready 'to witness the formulation and construction of the/a new Space-Time Era'. Martin's statement was quoted by Edward Lucie-Smith in his review of the exhibition ('Pragmatists and theoreticians') in *Studio International* (December, 1966) where the critic also noted that 'Barry Martin's machines have...an aggressiveness which saves them from whimsy'. Behind Martin's sublime optimism, that now seems so characteristic of the youthful spirit of England in the Sixties, lay his reading of *The Philosophy of Space & Time* by Hans Reichenbach (Berlin 1928; the English translation New York, 1957) while a student at Goldsmiths' (1961-66). He recently remarked that, in the light of devouring this book's ideas, 'much of the activity I found at St. Martin's Sculpture Department was Neanderthal in comparison and looked like a throwback to the Stone Age. With my machines I wanted to engage in a mental construct. An understanding of them could only be brought about by memory enveloped in an experience of pure movement'.

Reichenbach's classic study was written at a time of crisis in the relation between empiricist physical science, mathematics and philosophy. It explores the foundations of geometry, of time, the difference between Space and Time, the problem of a combined theory of *Space and Time* and some of the consequences of Einstein's Theory of Relativity. It raises the psychological problem of the status of visual intuition, between theory and observation. Long regarded as one of the clearest expositions in its field, Reichenbach's Space & Time is, nevertheless, the kind of book more likely

**The slowness of movement in *Tret* gives the piece a strange sense of menace**

to make sense to a student moving on from 'A'level mathematics, as Martin was; there cannot have been many well-thumbed copies in the art schools of London in the `Sixties.

Reichenbach assumes his reader to be familiar with the principles of geometry, as the closed and complete system established by Euclid in Alexandria in the reign of the first Ptolemy (323-283 BC), principles that retained their authority until the end of the 19th century. He begins by questioning their validity, as they are simply factual, not logical. In the 'Age of Reason' the philosopher Immanuel Kant (1724-1804) observed that the principles of geometry are certainties based on *a priori* knowledge, acquired independent of experience. For example, the axiom that two parallel lines do not intercept cannot be tested as they cannot be measured over an infinite distance. In the 19th century a theory of knowledge was built through systems of natural science rather than through philosophical speculation, as science and philosophy were regarded as two disciplines. The advent of non-Euclidian systems of geometry challenged physicists' use of mathematics, for Space is subject to the laws of optics and mechanics. Today, mathematicians distinguish between pure geometry and physical geometry, as two branches of science, the former dealing with abstract structures, and the latter with the empiricism of physics. Acceptance of not one but multiple geometries leads to the recognition of Space as having a twofold nature: physical space poses different sets of problems to those of mathematical space. Once the distinction is recognised, the physicist is challenged to measure the structure of physical space through experiments but he must adjust the very rules of measurement based on observed facts as his measuring instruments (be they rods or clocks) themselves expand and contract in Space.

Reichenbach's landmark publication helped to establish the empiricist concept of geometry and made the post-Einstein universe intelligible to many of its inhabitants. The greatest challenge to Einstein's physics and his dependence upon traditional mathematics came, of course, from Niels Bohr with his practical research into Quantum Mechanics. Between 1905 and 1927 Bohr revealed the fundamental anarchy of the universe at the sub-atomic level, where the behaviour of electrons is capricious, ruled only by uncertainty and chance. Half a century later, Stephen Hawking's *Brief History of Time* (1988) brought the biggest questions home to the general public but, strangely, he seems to have made little impact on the artists of his day, who must have other priorities.

In Martin's own heavily annotated copy of Reichenbach's *Space & Time* the first statement to be underlined is in the introduction: 'one individual is not capable of carrying on scientific and philosophical work at the same time'. He also notes Reichenbach's regret that 'the style of modern science has gradually adopted the hurried pace of technology induced by competition' resulting in 'this machine age knowledge which, in the minds of many people, will remain mere technology, but which, in its system as a whole, reveals a depth of insight that can only be reached through the teamwork of an organised group of individual scholars'. Martin's passionate young pen asterisks the observation that the philosophy of science should not 'stand like marble monuments before the gaze of generations, but should be considered...a fund of cooperatively discovered propositions'.

Reflecting on Einstein's theories in his chapter 'The Dependence of Spatial Measurement on the Definition of Simultaneity', Reichenbach noted how the measurement of space changes in systems moving at different speeds. He discusses how a measuring rod has a static dimension, its 'rest-length', and that its moving length is only assumed to be identical. The determination of moving length requires the use of time measurements. In kinematics, the precise length of a moving rod is the distance between the simultaneous positions of its endpoints; according to Einstein's formulation, this varies according to its velocity. If it sounds absurd that a rod can have two lengths, its rest-length and its motion-length, this is because the kinematic measurement is not of the rod but of its projection across a measuring system. In the same way, a photograph can record a moving car with its wheels slanted as the image depends on the speed of the camera's shutter. Reichenbach's account of the challenge of 'visualising the relation between space and time measurements' struck a chord with Martin, not least because he had already recognised the problem set by moving rods in making his kinetic sculpture *Metal Surface* in 1963.

From rods to the geometry of moving light, Reichenbach goes on to explain how light is curved by gravity, and the implications of this for the apparent behaviour patterns of Space and Time. To Martin, *The Philosophy of Space & Time* challenged him to create his own geometrical mechanical systems, to conduct his own experiments, not as a philosopher-physicist but as a young adult faced with living in a new unknown universe of infinite Relativity, one that the Space Race was making more real every day.

Martin's interest in the new frontiers of science and knowledge that the age promised to open up was not confined to making art. He acquired in

## Philosophy of science should not 'stand like marble monuments before the gaze of generations'

the mid-1960s several manuals for the training of astronauts. Particularly interesting to him were the sections dealing with the effects of sensory deprivation through suspension in water. Late in 1966 he made his own experiment at St. Martin's, subjecting fellow students Richard Long, George Pasmore, Hamish Fulton and Alan Berkley to sensory deprivation, stripped to their swimming trunks with hoods over their heads. The project was recorded on a film, now in the Tate Archives (as discussed by Adrian Glew in chapter 9). The sensory deprivation project evolved not only from the study of astronauts' manuals but also from Martin's interest in synaesthesia, the confused mind's ability to interchange sight, taste and sound, which he had encountered through the paintings of Kandinsky. The subject of mental perception advanced from the late 1950s through the mind-mapping research of David Hubel and Torsten Wiesel. The Nobel Prize-winning neuroscientists discovered how visual stimuli reaching the brain from the eyes are processed through columns of nerve cells, each recognising and responding to different information, such as corners or stationary vertical lines, before assembling and sending complex images to the higher brain cells where the visual impression is made and stored. Memories of images, as knowledge, are used to interpret and understand what is seen. Hubel and Wiesel established that the brain does not receive images like a mirror or movie screen but constructs what the eyes relay. The relationship between the subjective sense of self (which may be just a pattern of nerve cells) and the perceptual process, from observation via thought to understanding, would become a core theme of Martin's art.

*Double-Ringed Movement* (1966, Tate) is an intimate, sophisticated wall sculpture worthy of a horologist. It suggests the sensitivities, complexities and quiet, contemplative qualities of a laboratory test-piece. Two rows of nine aluminium discs, one set large, one set small, project from a mirroring aluminium surface. The aluminium rings are mounted on polished brass tubes of varying diameter slotted together to form axles within axles. Martin's invention of this mechanism enabled him to activate space in front of and behind each ring, and at different speeds. The axles are driven in and out by a Ferris-type wheel, akin to those used in barrel organs. The eighteen rings rotate in different directions at different speeds and

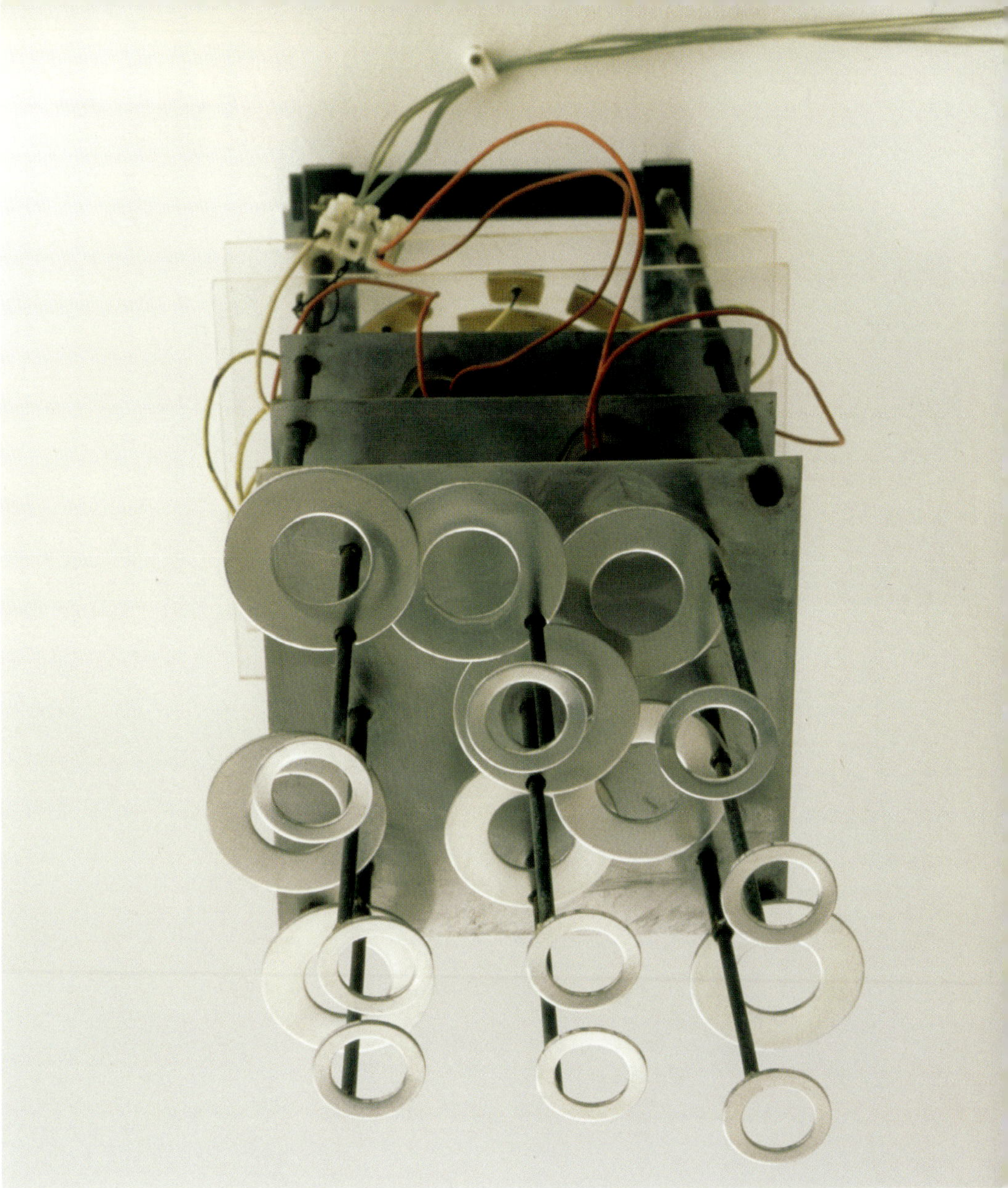

1966

*Double-Ringed Movement*

Aluminium, perspex, 3 motors with slow variable speeds, brass, steel

The forward rings could move independently of the back rings. Each pair of rings could move separately from each other although they were mounted on the same axle.
(Tate collection)

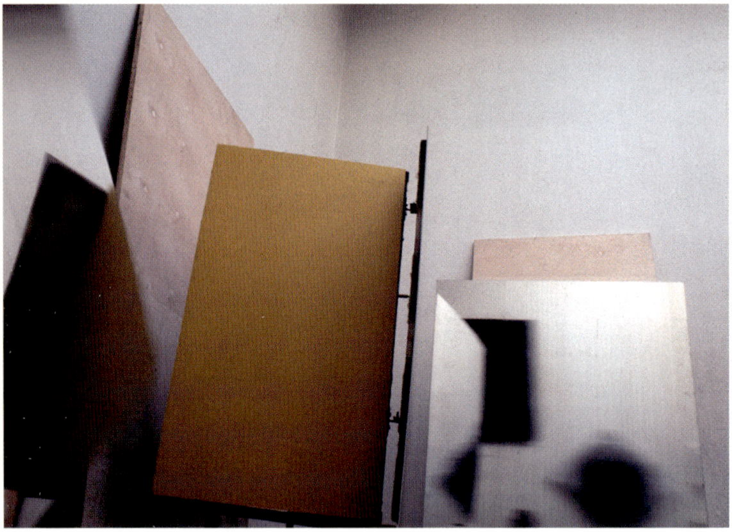

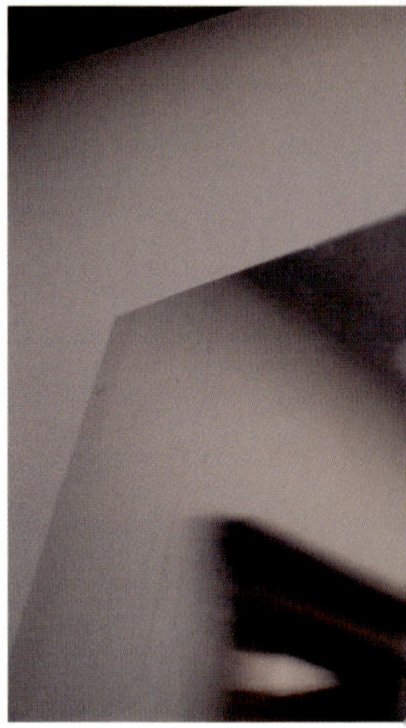





1968
*Triple movements, Spinning, Flapping, Tipping*
Aluminium, steel, wood.
300 x 480 x 120 cm

3 electromagnetic actuators, 2 motors programming machine with stepping motor

produce a fluidity of motion that, quite suddenly, stops as if transfixed for a split second of visual silence before continuing. The three motors generate a variety of movements and counter-movements of different quality that Martin compares to the way the paintings of Piet Mondrian explore contrapuntal composition by pushing opposites into equilibrium. Martin compares its 'score' to that of a musical composition.

*Triple Movements* (1968, destroyed) was one of Martin's most ambitious machines. Conceived more as a mobile installation than as an independent sculpture, it made maximum use of its environment at each venue. First shown at the Royal Academy in 1969, it was presented as part of the London Group exhibition, curated by Andrew Forge, along with works by members such as David Hockney, Leon Kossoff, Frank Auerbach and Ian Stevenson. *Triple Movements* ensured Martin's selection by the Arts Council as the young English artist for the four-man British show in 1970 at the Serpentine Gallery, where it was installed to very different effect.

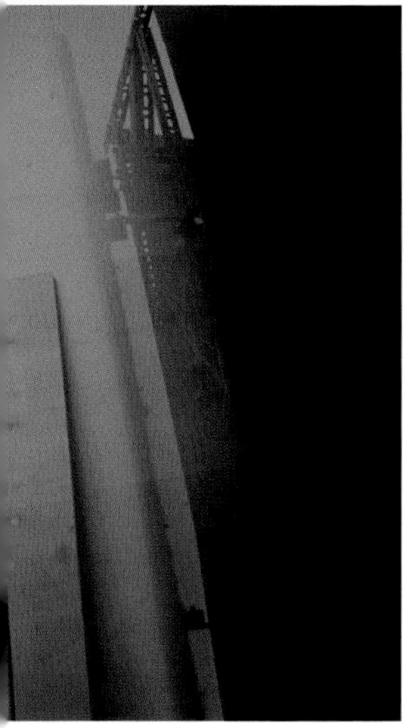 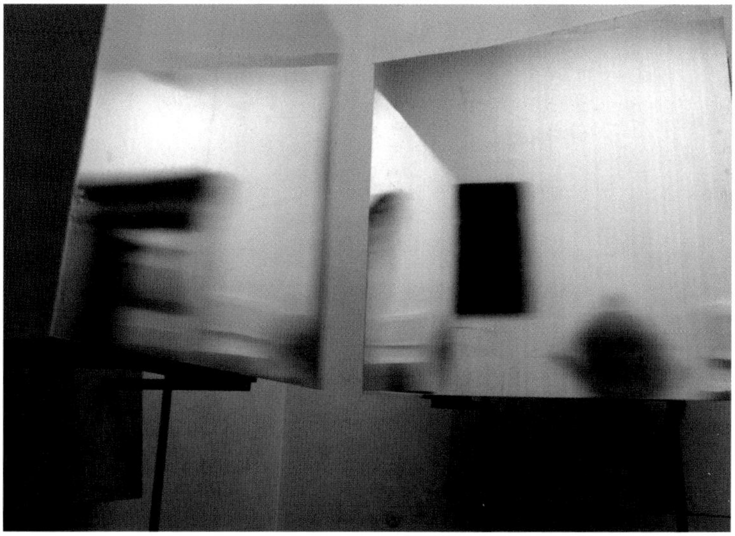





## *Triple Movements* was one of Martin's most ambitious machines

The sculpture comprised three planes of aluminium, each four by six feet, hung at a height of seven feet six inches, and two planes of wood, each eight by four feet, painted red and yellow ochre, mounted on vertical poles. *Triple Movements* was animated by the use of electromagnetic actuators that were originally designed to move landing flaps on the wings of Boeing aircraft. Martin had found them on sale, second-hand, in the Tottenham Court Road and succeeded in building his most ambitious machine to date with the assistance of the Engineering Department at Goldsmiths' College. The actuators made the aluminium planes not only flap but spin and tip in defiance of gravity and, apparently, any logic in a programme that lasted one hour before repeating.

With the aluminium planes polished to serve as mirrors, the piece seemed to swallow and spin the space it occupied, first playing with the geometry of the 18th century architecture of Burlington House and then with the extensive garden windows of the Serpentine Gallery. It challenged the spectator's sense of their physical relationship with their environment, distorting through the use of reflected space, whilst also forming compositions within itself by revealing and concealing the red and yellow planes in varying proportions with changing reflected light. *Triple Movements* also used the associative sound of the actuators, a noise familiar to anyone who has heard an aeroplane coming in to land. Right from the entrance to the exhibition visitors could hear the heavy-duty actuators, each capable of shunting half a ton of wing flaps, thrusting away. Long before finding the sculpture people wondered, as Martin recalls, 'What on Earth is making that sound? It did cause quite a disturbance'.

In the Hayward Gallery's vast exhibition of 1970, *Kinetics-International Survey*, most artists were not British or North American but were drawn from continental Europe. Of the 66 artists invited to participate by the curator Theo Crosby, 33 came from Europe, 16 from the U.S.A., four from South America, two from Canada and one from Korea. Among the ten British artists, Martin was the youngest, at the age of twenty-seven, the same age as Peter Logan. Apart from Kenneth Martin and Bryan Wynter, most of the British and Irish Kineticists were born in the 1930s: Malcolm Carder, Keith Grant, Robert Janz, John Kaine, Michael McKinnon, William Pye and Stephen Willats. Barry Martin was represented by Tret (1965) and by a new work, Moving Sculpture, which was installed prominently on the terrace outside.





*Moving Sculpture* stood fourteen feet tall and reached eighteen feet across. High on the terrace of the Hayward Gallery, with the wind blowing across from the Thames, the sculpture forced you to look up, to see it against the moving clouds and changing tones of the London sky. It was so tall that you lost the sense of standing next to art, of any physical relationship between your body and the sculpture, of occupying any shared space. The sense was more of being released from gravity, almost flying, like that dizzying feeling you get from watching seagulls swirling overhead.

The potential of creating free-standing sculpture on this level first came to Martin in a static piece, *Vertical Upright with Horizontal Slab* that he made in the sculpture yard at St. Martin's between 1966 and 1967. By then, older contemporaries such as Anthony Caro and Philip King were making the most of taking sculpture 'off the pedestal' but, as Martin recalls, 'no one at that time was creating free-standing abstract sculptures that started above head height, in the open air'. Overhead outdoor sculptures could be like mobiles, suspended from the sky.

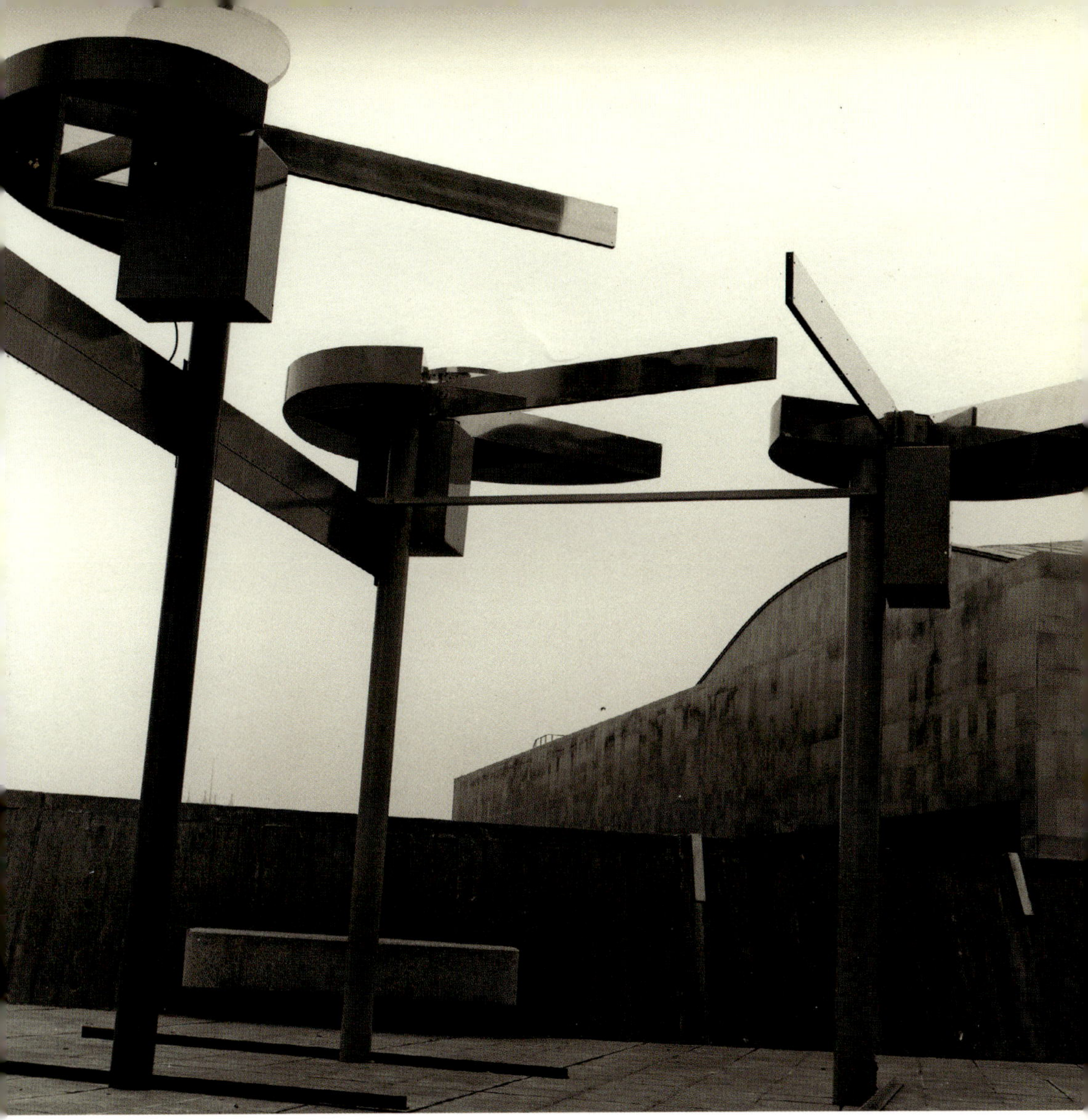

1969-70

*Moving Sculpture*

Steel, aluminium, stainless steel, perspex, laminated wood, 5 heavy duty electric motors. Colour: blue, orange, green, yellow.

422.5 x 544.5 x 600cm

Five different types of movement and different speeds allowed sections to interlock. A programmer and stepping motor controlled movement variations. Light was reflected from the sculpture to form units of light that penetrated the immediate environment. This both structured and destructured the composition and immediate environment to the sculpture core.

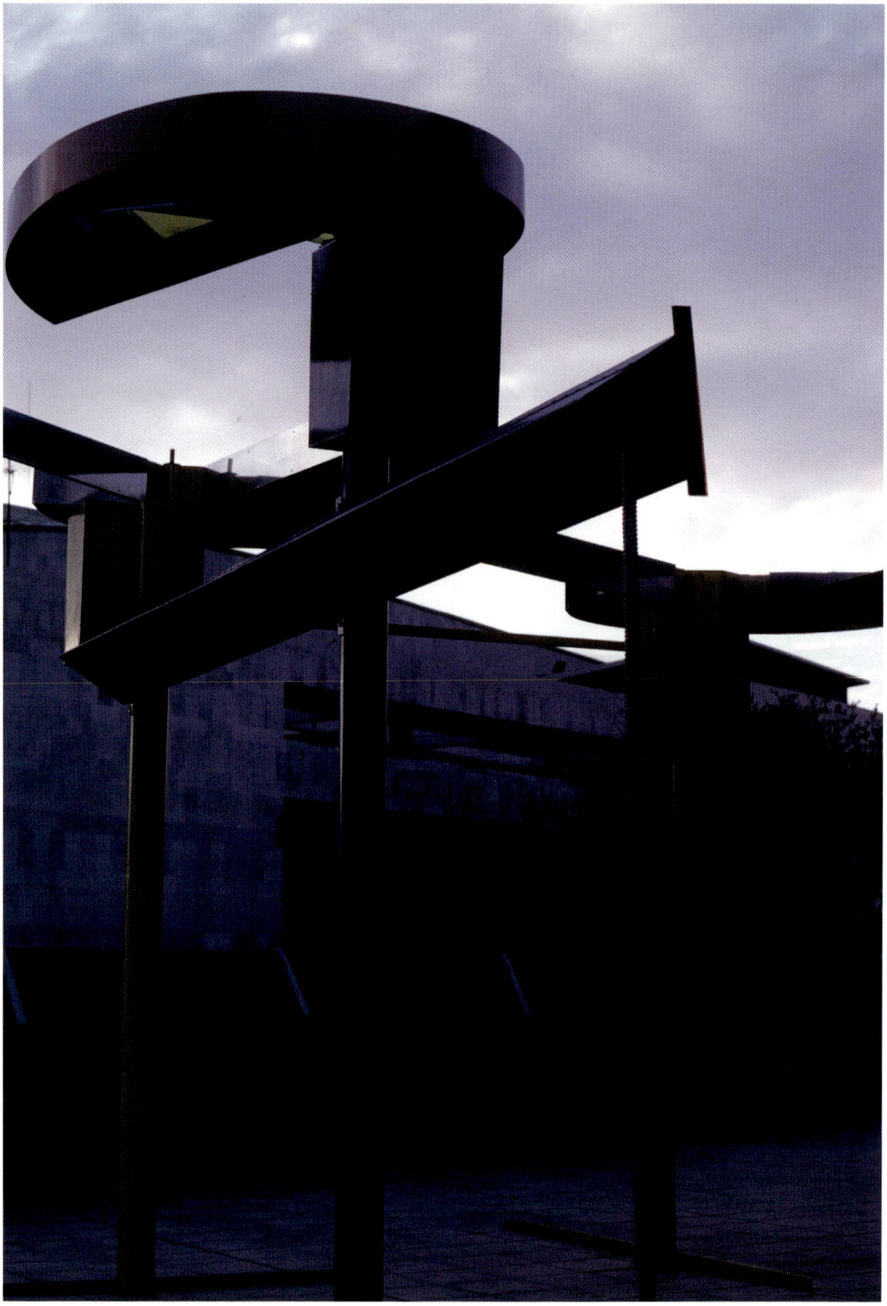

1969-70

*Moving Sculpture*

Steel, aluminium, stainless steel, perspex, laminated wood, 5 heavy duty electric motors. Colour: blue, orange, green, yellow.

422.5 x 544.5 x 600cm

1969-70

*Moving Sculpture*

Model and working drawing

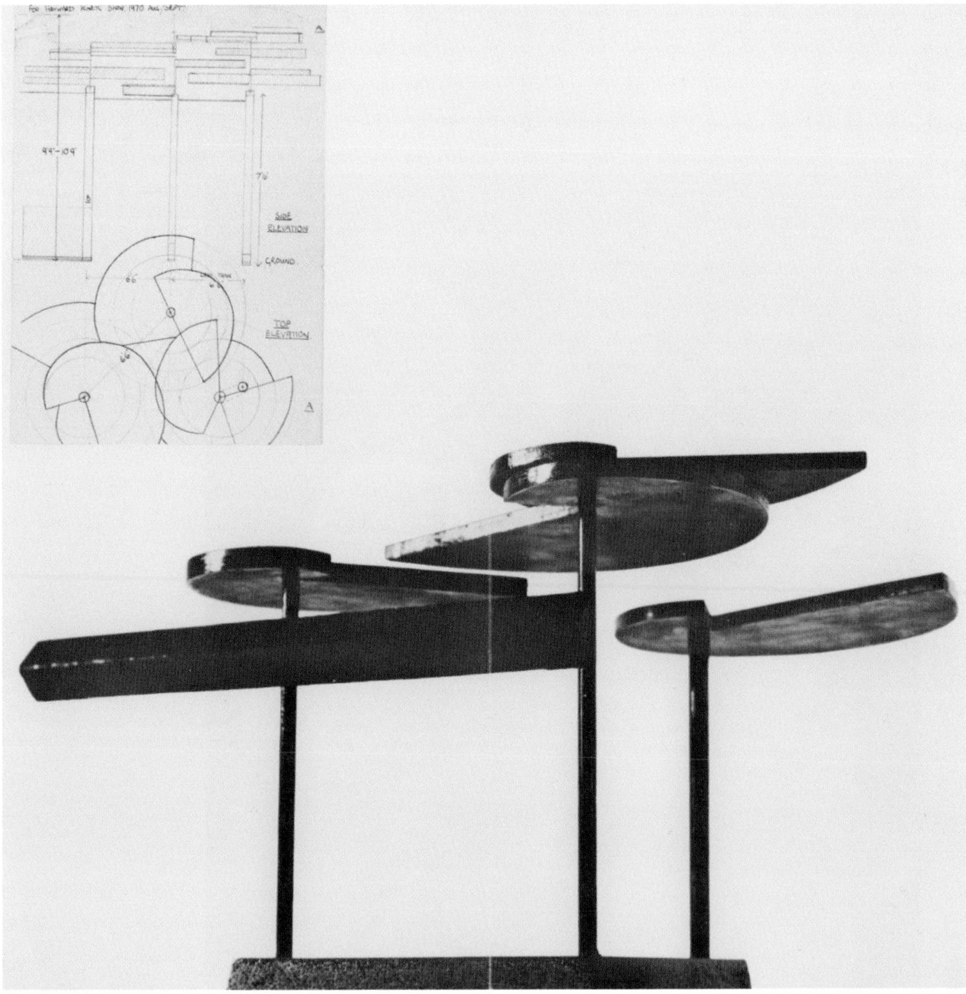

The three units begin with three coloured poles: red, blue and yellow. Each pole supports a reflector of matching colour. Each reflector consists of an horizontal oval drum-like unit with one segment removed; the segment of space is lined on one side with a mirror surface and on the other with coloured Perspex. Mounted at staggered heights and driven at different speeds by their motors, the ovoid reflectors rotate, coming together and going their separate

1969

*Programmed Shape Development*

Aluminium, polish, electric motors.

76 x 84 x 46cm

Statically developed shapes generate new classes of shapes and forms in movement. The aluminium shapes were thought of as fragments of the space they inhabited.

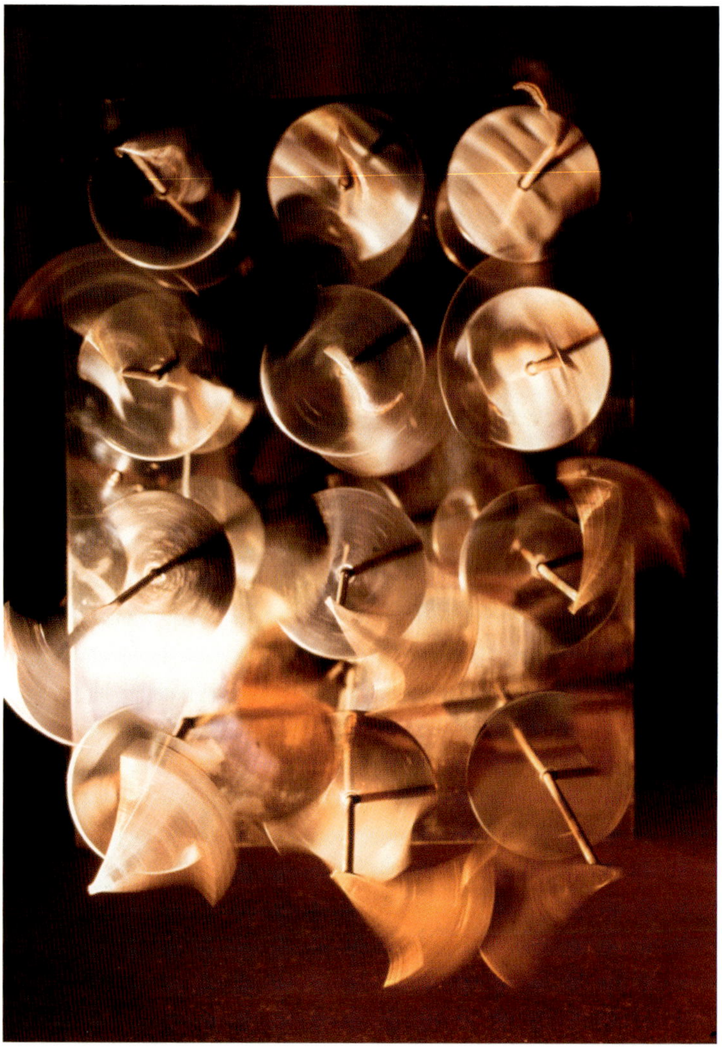

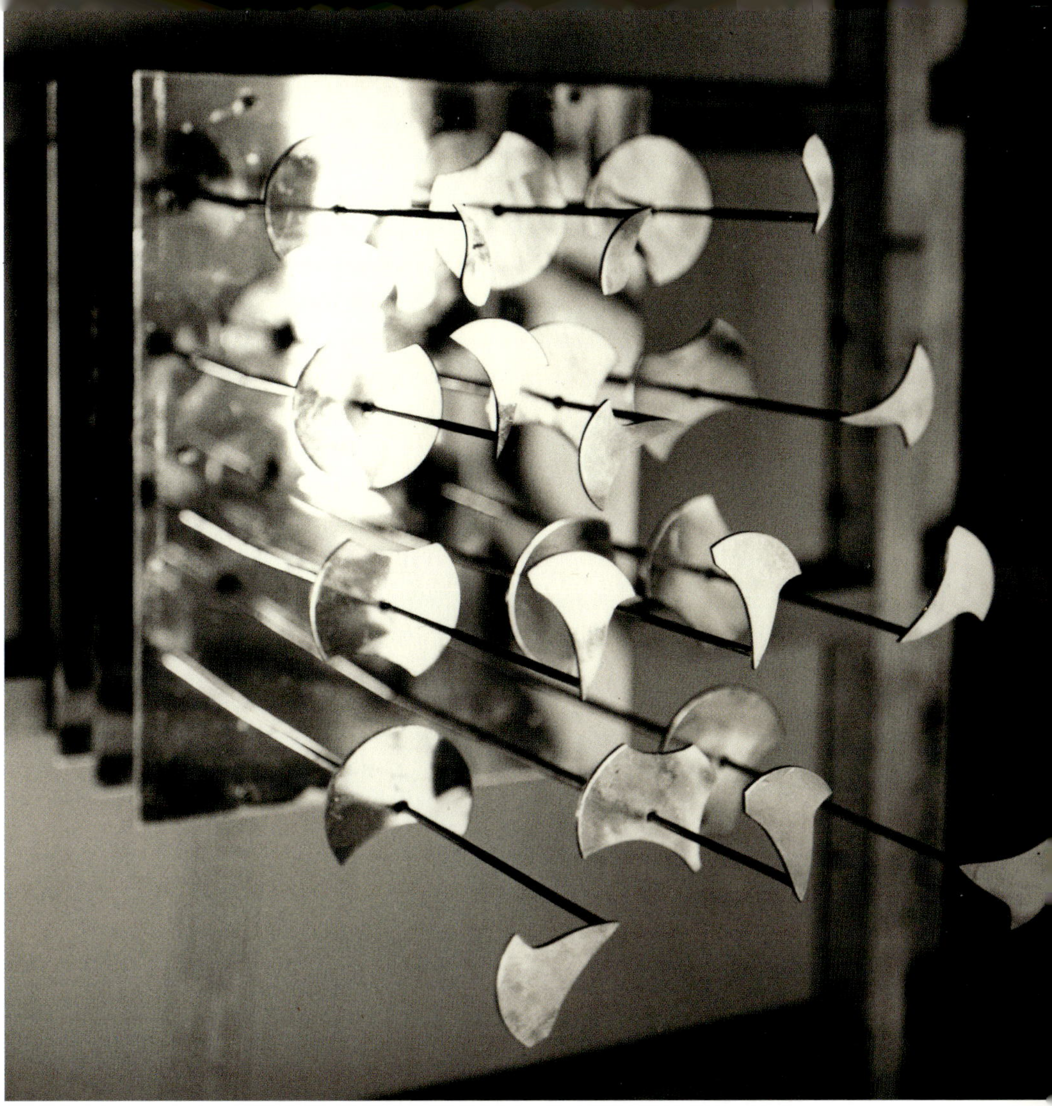

ways. All they reflect is daylight, but the stainless steel is so polished that the reflectors respond immediately to London's changing sky. One minute they scoop up and send out dazzling shafts of tinted sunlight that slice into their setting. Then they pass on a soft tinted light that pools on the ground and models with shadows. As you walk beneath the poles colours overlap and interfere. Martin had achieved similar effects with electric lights in his Chelsea pavilion piece (as explained in chapter 3) but now the light, shadows and movement are natural and random, and the open-air setting is limitless. The English climate has traditionally been considered unsympathetic to sculpture, offering none of the crisp silhouettes and strong shadows cast by Southern Mediterranean skies. On the Hayward's terraces Martin's sculpture was at home against the grey amorphous skies and puddles of the Thames that Turner and a nation of watercolourists knew how to use.

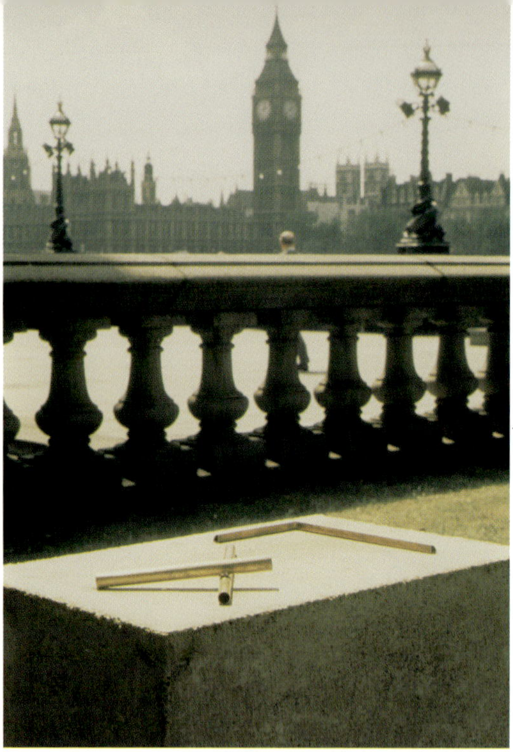

1977
*2 piece - time piece*
Brass, cement and the Big Ben
Exhibited St Martin's 125th anniversary exhibition, South Bank, London, july 1977

In the catalogue to the Hayward Gallery exhibition Theo Crosby described Kinetic Art as 'a world movement' rooted in Cubism, the Bauhaus and the Italian Futurist Movement that was now 'linked to almost every kind of contemporary art activity, from constructions to happenings'. He admitted

**Their art could not be photographed meaningfully for illustration in catalogues, readily bought and sold by dealers as self-sufficient commodities**

that, as a selector, he had concentrated on the theme of mechanical movement and had invited 'the heroic figures of the post-war resurgence of kinetic art...to provide a basis for comparison with the work of the new generation'. The catalogue quoted Martin in equally optimistic mood: 'I am moving into new areas of investigation which need a fresh vocabulary, not only to escape the tired clichés of Neo-Dada, and the atmosphere of apathy and acceptance or confusion which surrounds art today, but more important, because I feel that movement is the only direction in which further positive progress can be made'.

Jonathan Benthall ended his introductory essay in the catalogue on an assertive and ambitious note. He predicted: 'Kinetic art to date will be seen by artists of the 1970s as a powerful springboard' fuelled by its 'propulsive force' and that 'such distractions as the dead-end kid of Conceptual Art can be left behind to splash and piddle in a stagnant art-world'. However, by the 1980s as a major movement in Britain Kinetic Art was running out of steam. With hindsight, one could argue that the society that sustained it had changed. The optimism had gone with the passing of the living science-fiction age that had seen six manned landings on the moon between 1969 and 1972, the age of Arthur C. Clark and Stanley Kubrick's *2001*, when every schoolboy's comic was filled with artists' impressions of life on Mars. These were the promises that the Cold War could not keep.

Today, Kinetic Art has almost disappeared from the story of British sculpture, both as a chapter in its history and as an option for working artists today. As generators of art, what Martin's younger generation of

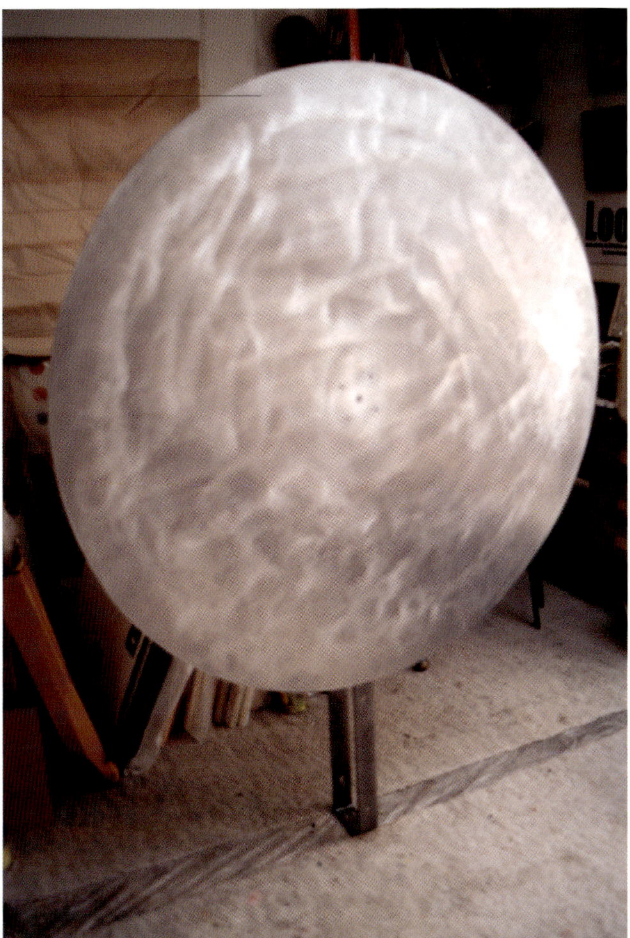

2000
*Universalis*
Steel, electric motor.
183 x 152.5 cm

British Kineticists produced only really existed as installations, as events in time and space. Their art could not be photographed meaningfully for illustration in catalogues, readily bought and sold by dealers as self-sufficient commodities, or simply lent between museums for exhibitions. Theirs is an ephemeral medium, a performance art without people, one that is especially allusive and elusive when striking up its own relationship with each viewer. It can also be technically challenging, and expensive, for an artist to make, install, operate and maintain. Indeed, unlike other art media, Kinetic Art can, quite simply and literally, break down. Works can also seem 'dated' and clumsy due to technological advances, particularly with the advent of personal computers. Unfortunately, Kinetic sculptures such as mobiles also proved easy to copy for sale in the domestic furnishings sections of department stores. Countless imitations made their way into the Modernist home and into the smart office in need of 'executive toys'. Consequently, the Kinetic medium has proved less sustainable, less able to make the transition from positive art criticism to a place in museums and art history.

Thirty years on from its survey exhibition of 1970, in 2000 the Hayward Gallery revisited Kinetic Art with *Force Fields: Phases of the Kinetic*. The equally ambitious show reminded the public that creators of Kinetic Art do not simply make art that moves, but are united in their 'cosmic speculation', in their awareness of Space, Time and the relationship between the individual mind and its perception of the universe, a dynamic that can be expressed through the artistic language of movement. The exhibition's curator, Guy Brett, presented Kinetic Art as a global movement, most active between 1920 and the 1970s. His selection included 25 artists from Europe, seven from the U.S.A., five from South America and individual artists from Japan, China, the Philippines, and New Zealand. However, thirty years on only one British artist was included, John Latham (1921-2007) who showed two 'one-second drawings' from 1970 and 1975, the fruits of one-second bursts of paint from a spray gun onto off-cuts of wood. One might have thought that Kinetic Art had made no impact in Britain.

In October 2006 Britain's first museum devoted to this art form, the Kinetica Museum, opened in London's Old Spitalfields Market with a show of thirty interactive computer-controlled robotic sculptures 'creating an anarchic technological spectacle'. Robotics and computers certainly open up new possibilities for Kinetic Art in the 21st century but they are only the means, the tools, not the principles that make Kineticism an essential artistic language of movement. The enduring influence of Kinetic Art, since it flourished in London in the 1960s and early 1970s, goes far beyond the characteristic machine-generated spectacle. The global movement unlocked the potential of the artist, beyond being a painter or sculptor, to become a creative force free to work simultaneously across all media. In addressing the fundamental issue of the relationship between Space and Time through movement, Kinetic Art helped to raise artists' ambitions beyond Formalism and Pop Art and encouraged them to think about the way we think. Barry Martin's metal machines and the exploration of other media in his subsequent career can be seen as a campaign of research into this question.



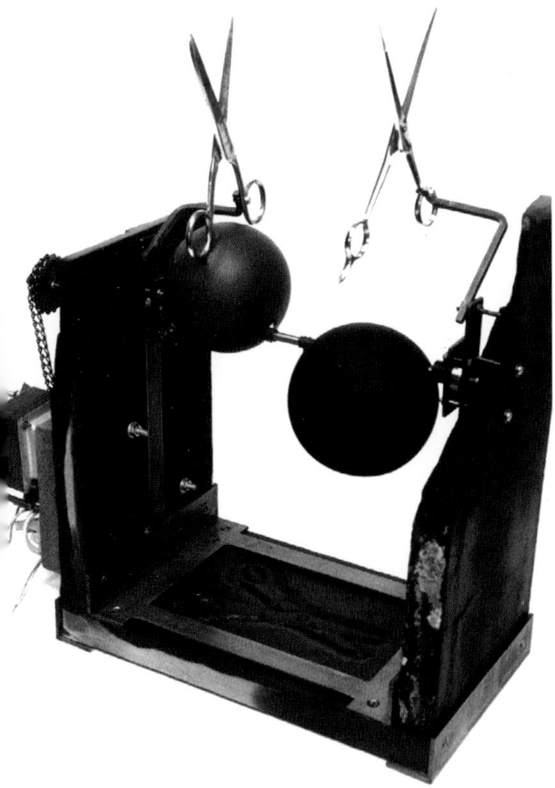

1999

*Babel*

Steel, slate, electric motor, scissors.

92 x 53.5 x 61cm

This work, like several others, is inspired by movement contained in game-play.

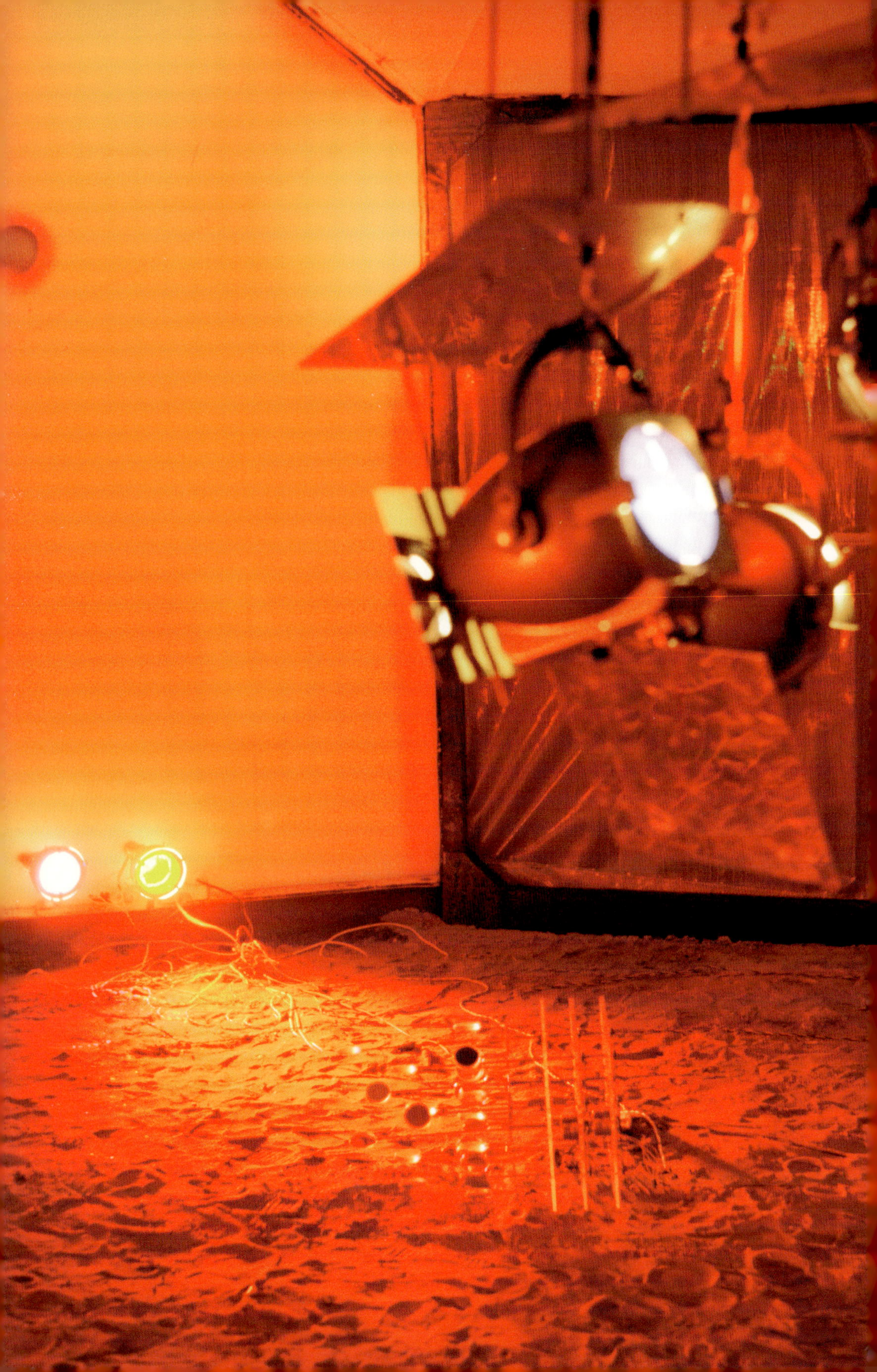

# 3 Light Sculptures





Spectacular light shows became a familiar feature of rock concerts in the early 1970s, particularly for Progressive rock bands with a love of theatre, most notably *Pink Floyd* and the Science Fantasy cosmos of *Hawkwind*. Since the psychedelic 'Sixties, thanks partly to Andy Warhol's *Velvet Underground*, the use of images, coloured oils mixing on sliding filters and stroboscopic effects through dry ice had extended the art of projection at concerts to simulate and enhance the effects of hallucinatory drugs. With the availability of laser technology the void above the audience's head, in concerts and discotheques, could also be filled with light, as a plastic medium.

1967
Pavilions in the Park, interior view with Central *Hanging Light Piece* and *K. N. 38* (bottom-center)
Chelsea

In recognising the potential of electric light as sculpture, independent of any projection surface, Barry Martin opened up new possibilities in Britain. As an ephemeral medium, light sculptures cannot be owned or illustrated and so have been forgotten by all except those who were there, who experienced them when they were new. Some of the earliest experiments in 'lumino-kinetics' were conducted at the Bauhaus between 1921 and 1923, using colour organs and projection techniques. A classic example in the history of Kinetic Art is the film produced by Moholy-Nagy using his *Light Prop for an Electric Stage*, also known as the *Light Space Modulator* (1928-30, Busch-Reisinger Museum of Harvard University, U.S.A.), a device made by a Berlin architect sponsored by Germany's largest electrical supplier, AEG. Grander historic precedents include the architectural use of military search lights as mass spectacle for Nazi rallies, as in *Cathedral of Ice*, a vertical luminescent construction devised by Albert Speer in 1934, comprising 130 searchlights set in a square reaching 20,000 feet into the sky and ensnaring the occasional passing cloud.

**Today, to appreciate the sense of participating in it in three dimensions, one has to engage the imagination**

The use of coloured fluorescent lamps by Dan Flavin (1933-96) from 1961 to make Minimalist sculptures that glow may seem related but these are fixed, linear works defined by their commercialy available components. The similarity to Martin's work lies in the clouds. When Dan Flavin was twenty he studied at the U.S. Airforce's meteorological training school in Ilinois. Martin also discovered clouds, but from the inside, when he qualified as a glider pilot as a teenager. Both artists experienced space as light, rather than as something revealed by light. Both learnt first-hand how light is the most unstable, impermanent medium, the one that only exists in time that has its own energy source, defies gravity and controls everything we see.

The first light sculpture produced by Martin, *Central Hanging Light Piece* (1967) has been partially recorded on a film, now in the Tate Archives. This was his first environmental installation to use light as the primary agent. Today, to appreciate the sense of participating in it in three dimensions, one has to engage the imagination. The first of Martin's series of light machines formed an installation in Chelsea in the summer of 1968. Walking along Oakley Street, where the terraced environs of the King's Road open up before the Thames at Albert Bridge, you came to a gap, one of London's many derelict bomb sites that still remained from the Second World War. Passing through a gate, you found three domes, each about 25 feet high, like giant mushrooms or igloos, ready for life on the moon.

'Pavilions in the Park' was an independent initiative by the exhibition curator Su Braden with architects Keith Critchlow and Keith Albarn to find unusual sites in London where artists, musicians and poets could present new work within temporary structures. Martin's pavilion



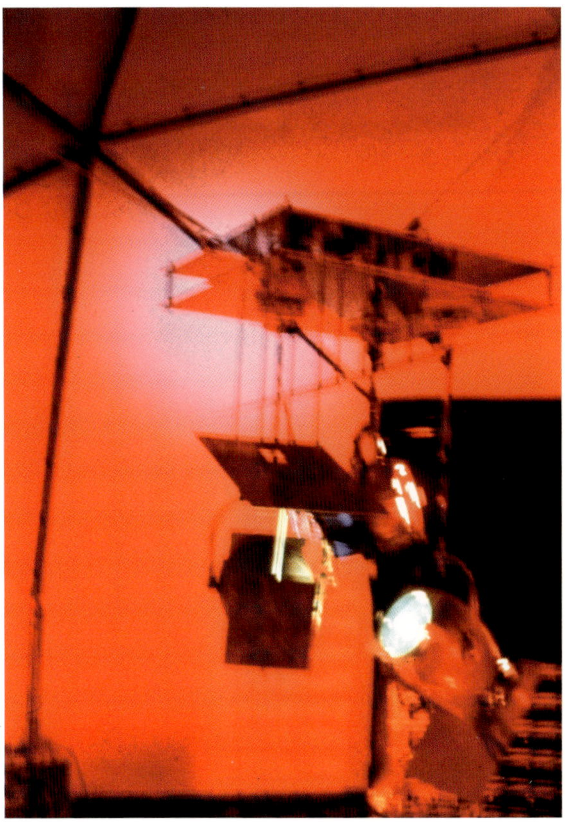

1967
*Pavillions in the Park: Interior views with Moving Light Sculpture, Chelsea*

in Chelsea was the first to open. Contrary to popular notions of 'Swinging Sixties London' as a place of freedom to experiment, Martin recalls that there were no enterprising collectors such as Maurice Saatchi and dealers like Jay Jopling who kick-started the Young British Artists movement in the 1990s. The contemporary art trade in Cork Street was, in Martin's opinion, conservative. 'Major dealers like Marlborough Fine Art only wanted things they could sell, paintings, prints, drawings and sculptures, not experimental installations'. The 'Pavilions' scheme was aimed at breaking down 'the stranglehold that both the Bond and Cork Street galleries had over the type of art being shown'. Art school degree shows still followed the national curriculum that required traditional figurative drawing, painting and sculpture. He recalls: 'until 1965/6 all art schools were still under the auspices of the old National Design Diploma scheme. Only post-graduate courses, like at the Slade and the Royal College, encouraged experiment'. Beyond the Institute of Contemporary Arts, few opportunities could be found to show challenging new work.



Conceived in the tradition of Buckminster Fuller's Dymaxion House project (1927), Keith Critchlow's Chelsea pavilion, the 'Octahedron House', was in fact a fibreglass and reinforced card prototype solution to the need for temporary housing in the Middle East. Martin had it customised. Stepping inside you first find the door is covered with shiny black PVC, in contrast to the creamy white dome. The floor is a sea of yellow sand combed with footprints. Colour fills the space, pouring forth from a brace of three powerful (2,000 watt) theatre floodlights, red, blue and green, each driven by its own motor and fitted with reflective back-planes. Tail units on each lamp, specially devised by Martin, continually alter the colour segments in a slow, panning, blending rhythm. They project across the room and into the dome, inviting the viewer to pass through the floating colours that form a cloud-like envelope in the centre.

As you step inside the light sculpture so your shadows change colour. You notice how projected coloured light behaves differently to colour pigment, as the primaries red and green, for example, produce yellow. The floor is raked by another set of lights set at ground-level to spread wave-like oscillations across the sand. During an hour-long programme the lamps are orchestrated to play their beams across the space, each altering in turn its speed, direction of throw and circle of inclination. When one light pauses its sweep another beam passes through it causing coloured shadows. The light beams make coloured spheres blossom in space that vary in shape, in chromatic intensity and hue, enticing the spectators to participate. Around the walls four metal machines, including *Tret*, catch the light, quietly making their own accompanying movements.

If it all sounds like a scene from Michelangelo Antonioni's *Blow Up* (1966) that is because it nearly was, or at least, a sequel. Martin recalls how the actor Terence Stamp loved the show, introduced himself and returned with Antonioni. The film director, actor and artist all stood there in the Pavilion 'with the lights coming up our legs, for about an hour, wondering what to do next'. Another admirer, the sculptor Bernard Meadows, came to the Pavilion to purchase one of Martin's works on behalf of the Arts Council, and regretted that he could not make the most 'adventurous' acquisition, of the light-piece itself, and so settled for part of the support act, *Tret.*

## As you step inside the light sculpture so your shadows change colour

*Inter* (1968) was chosen by the writer Edward Lucie-Smith for inclusion in the exhibition 'Poet's Choice' at the AIA Gallery off Piccadilly in 1968, along with other works by Martin. The selection committee also included the poets Adrian Henri, Stephen Spender and Roy Fuller. *Inter* comprised a pair of identical machines, suspended six feet three inches above the ground, hanging parallel, and the space ('inter') between them. Each one sandwiched between two mirror-finished aluminium sheets (measuring four feet six inches square) a rotating leather belt to which were affixed three back reflector lights. The ensemble seemed to float just above and below eye level, hovering in its own radiance, the back-reflector lamps (each 240 watts) shining into the aluminium squares and onto the rear wall as they rotated around each square. One clock-wise, the other anti-clockwise, the sets of lamps rotated slowly and switched on and off. As with the Chelsea Pavilion installation of the previous year, *Inter* addressed the space between the light sources, but did so more emphatically by defining it with geometrical precision, as if in a laboratory experiment. Through light, reflections and contrapuntal movement the interval became the heart of the sculpture, as in the way the mind takes in the world through binocular vision and hearing. Inter invites appreciation of space as sculptural form, both when confined by an artist's setting and when occupied at large by the viewer. Inspired by vast belt-driven machinery that Martin had admired in the Science Museum, *Inter* was, quite literally, highly dangerous to make, operate and view.

Martin's installation at the AIA Gallery in 1968 inspired Edward Lucie-Smith to pen verse:

*On Light (for Barry Martin)*

*The voyager that*
*travels the furthest:*
*light, ambassador*
*of all that we find*
*most remote from us*
*(slowly pulsing, the*
*brightness of a star).*

*It is the nearest*
*we get to knowing*
*how the world moves, what*
*grips it, what forces*
*impel it towards*
*the last boundary*
*at the end of light.*

When *Inter* and other new works went on show in Glasgow, at the Compass Gallery in the summer of 1968 Edward Lucie-Smith had difficulty describing Martin, in his review for the *Glasgow Herald*, as 'a relatively unestablished and indeed unclassifiable, artist of this kind'.

The scale of Martin's work at this time was constrained by the size of his studio (a flat at 227 Cromwell Road, South Kensington), by the demands of teaching at Goldsmiths' College, and by his modest income. In 1969, however, a commission from a collector of Martin's work enabled him to light up a lighting shop in the New King's Road. The proprietor of 'Mr Resistor' gave him the materials and space he needed for a more permanent installation. Above a stairwell, eight coloured spotlights were assembled into two rotating units driven by five electric motors. In developing a programme that would alternate the inclination of lamps

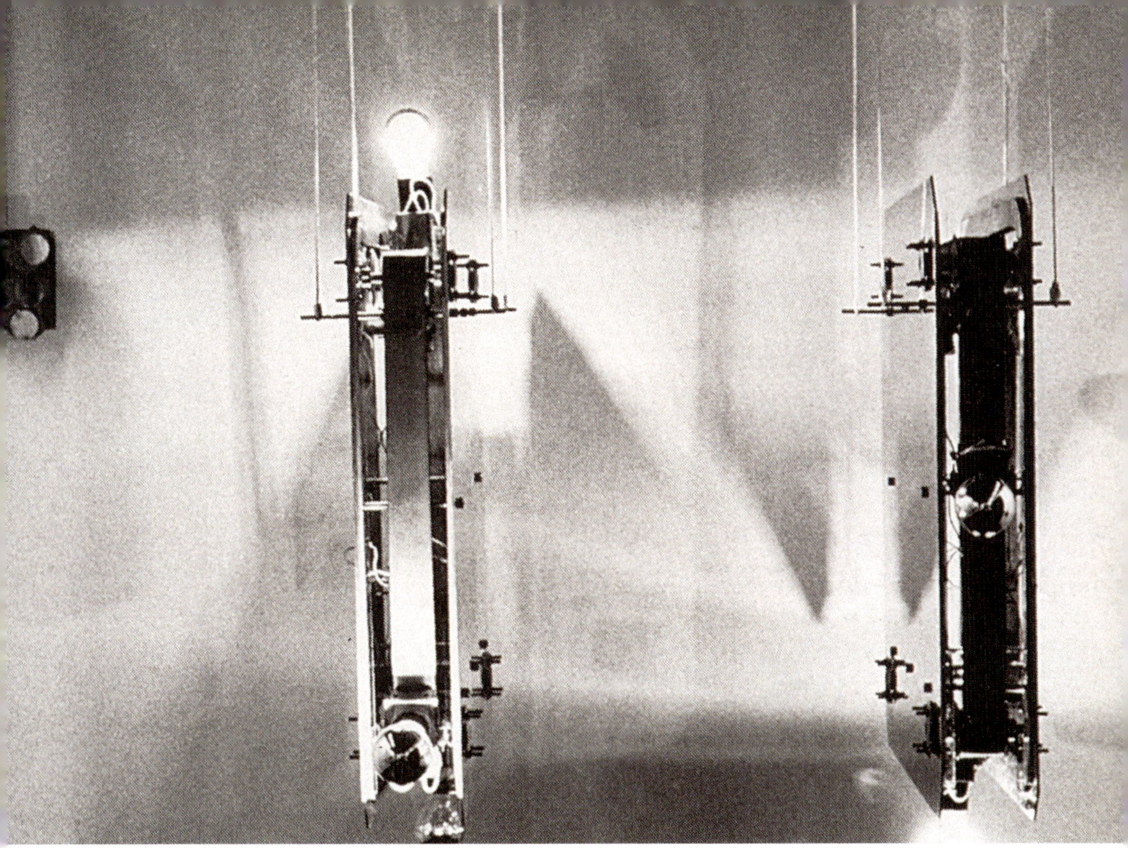

1968

*Inter* and *Nine Revolving Disks -Small (left)*

*Inter*

Aluminium, steel, leather,

2 electric motors, 6 back reflector

lights, programme.

Two 137 squares suspended 190.5cm above the ground. The leather belts slowly move the lights around the circumference of the aluminium. Planned pauses used.



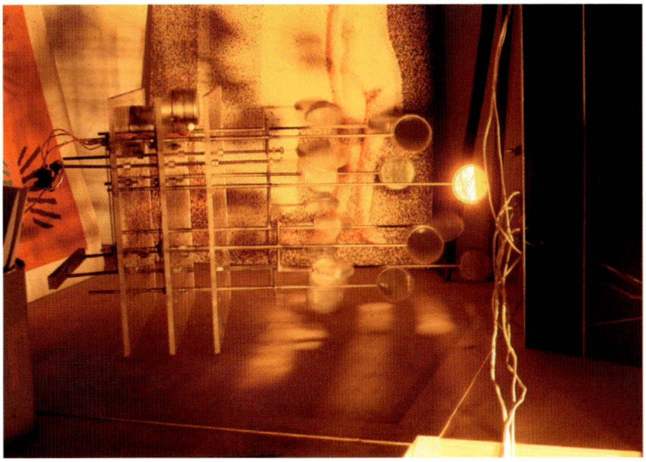

1968

*K.N.38.*

Perspex, Glass, Brass, Aluminium,

2 electric motors driving the front

and back mirrors independently.

Numerous coloured spot lights.

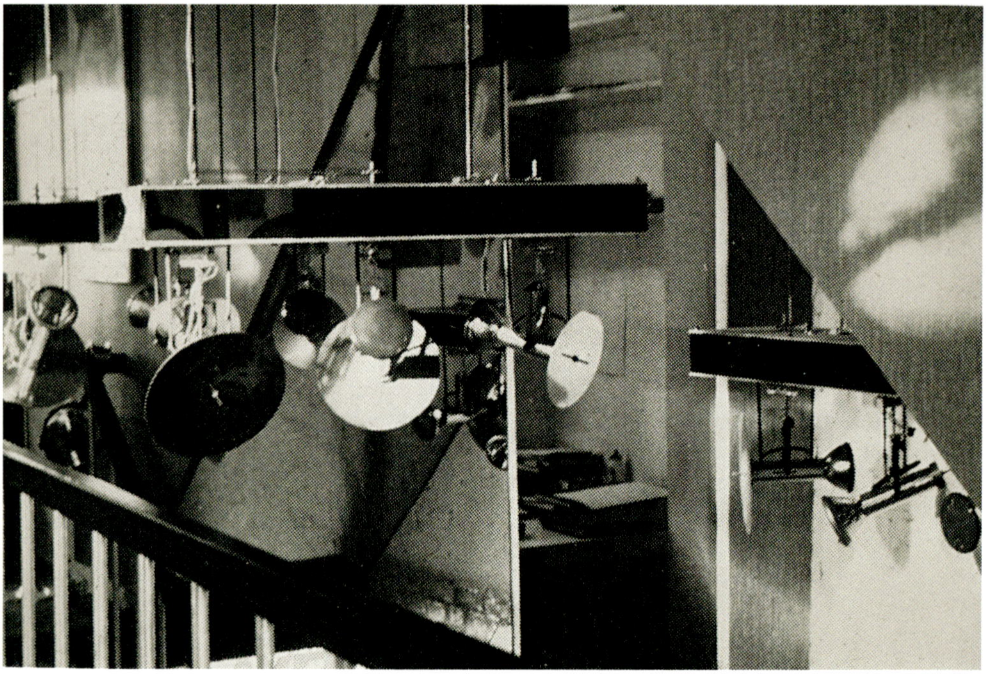

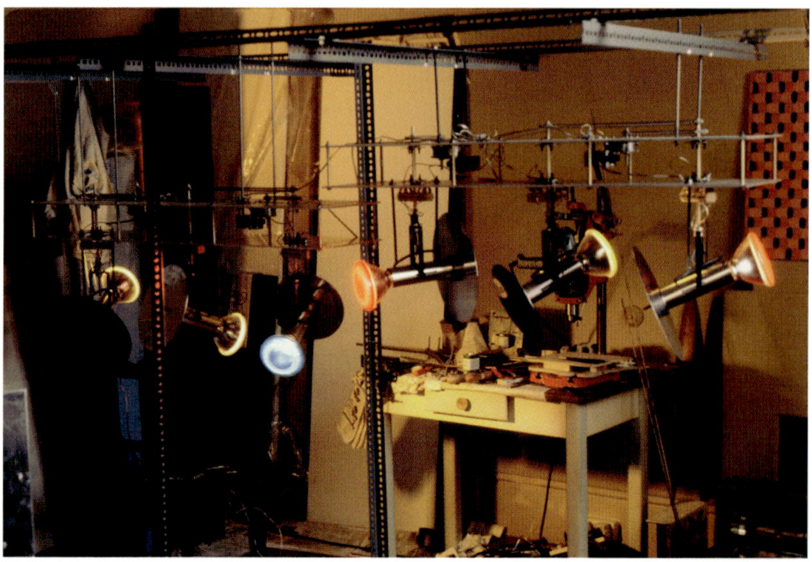

1969
*Installation for 'Mr Resistor'*
A new lighting shop, King's Road, Chelsea

Aluminium, Perspex, brass, 6 par. 38 coloured spot lights, 5 electric motors. The lights could rotate, alter their direction and angle of throw. Speed was variable. The two units were hung in a line over the stairwell.

1968-9
Studio Workshop Bench
Installation for '*Mr Resistor*'
under construction
227 Cromwell Road,
London SW7

Martin made a technological breakthrough. With the support of his patron, a prototype was developed, *the Patented Light Machine* (1969, Science Museum, London).

Martin's invention consists of three coloured lamps supported on interlocking tubular axles rotating in different directions, as inner and outer tubes, the outer one having a ring and rod affixed to a lamp (a precise specification is given in the patent documentation). The machine gave unprecedented sensitivity and flexibility to the operator in directing coloured light. From the shop in Chelsea the artist, models and drawings swiftly travelled to Glasgow, to the factory of Andrew Chalmer, and thence to Her Majesty's Patent Office. It was his first taste of the high life: flying monthly first-class to Scotland for business lunches, a brief meeting with the Scottish boffins and then straight back to London, the worse for champagne. But for all the patron's investments, the *Patented Light Machine* made no one's fortune and Martin remained a struggling artist. To make ends meet, he came closest to a commercial application of his light inventions by hiring out his Chelsea Pavilion piece to provide light shows at private parties in Chelsea, Mayfair and Belgravia between 1968 and 1970. The idea caught on and the enterprise took off, becoming part of a well-known mobile discotheque for London's jeunesse doré, only without Martin. To this day he remains convinced that the world is the better for his disco light show, but laments ' By now I should have a fleet of Rolls-Royces and a castle in every civilised country'.

Fortunately he had other irons in the fire. In 1970 the Institute of Contemporary Arts commissioned Martin to create an installation for their foyer, as the entrance to an exhibition. Under the chairmanship of Roland Penrose the ICA conceived its *Electric Theatre* show of 1971, sub-titled '25 artists working with lights, sound and space', as a response to the Hayward's *Kinetic Art: International Survey* of 1970. The ICA's scientific adviser introduced Martin to the new technology of the photo-electric beam. The untitled installation consisted of an iron rod suspended horizontally above head height over the entrance stairs. Two electric motors controlled the rod's elevation and rotation. Nine theatre lights, both spots and floods, of different colours and strength, were positioned to illuminate the rod. As visitors passed beneath the moving rod they broke the two photo-electric beams and activated the motors and the lights. The rod rotated and descended, casting coloured shadows in response to the viewer's own actions. As an interactive sculpture made of moving light, the work existed only in each visitor's actions and reactions at a moment in time. There were also practical reasons why light sculptures were short lived. Martin is convinced that today such an installation would be prohibited by the Health and Safety Executive.





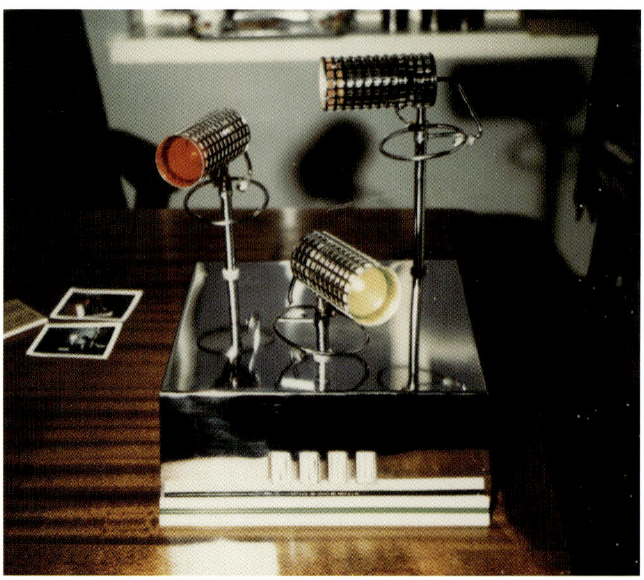

1969

*A Patented Light Machine*

Steel, 7 electric motors, light, eletricity, coloured light filters

20 x 25cm.

As an interactive sculpture made of moving light, the work existed only in each visitor's actions and reactions at a moment in time

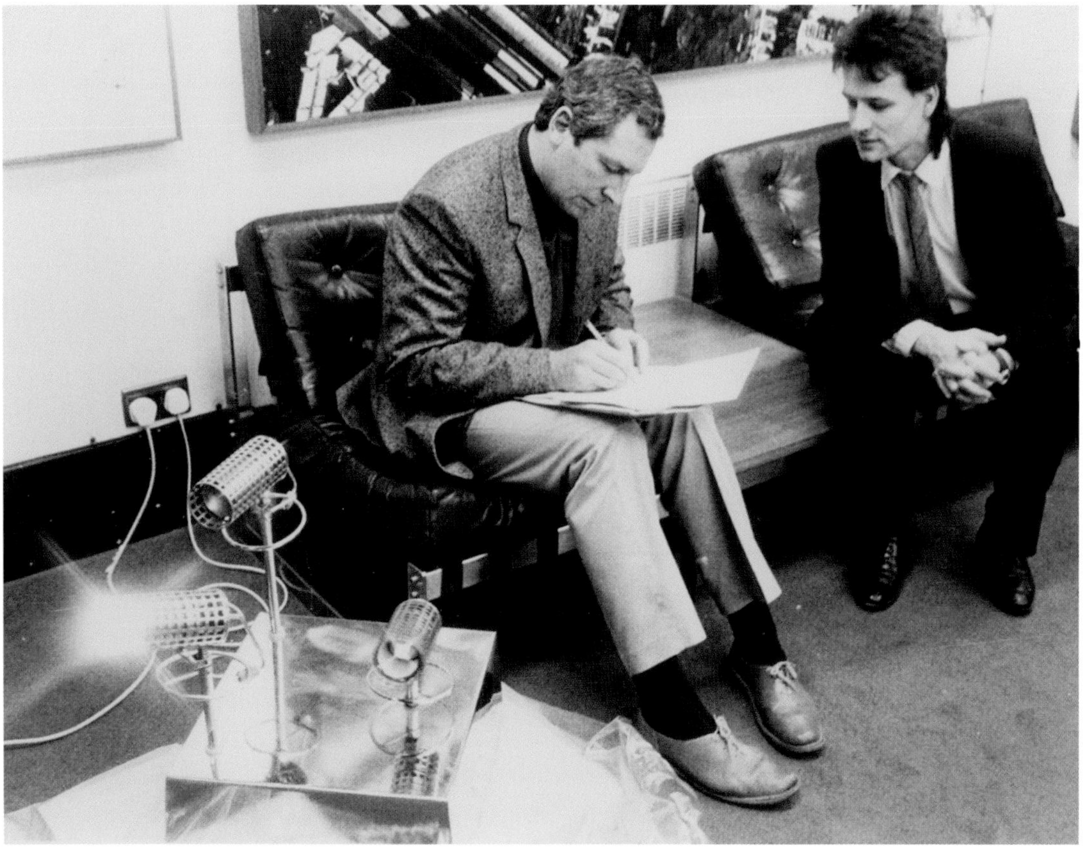

1969

The artist (left), signing the Science Museum's acquisition form with the museum 's lighting collection curator. The light machine in working mode is bottom left

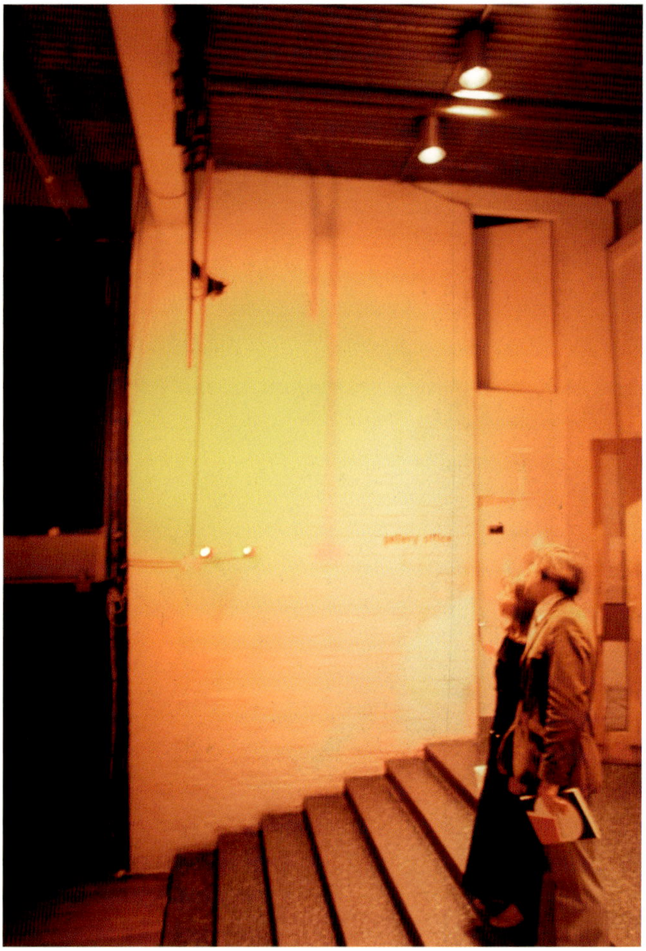

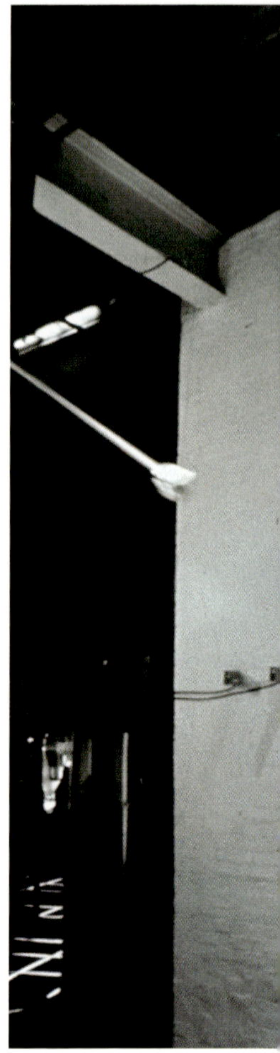

1971

Installation for '*Electric Theatre*'

exhibition, ICA, Nash House, London, entrance stairway

Photo-electric beams, 9 projectings coloured spot and flood lights, 500-2K watts, electromagnetic actuator, electric motor, steel, stepped moter and programmer. The postion of the rod triggered two electro-photo beams that switched on or off the different individual coloured light.

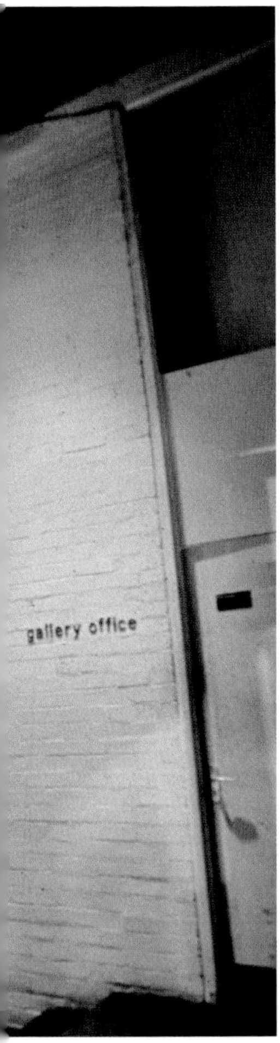
gallery office
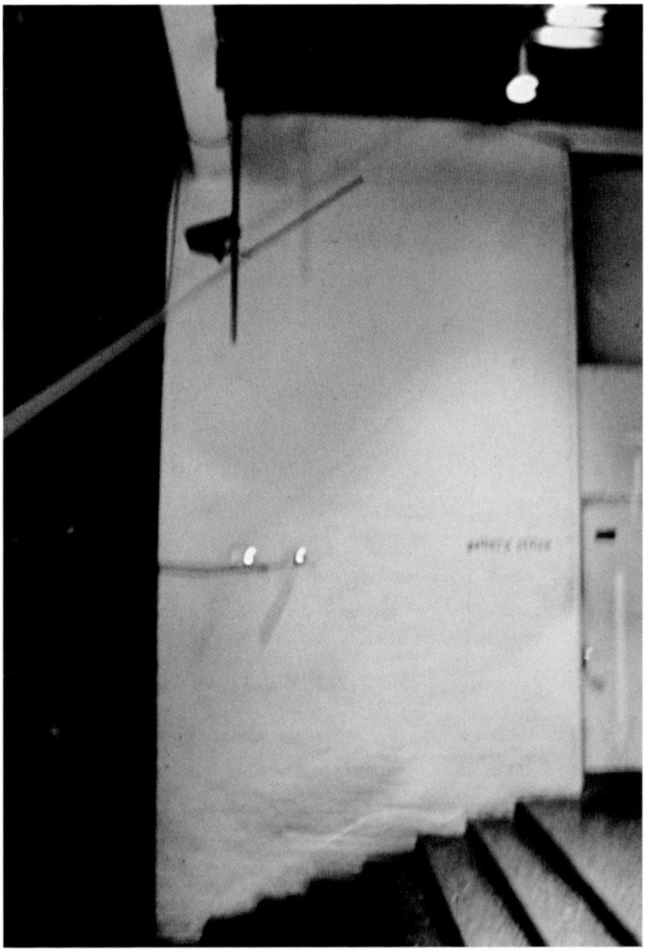

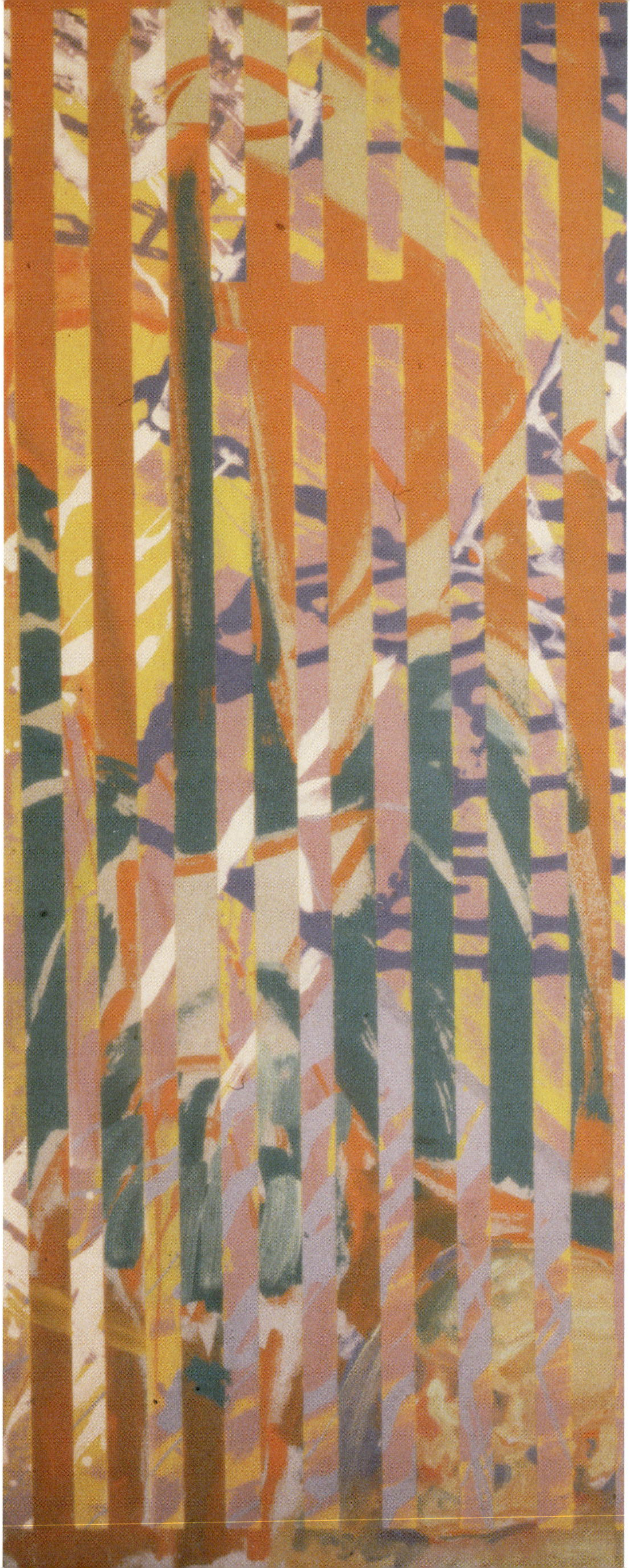

*Abstract expressionism:*

# 4 A crisis in colour



Throughout his career Martin has never seen himself as a member of an artists' group or colony, despite the successful attempts by exhibition curators to include his work in thematic shows. In 1982 his individualism came home to him when he participated in an intense two-week creative gathering of artists. The Triangle Workshop was held at Mashomack, Pine Plains, about 100 miles north of New York City, in a group of barns and farm sheds belonging to Robert Loder, a friend of Anthony Caro. It was the artists' equivalent of an academic conference. The name of the workshop came from the confluence of artists from England, Canada and the U.S.A. But it also reflected three generations of painters, from Abstract Expressionists to the Colour Field Painters.

1974

*Whole with Machine Intrusions*

Acrylic on canvas

183 x 77 cm

Martin discussed his work with visiting critics and painters whom Caro had invited, including Clement Greenberg, Larry Poons, Kenneth Noland, Helen Frankenthaler, Darby Bannard and Jules Olitski. Martin recalls: 'the freedom of exchange of ideas about critical value, of what is excellence, or how can we achieve it, or how we can compare each others' notion of excellence was extremely constructive'. He also recalls with pleasure drinking late into the night and deep into the whisky bottle on more than one occasion with Greenberg, and comments he made on artists that cannot go into print.



With the hindsight of history, we may assume there to have been a more pressing motive for the gathering. Months earlier, in March 1981, Greenberg had participated in a conference of art historians in Vancouver. The most influential art critic of post-war America, Greenberg had come under regular attack in the 1970s as Formalism came to seem as elitist as traditional connoisseurship to those seeking socio-political content in art and to advocates of Conceptual Art. The aesthetic autonomy of the art object and authority of the critic as man of taste seemed untenable to art historians who, in the 1970s, embraced feminism and economic determinism. To some Marxist and feminist art historians Abstract Expressionism and the language of its champions smacked of macho American cultural imperialism. At the conference at the University of British Columbia, Vancouver, Greenberg met his match in Professor T. J. Clark. The papers and discussion were published, verbatim, as *Modernism and Modernity* in 1983 (a seminal work, republished 2004). Clark seems to end Greenberg's reign with the polite observation 'you unfortunately have become- I really do say this with respect...a spokesman for a kind of devastating artistic self-satisfaction and laziness...your vision- the crisis- the extremity of the situation of art in our time is presented now in such a stripped-down form that it gives license to those who say there is no problem, it's the aesthetic realm, let's get on with the job, don't talk, painter paint- all the clichés, and this is a danger'.

This crisis in Modernism must have been an undercurrent at the Triangle Workshop in 1982 but Martin does not recall any overt reference to the Vancouver conference. Perhaps Greenberg, as a wounded old lion, found reassurance among productive painters and their own debates about making paintings work.

In retrospect, Martin feels that the meeting of 'second generation' New York Abstract Expressionists with their 'first generation' British counterparts that summer was not as fruitful as others have since maintained. He sensed that the younger Americans had allowed some of the sublime depths of meaning, the 'sense of authenticity' to drain out of Abstract Expressionism as they simplified abstract painting to something almost formulaic, even decorative, without real identity. He feared that the British artists were too keen to emulate the younger Americans in approach.

Another debate that Martin recalls at the Workshop was around the use, initially by Larry Poons, of 'cropping', of reducing all-over Colour Field paintings after they had dried to improve their general effect. One evening it was Martin's turn to present slides of his own new work, made in England, to lead the discussion. His paintings in oil, inspired in part by his studies of Egyptology in the British Museum, would not submit to the new love of 'cropping'. To Martin, this seemed a pointless fashion, one that diminished the integrity of the creative process as one of problem-solving and hence of the *finished* painting. Listening to the debate, he knew he had moved on from Formalism as an end in itself, whereas the North Americans were, to him, going nowhere. Subject matter mattered to Martin, not in the sense of narrative content (as in figurative painting) but as the issue of the perception by the individual of the external world, the big issue that he knows for him is best thought-through in paint on canvas. This Romantic quest, this spirit of intellectual exploration, is something he found absent among artists he saw painting almost automatically, mindlessly, knowing they could crop it down later into something visually satisfying. Martin blames big international art dealers for encouraging painters to work this

He feared that the British artists were too keen to emulate the younger Americans in approach

way, to meet demand with supply, to paint almost literally 'by the yard' and so be over-productive. It is an issue he sees as very much alive in London, here in the 21st century.

One reason for Martin's frustration with the second generation of New York Abstract Expressionist painters lay in the fact that he felt he had already 'been there', he had explored to his own satisfaction the qualities of painting 'all over' the canvas, and of building up the paint layers until the raised surfaces could accept incised, directional marks. For once, he felt sure, London was ahead of New York ('it was like taking coals to Newcastle') yet there seemed to be an expectation at the Triangle Workshop that the

British would now adopt the American mannerism. Martin had first met Greenberg in London in 1976, when he came to a collector's house in Clapham to see, hung in a former coach house, some paintings that Martin made the year before. Greenberg's observations are recorded in a letter he wrote to Martin, now in the Tate Archives (as quoted in the chapter by Adrian Glew). The works were from two series of new paintings that Martin had shown at the Hoya Gallery in London in 1975, paintings so big and powerful that they seemed to fill the space with sunshine.

The *Agapes* series (now divided between private collections in Los Angeles and Berkshire) consists of three bright yellow paintings, each ten feet tall by seven feet wide. The paint is applied in thick, encrusted layers forming cracked, blistered ridges of parallel lines stretching diagonally; visual support is given by triangular columns in the same paint at the base of each canvas; counterpoints come from blue strips inserted at the corners. This was Martin's rich blast of a reply to the American Colour Field painters, the kind of blinding sunlight that J. M. W. Turner used to paint in order to paint his rivals into the shadows. The series title is taken not from the wide-eyed expression of wondering expectation, but rather from the name for a 'love-feast' held by the early Christians in connection with the Lord's Supper (as defined in the *Oxford English Dictionary*). In the same exhibition, the *Rootaries* series presented a set of twelve small studies, each only 7 inches tall, that ran the full waveband from palest yellow to a deep, Burnt Sienna, orange. In scale, they resembled pages from some fragmented book of illuminations but in subject they sought to embody the raw energy of sunlight in the same way as their giant neighbours. Their title emphasised the artist's wish that they serve as a source of nourishment and as evidence of its paths, like the garden features of the same name.

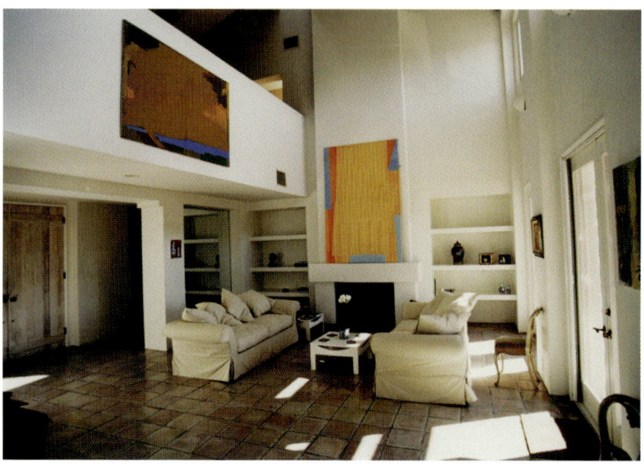

1975
*Agapes* (centre)
Installed in a Hollywood house,
Los Angeles, U.S.A.
(Private collection)

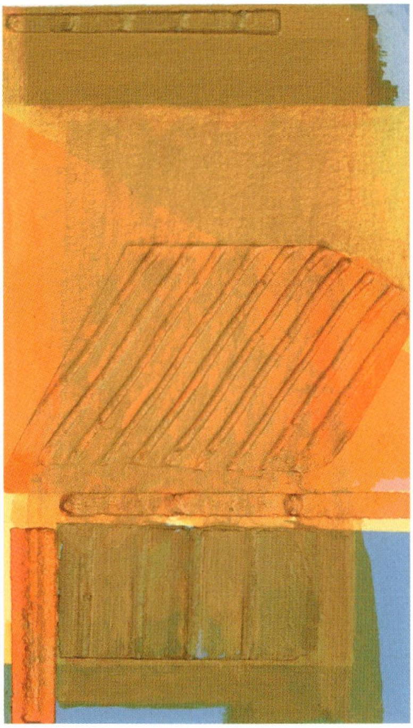

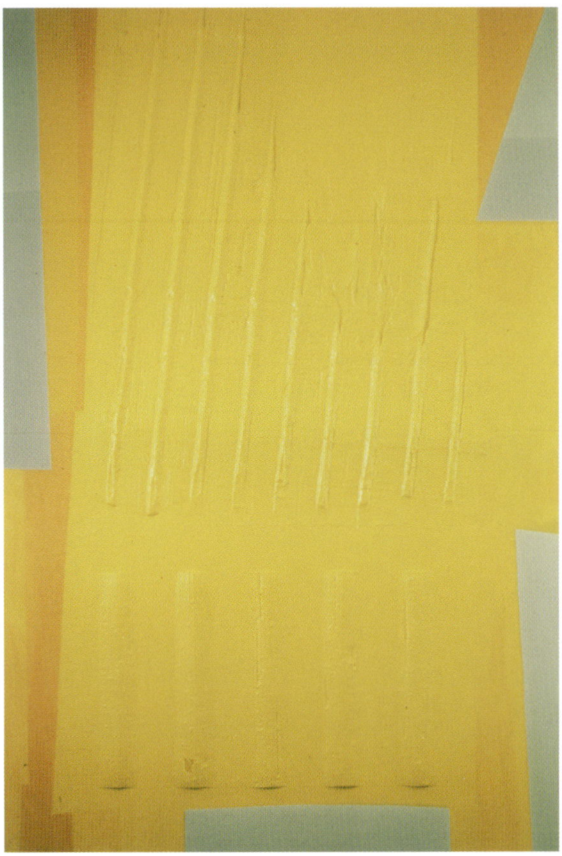



1975

*Rooteries* (Two from series)

Each Acrylic paint Aggregates

on paper

25 x 15 cm

1975

*Agapes*

Acrylic and Aggregates on canvas

305 x 190 cm

2 canvases on separate stretchers

joined together

In structure, like the earlier Kinetic sculptures and light pieces, the series of paintings worked as a single installation; they changed from one to the next as the eye and body shifted to apprehend them. As well as movement, memory was called into play, to recall before and after, in order to perceive the whole.

To understand Martin's ambitions as a painter and how the paintings relate to his Kinetic sculptures one needs to return to the early works. *Red and Blue Modulations* (1965) envelopes you the closer you stand to the canvas. As it stretches almost five feet tall and five feet wide, the golden ground fills you with warmth, the alternating colours seem so random but the mind races to construct patterns, groups, circles, arcs, even swells that are not there. In the same milli-second of encounter another side of the brain offers ideas, associations, to help prevent a sense of bewilderment: are they bees, swarming against sunlight, or people far below on some vast dance floor, couples circling, embracing, separating, or is this some biological structure, a diagram of genes, a molecular model? The guessing game goes on until a superior, management side of the brain calls a halt to the guesswork and decides what it is. Oh yes, modern art, very good, now move along please.





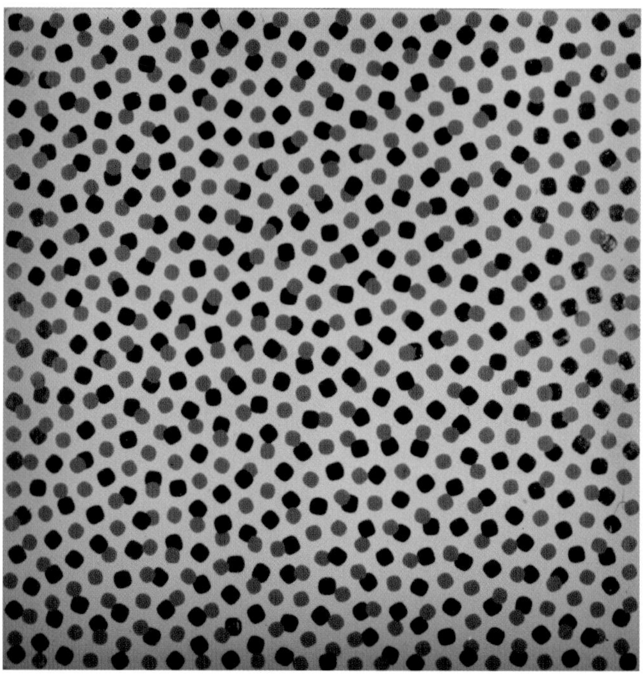

1965

*Red and Blue Modulations*

Household paint on board

150 x 150 cm

*1970*

*The Serpentine Series - 4 : 5 : 6*

each 41 x 36 cm

Silk screen

3 editions of 25 on Imperial hand pressed Arches paper.

(Government Art Collection)

The following statement by the artist was placed next to the prints when they were exhibited alongside his kinetic sculptures at the opening exhibition Serpentine Gallery 1970, London. This is a set of three silk-screen prints, each of which depicts in their lower portion an interior filled with shapes. The interiors are of the Serpentine Gallery, London, the Arts Council of England's building in Kensington Gardens. Each space in it was photographed before the building's completion as a gallery. Thus ladders, planks etc can be seen in each of the rooms.

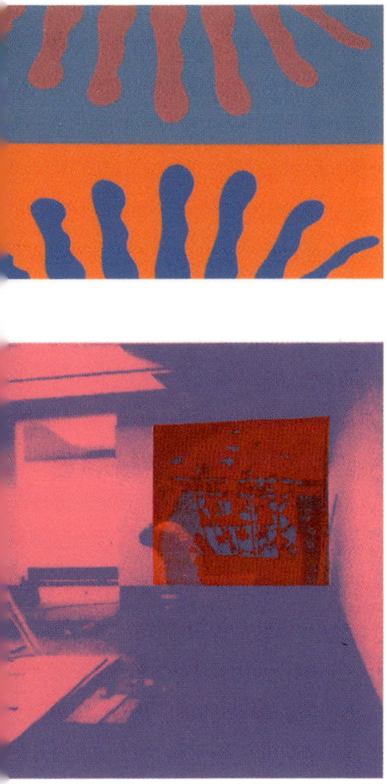

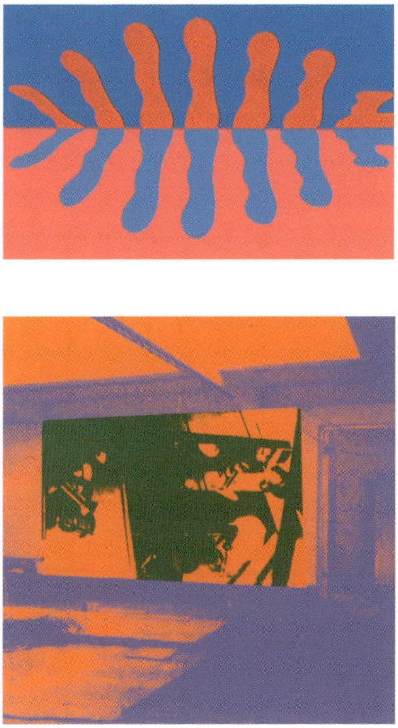

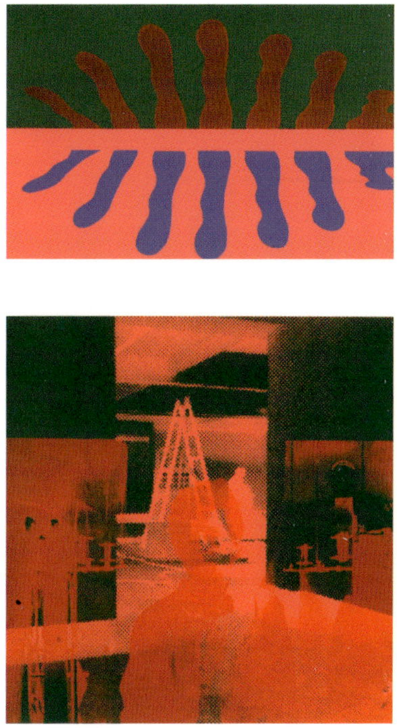

move along please.

As a painter, Martin has never identified himself with artistic camps or definitions. Movement, the interaction of Space and Time, is, simply, his central concern, not as a visual and artistic theme but as the fundamental intellectual issue that connects the self-conscious individual to the physical world beyond. Martin sets and tests his hypotheses not in words through logic and poetry, nor in numbers through calculations ending in balanced equations. He questions and reasons in paint, light, materials and

**His paintings challenge the relationship between the eye and the mind**

colour.

The kinship between his paintings and those by artists seeking to create optical illusions lies in the required movement not of the spectator but,

He leads us into the unknown world we inhabit in that constant succession of ideas before we interpret them

at the subtlest level, of their eyes and outlook. Martin's goal is not simply visual, for his paintings challenge the relationship between the eye and the mind, the cognitive process that translates received impressions of colour and light into the perception of form and space. In that process of digestion, analysis, identification, the mind draws on previous experience, testing against memories and associations before deciding what the eyes are seeing. All this happens in milli-seconds, the body functioning so efficiently that there is, usually, no need to bother the conscious mind unless, for example, one is driving in the dark in the rain. The essential kineticism of Martin's paintings lies in their attempt to capture that milli-second experience of cognition. He is painting at the very frontier, the view from the bridge between the individual and everything else. The view is not simply some kind of ultra- Impressionism for it involves two-way traffic from the mind, that jostling sea of associations from past experience that are being tested, filtered down as options before the process of identification can be concluded.





Diving into another of Martin's paintings, we place our eyes and minds in the artist's care; he leads us into the unknown world we inhabit in that constant succession of ideas before we interpret them. The view from the bridge is glorious before the painting entitled *Movement with, orange, yellow and blue-violet*. Structured like a chessboard or woven patterned fabric, the painting offers no dominant features on which to focus the eyes as a starting point. Instead, before we know it we are reading it as if a text, from top left in horizontals (assuming we have leant to read in the Western world). Meanwhile, associations pour in as we try to find motifs and distinguish objects from background. The automatic procession of cognition works ahead of any desire we may have to arrest it momentarily. We seem to be offered a golden sky above a blue ocean, until the horizon proves too elusive, for the transition from blue to gold, from top to bottom, has no break. The units seem to be stretching as they descend, as if drawn by gravity. Reversing, reading upward, the surface seems to swell and dent, like a ruffled carpet or screen hanging in the wind. Colour brings

paint gives each unit a softness we now enjoy, safe in the understanding that it is only an abstract painting before us.

Martin's artistic journey can be traced back to his early exercises in the life class at Goldsmiths' College. The Pointillist studies, in the manner of Georges Seurat (1859-91) record the artist's growing awareness of the unmediated world of light, colour and movement that we inhabit, before the mind sets them into forms and hierarchies of significance. Martin understood Seurat's application of scientific principles to painting in a way that may not have interested many Neo-Impressionists. The surface effects of oscillation that result from placing pure primary colours adjacent in dots does not become an end in itself. As a well-read artist, Seurat provided Martin with more than visual lessons. Seurat's paintings were informed by academic theories of the colour circle and colour values, by the latest scientific research into optical phenomena, and by his own study of the use of colour by Delacroix. Seurat also read and used current thinking about the expressive value of colour and line. For example, he knew that downward lines and cool colours have an inhibitory, calming effect whereas warm colours and flowing vertical lines are uplifting, even joyful. Seurat employed his research to the full in ambitious, large-scale canvases in which different types of brush stroke are used in different areas in a systematic way. When viewed from close-to, Seurat's harmonic pairs of complementary colours seem highly organised, but when seen from a distance they seem to oscillate and merge through optical fusion. This visual flux is something Martin explores more empirically, enjoying as he goes the surface qualities as ends in themselves, preferring to capture moments of ambiguity rather than to define form through Seurat's Pointillist technique.

Martin's early life-class studies also embody his growing awareness of the gap between the self-conscious individual and everything else. If the life-model seems to be going out of focus, or fragmenting, it is because the artist saw her in just those terms. As he painted so he wondered. His thoughts were stimulated by his reading of the eighteenth- century British philosophers George Berkeley (*An Essay towards a New Theory of Vision,* 1709) and David Hume (*An Enquiry Concerning Human Understanding*, 1748). The most influential of the British empiricists, Hume expressed his scepticism about the existence of material objects beyond only the experience of them and the mind's idea of them. For Hume, the difference between an impression of something and the idea of it was their respective 'force' or 'liveliness'; the idea is a memory that lacks the force of its first

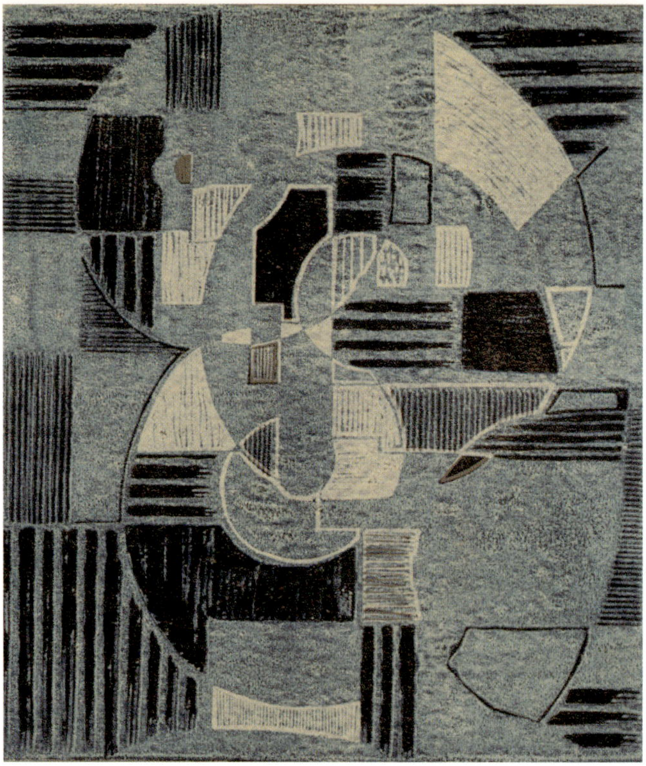

1961
*Three Interlocking Spirals with differe[nt]*
*rates of Acceleration*
Lino print
(Tate collection)

This theme was developed by the artist nearly a decade later in a large three dimensional kinetic sculpture, entitled *Moving Sculpture*.
This was exhibited in the Arts Council Of Great Britain's international kinetic exhibition at the Hayward Gallery.

arrival as an impression. All ideas, all understanding, to Hume, depended on empirical, sensory experience. Hume also challenged the assertion of the French philosopher, Rene Descartes, that the self is a certainty ('I think, therefore I am'). Hume saw the 'self' only as a relationship of ideas, impressions and memories, not one definite essence.

Fortunately Hume's radical scepticism was answered by the German philosopher Immanuel Kant who saw Hume's world, of sensations received by individuals who were nothing more than memories of sensations, as a world of incoherence. His *Critique of Pure Reason* (1781) answered the bold assertion from the new world of science that all human knowledge derived only from experience. Defending metaphysics, Kant showed the limits of knowledge for, as a synthesis of impressions and ideas, of experiences and concepts, knowledge is formed in a process that itself cannot be observed, that is 'transcendental'. As experiences are received, so the mind sorts them into categories that must already exist, so the mind must already have a notion of the external world as one of order, of space and time. This is the reassurance Martin no sooner found, than he felt blown away by reading Reichenbach, and finding himself in a modern universe of Relativity, in a new Space-Time era.

Martin's colour paintings seem to capture that moment of moments, when

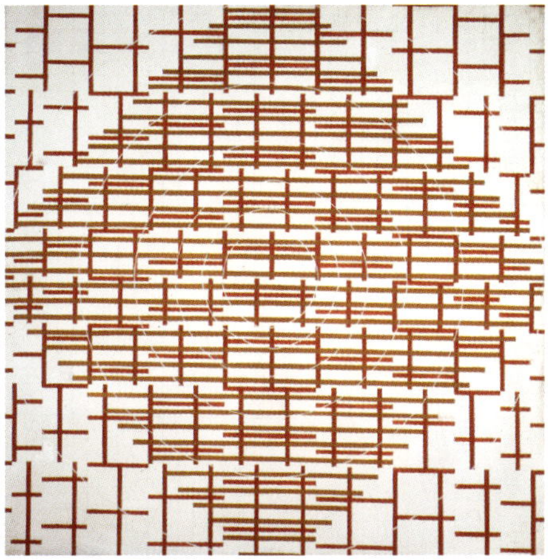

1963
*Constructed Painting with interior circles*
Oil paint on canvas
111 x 111 cm

an encounter sets off a race between the eye and the mind, when the eye is scanning a scene and electrical impulses race across the brain trying to make sense of the received impression. His paintings also have linear themes that convey a similar sense of cognitive distance, of the world existing only in the traces of energy, in lines that are the trails of atoms or the fragments, the splintered edges of lost forms.

In his early unique linocut *Three Interlocking Spirals with Differing Rates of Acceleration* (1961, Tate) he uses a compositional theme that later informs his metal machines: the theme of vectors in rotation. The way the spirals rotate inward and outward, like springs, also suggests the mind of the eighteen year-old artist flexing its muscles, testing his inward and

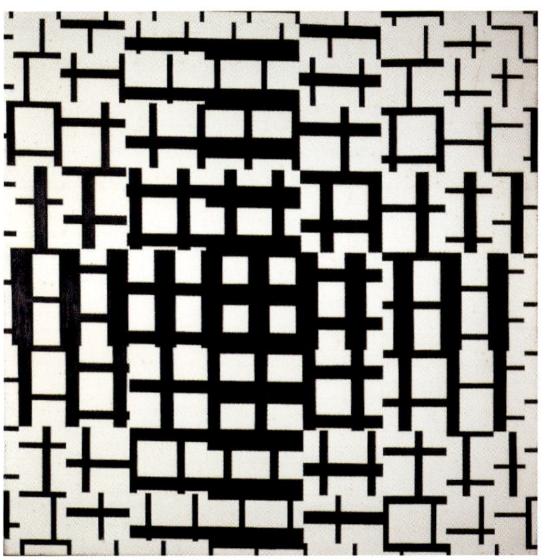

1963
*Black and White Canvas*
Oil paint on canvas
107 x 107 cm

Different rates of acceleration in anumber of directions simultaneously

of the eighteen year-old artist flexing its muscles, testing his inward and outward environments. On the Tate's website the work is compared by a young woman curator to Marcel Duchamp's *Large Glass* where 'the grinding action of the *Coffee Mill* is a metaphor for masturbation...Martin seems to be attempting to use a similar metaphorical language'. This is not a reading Martin wishes to endorse.

The *Black and White Canvas* (1963) Martin describes as a study in presenting 'different rates of acceleration in a number of directions simultaneously'. The eye is immediately drawn to the boldest unit, the central crossed square, as if it were the point of impact from which the rest of the canvas reverberates. But as the eye moves outward sub-divisions

**There is a sexual allusion made by the sculpture**

appear in geometric order, the invisible, implied lines of each unit forming edges. The mind cannot reconcile the play between symmetry and chaos. If first memories of that fragmenting ceiling above Martin's infant cot lie behind this work the central impact and reverberation is even more powerful in *Constructed Painting with interior circles* from the same year. The inscribed concentric circles of varying width suggest a target or sound waves that are about to shatter the ordered linear mesh.

The correspondence between Martin's paintings and machines in the 1960s is closest between his *Black and white Relief* (1965) and *Constructed painting* (1964-5) (see page 89). In the relief, each plastic sphere is mounted on a watch spring to extend it from its black circle on the painted wooden surface. The visual effect is both random and repetitive. In the painted equivalent of this conception the spheres seem to invert, their backgrounds suggesting holes in a perforated steel sheet, yet none of them are painted from a consistent viewpoint. Consequently, the surface seems to flow and distort. This is the closest Martin came to making Op Art, as it left him with no love of patient, mechanical, repetitive painting.

The challenge of transferring compositional concerns from kinetic sculptures to graphic works also produced a pair across media. As one of a series of silk screens, *4:5:6* (1970, Government Art Collection) revisits visual ideas that Martin assembled six years before in his only 'mobile', *Spiral Sculpture with Male and Female Ends* (1964). At the simplest, formal level, as the pure white shapes rotate against a black background they seem to melt and merge, distorting the lines of black space between them. In the

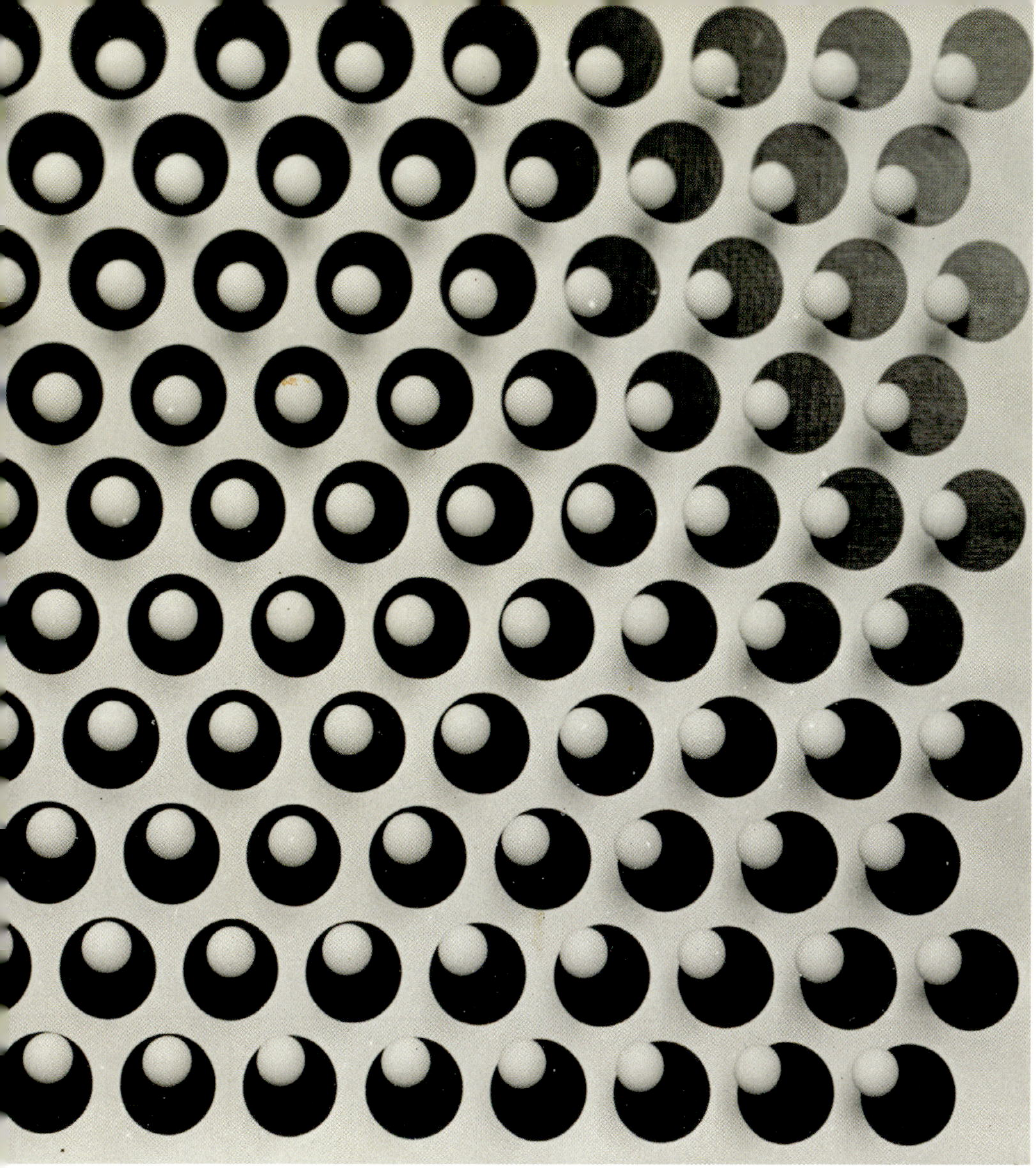



1965

*Black And White Relief*

Household paint, wood , plastic, metal.

130 x 127 cm

The spheres were extended from the surface and could move in two directions.

(Collection: David Talbot-Rice)

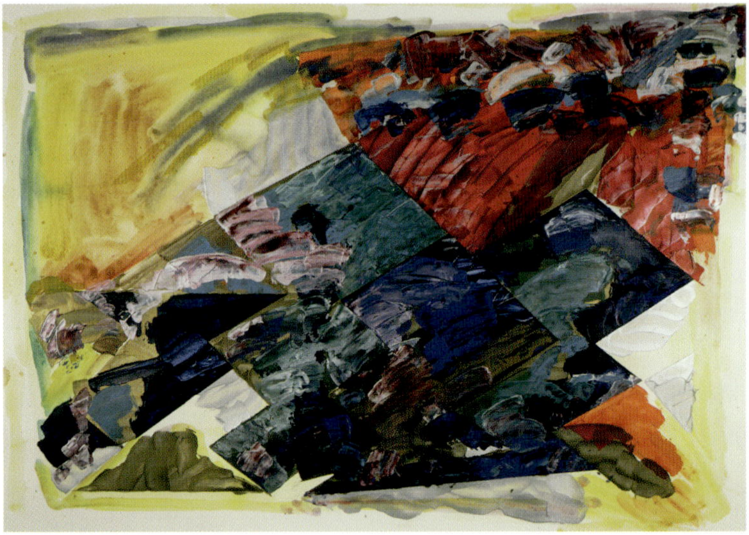

1979

*Spanish Series No. 16 - Especially Nice Night in Kingley Street*

Acrylic and Liquitex on Arches Paper

70 x 100 cm

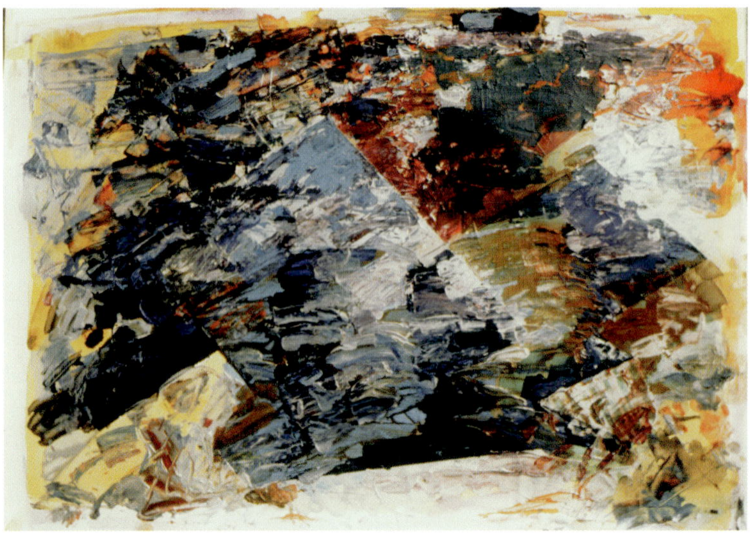

1979

Spanish Series No. 18 - Especially Nice Night in Kingley Street

Acrylic and Liquitex on Arches Paper

70 x 100 cm

(Private Collection)

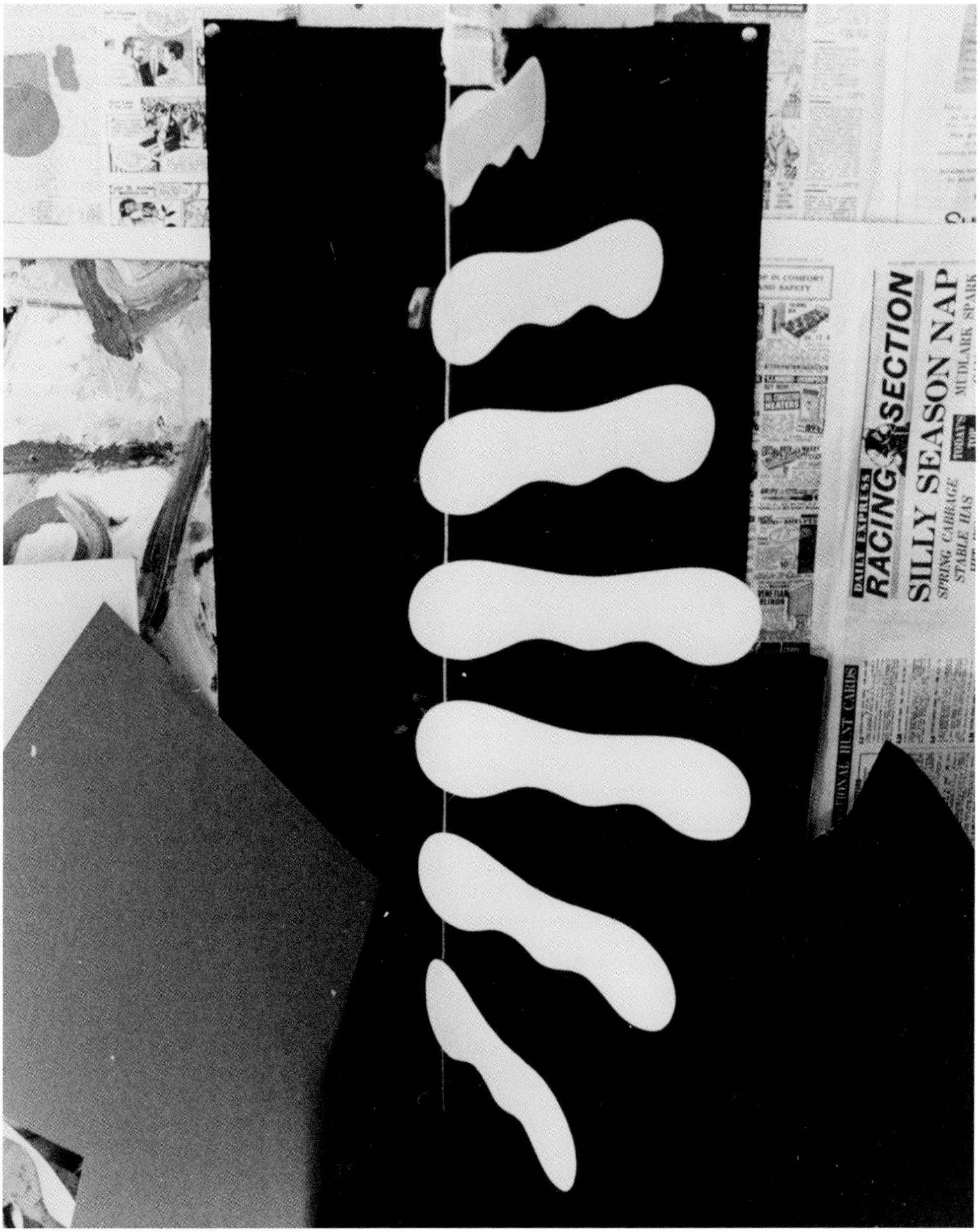


1964

*Spiral with Male and Female Ends*

80 x 30 x30 cm

White card, paper, wire

coloured stripes which seem to rotate and recede as we follow them from left to right. On another level, the sexual allusion made by the sculpture can make it seem like an object inviting gentle contemplation, a quiet point of focus for meandering thoughts on sexual identity as an illusion, choice and fact.

*Red and Blue Undulations* (1965) is also based on the rotating mobile of the year before. It addresses the same question of the exchange between the mind and the eye as to what we see automatically and what we choose to see. At first sight, to most people, the acrylic on canvas is a series of alternating maroon and blue horizontal stripes. The white mobile against a black background has been translated into warm and cool colours. Then you notice, if accustomed to reading from left to right, that the red stripes are of a different shape. They begin like fully-laden rounded brushstrokes at the far left and gradually trail off, becoming animated as they seem to shed their load and reach the right side of the canvas, where an upward force (like the lifting hand) runs throughout. This form of each maroon stripe was suggested by the rotating mobile, so could seem to exist in space, as a twisting and receding line, repeated in rows against a blue background. In art-school teaching, blue recedes (like the sky) whereas red is dominant. But this is an age-old assumption, one maintained by the first president of the Royal Academy, Joshua Reynolds, in the 18th century, when it prompted his rival, Thomas Gainsborough, to paint the picture we now call *Blue Boy* (1770, Huntington Library and Art Gallery, San Marino, U.S.A.), a portrait in which the boy in the foreground is dressed in blue.

As you look closer at the varying thickness of the paint (for the best paintings are the subtlest of low-relief sculptures) you see that each maroon layer is so thinly painted that they reveal the texture of the canvas beneath, whereas each blue stripe is so thick as to hang heavy, swelling into ridges at each lower edge. On noticing this, your mind decides that the blue stripes hover over a continuous maroon ground, despite the shape of each maroon bar implying that they are the actual strokes over the blue. Similar things happen when you look over a rich russet Turkish carpet, where the large scale of the visual field causes interference between the point of interest and focus and the dynamic alternative options offered by peripheral vision. Looking at the top and bottom of the painting, there is continuity in shape, as if one were studying a single repeat from an infinite pattern rolling over in a continuous loop.

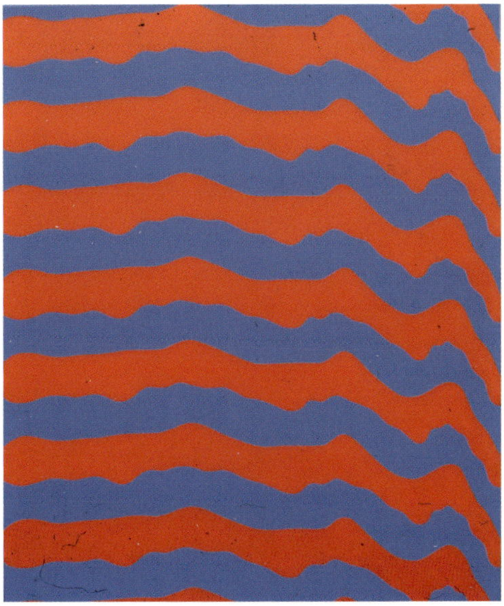

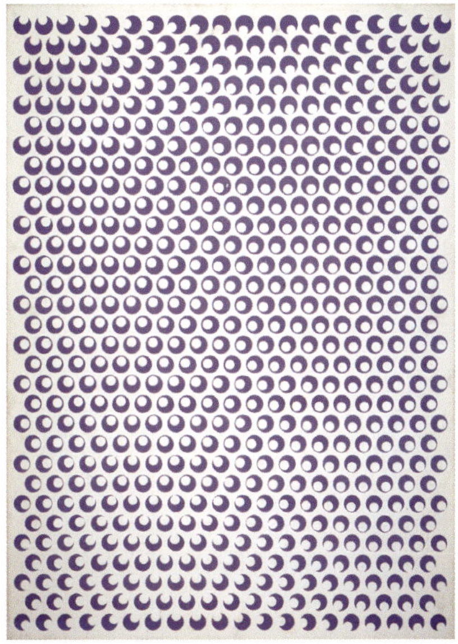



In another painting from the same year, *Movement* (1965) Martin plays with the pictorial conventions of suggesting space on a flat surface. In a freely-painted series of squares, the top third appear to be set against a yellow or orange area while the bottom third has a violet background. The mind finds sky above and earth below, as in an infant's first painting or a medieval Biblical panel. At the point of merger and transition in the centre, a sense of recession and depth occurs, as in the illusion of perspectival space created first through mathematics by Renaissance artists. But then the viewer may choose to read the picture not as square units descending over grounds, but as a series of horizontal stripes, weaving in and out of each other, as in some Islamic fabric. Looking at the four sides of the canvas, you notice that the colour continues around the edges, so emphasising the physicality of the whole object and suggesting that each square is actually a cube, and hence that the whole is but a slice from some vast laminated log of coloured strips. Is this a painting or a sculpture?

As both a painter and a sculptor at a time when artists defined themselves by their materials, Martin brought a

1965
*Blue and Red Undulations*
Acrylic on canvas
122 x 92 cm

1964
*Contructed painting*
Oil paint on canvas
145 x 105 cm

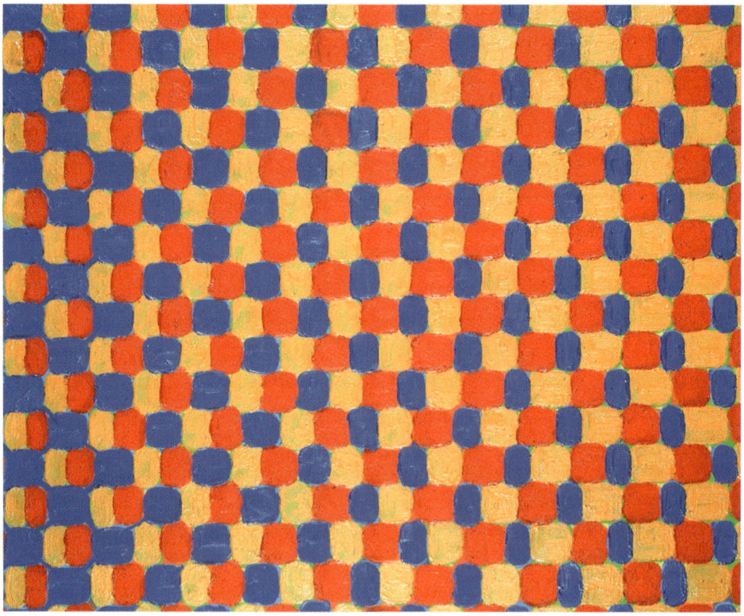

1964-5

*Movement with blue, red and gold*

Oil paint on canvas

45 x 65 cm

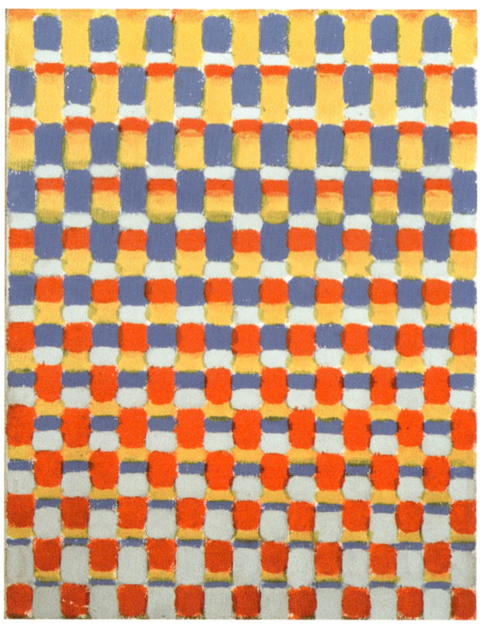

1964-5

*Movement with red, blue, yellow and grey*

Oil paint on canvas

45 x 30 cm

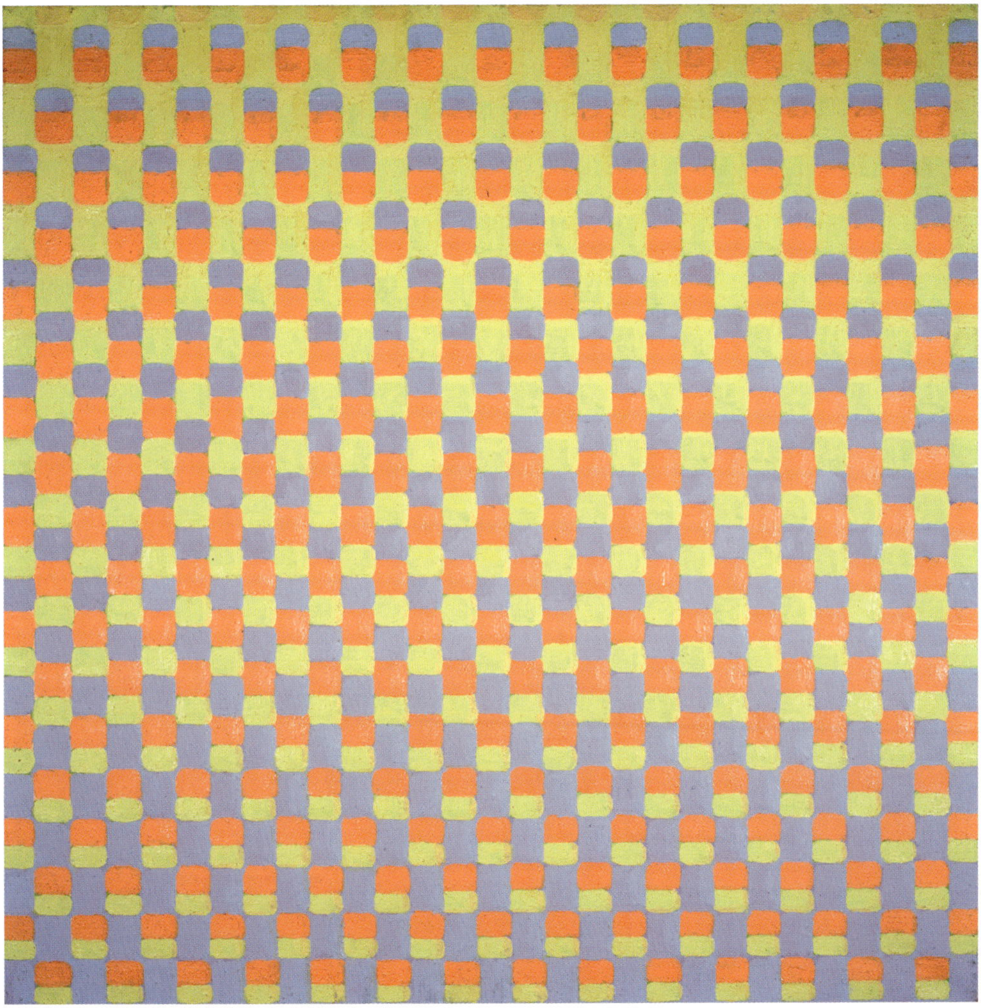



1964-5

*Movement with orange, yellow and blue-violet*

Oil paint on canvas

120 x 120 cm

fresh eye to the artistic ambitions and competitive business of producing modern sculpture at St Martin's. In a series of six standing sculptures, made at St Martin's between 1966 and 1967, Martin used colour in planar compositions in a way that anticipated its use by his contemporaries. Fresh from writing his thesis on Piet Mondrian (1965; published as a book in 1984) Martin built sculptures from rectangular sheets of wood and metal that he painted in the primary colours blue, red and yellow. If these sculptures have a kineticism it is in the destabilising effect that colour relationships bring to geometric composition, as Martin learnt from Mondrian. Anthony Caro had been making single-colour sculptures for several years (for example, *Early One Morning*, 1962, Tate) but Martin's use of primary colours for component parts was something new in British sculpture. Beyond Mondrian, it recalls the Red Blue Chair by Gerrit Rietveld, which became an icon of Modernism, and Rietveld's house in Utrecht for Mrs Schroeder (1924).

Each of the series of sculptures teases the observer by appearing lucid, ordered, and perfect in execution yet on the very brink of collapse. *Vertical Upright with Horizontal Slab* (1966-67) is built beyond human scale and forces the viewer to look up to what is, painted black, visually the heaviest component: an elevated plane seemingly floating in space. In these

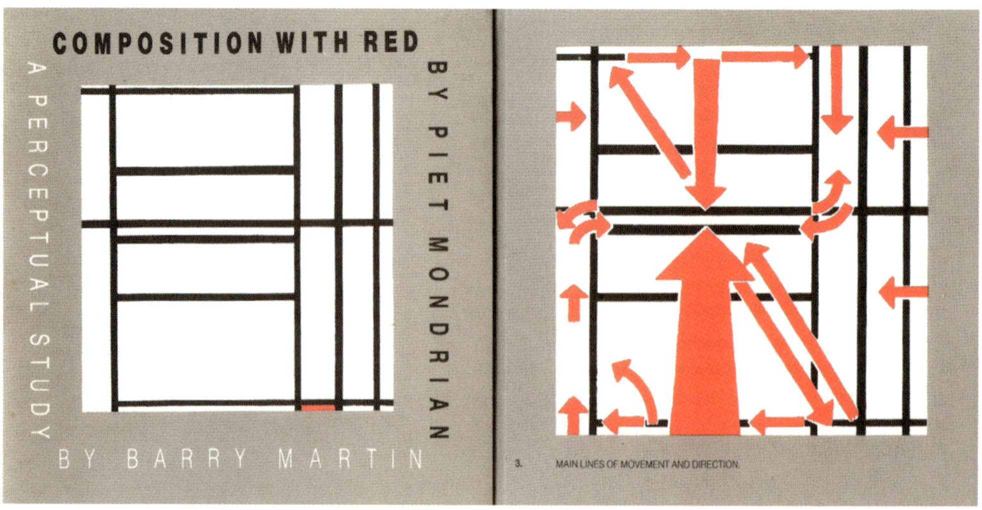


1965

*Composition with Red by Piet Mondrian*

*A Perceptual Study* by Barry Martin.

Published 1984

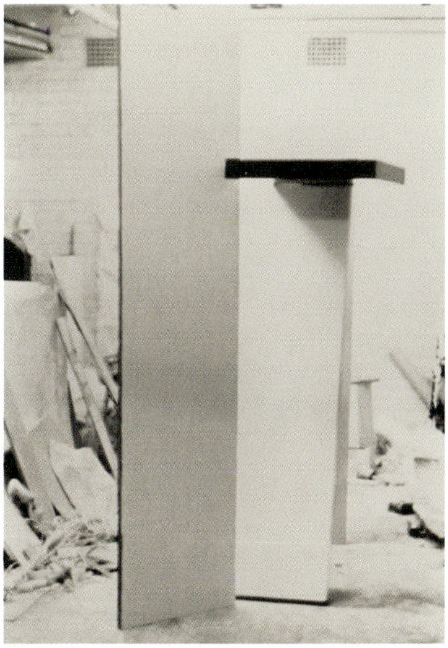

1966-7

*Vertical Upright with Horizontal Slab*

Wood, metal, colours: white, yellow. black, blue, red edge and blue edge

259 x 336 x 183 cm

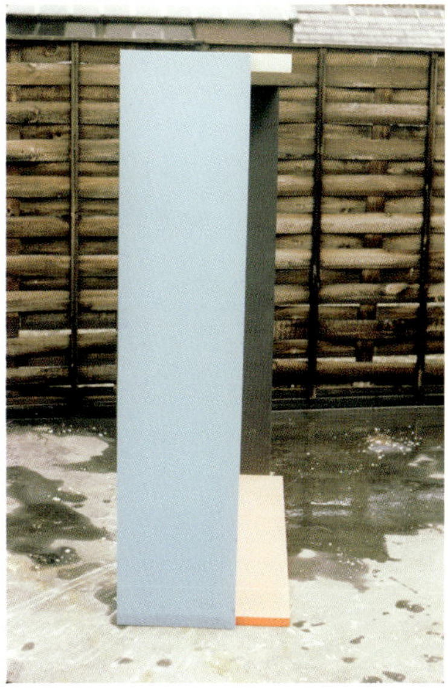

1967

*Enclosure*

Spring wood, metal, colour. Colour: blue, black, uprights, grey, red, horizontals

191 x 203 x 70 cm

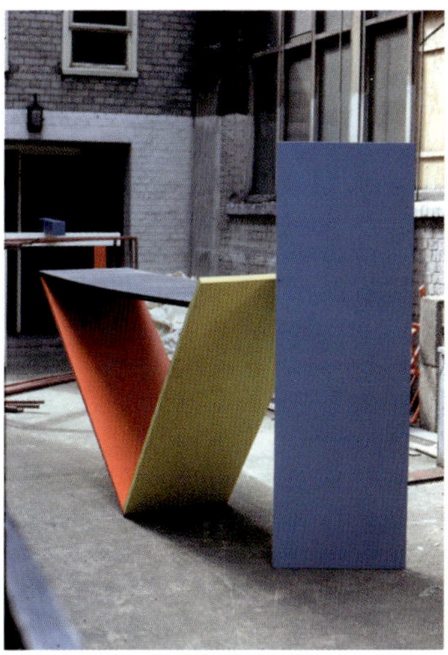

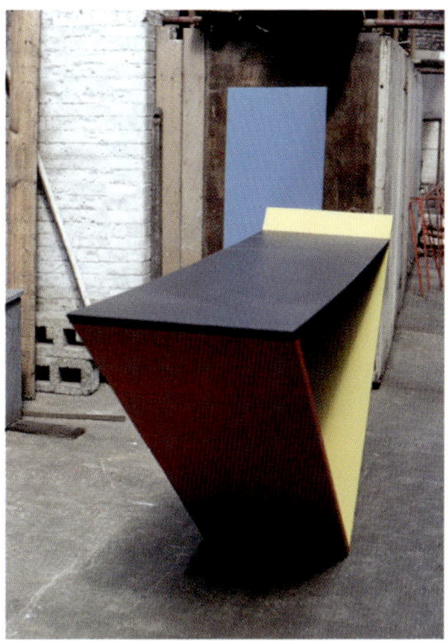

1966-7

*Vertical Upright*

Wood, metal, colour, coeruleum, blue, black, bright, yellow, full chromatic red

198 x 320 x 125 cm (top of horizontal plane)

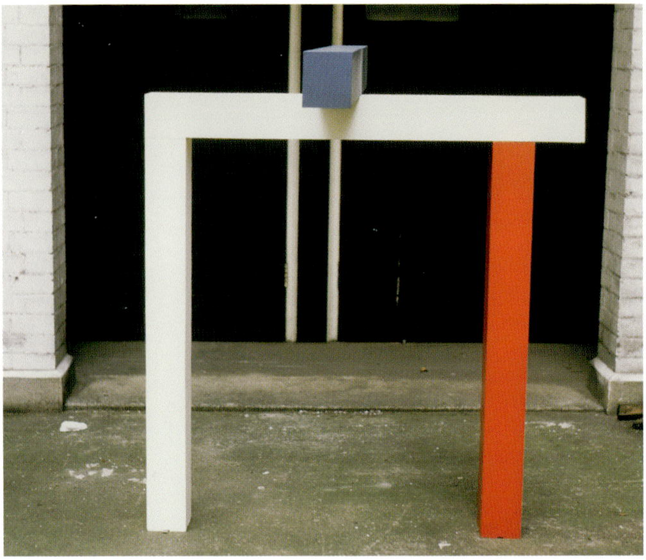

1966

*Red Vertical*

Wood, paint

129 x 120 x 120 cm



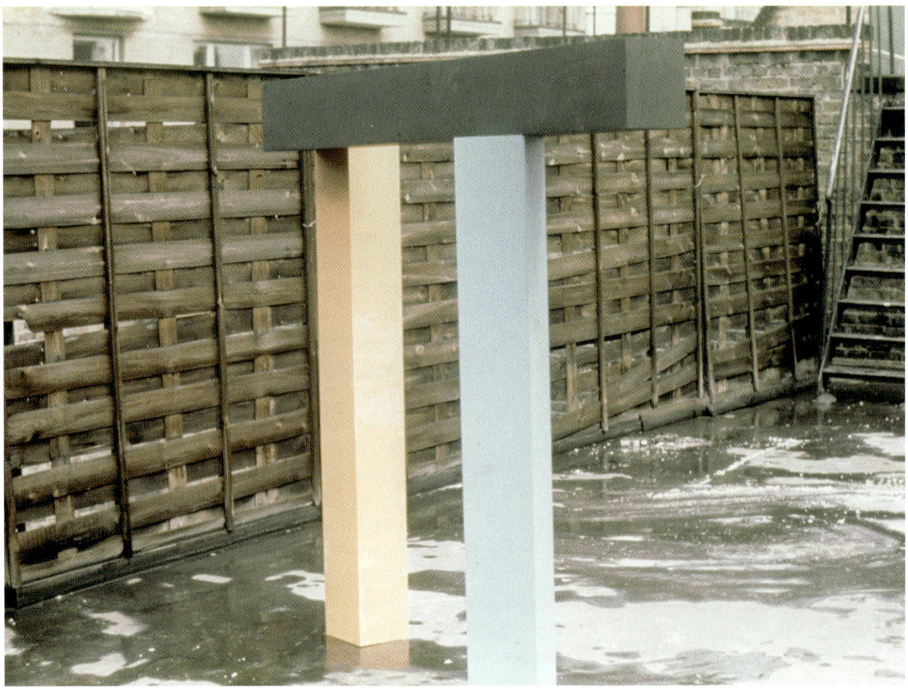

1966-7

*Black Horizontal resting on Blue End*

Wood, metal, colour. Black with blue and orange verticals

198,25 x 305 x 55 cm

minimalist works Martin combined geometric shapes of pure colour into compositions that let us feel we are walking inside a painting by Mondrian. A sense of imminent movement arises from the way he assembles his structures, for the random element is always present, either as a threat or promise. This seems to be a theme running through all Martin's media.

In the 1970s Martin concentrated on painting and collage. In a series of tall canvases he created a distinct, personal idiom through evolving a way of producing two abstract paintings occupying the same canvas, as if in alternating strips. Perhaps the best of these is *Whole with Machine Intrusions* (1974) (see page 72) in which the viewer can make out two paintings of contrasting character. One, broadly washed in red and green, subtly varies the khaki tone of the unpainted primed canvas from warm to cool. The other, with a palette of mauve, yellow and blue, uses poured paint and seems to flow in and out of the other painting. The contrast suggests a male/female or autumn/spring dichotomy, as the two paintings emerge from a chaotic first impression, then separate but compete for primacy as they intersect and overlap. Finally, the patient observer is rewarded on finding how they interweave, merge and blend into one whole. The mind and eye can read the two paintings as rivals, on two visual levels but, as the

1965-6
*Movement Types*
Acrylic on canvas
183 x 183 cm

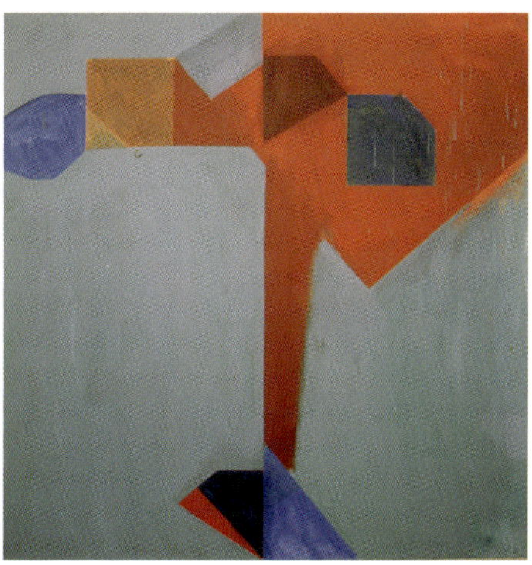

1965
*High Edge*
Acrylic on canvas
183 x 183 cm

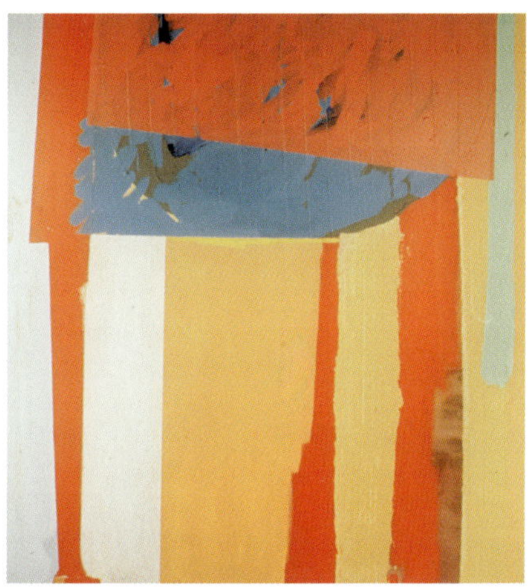

title asserts, the challenge is to find how they link into the whole. In his interlacing of poured paint and staining techniques, Martin synthesised two approaches He describes the double painting as a response to the debates over the choice between abstraction and figuration; in Martin's art, multiple approaches may occupy the same space

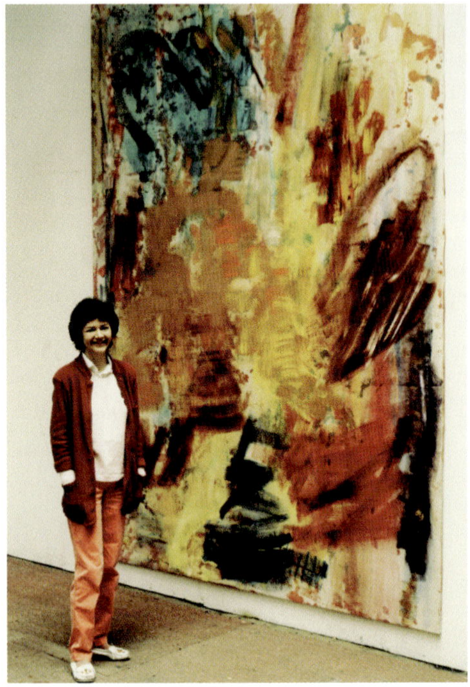

1979

*43 Movement Types*

oil on canvas

420 x 240 cm

Installation view

In an interview for a documentary film made in 1968, when he was twenty-five, Martin identified the key link between his metal machines and his work in colour on canvas, paper or wood, in humanist terms. He saw all his concern with movement as reflecting the uncertainty of human relationships, and as a search for security in the physical environment. As an artist he felt driven to 'make more concrete statements...which would always exist, and which didn't rest on shifting ground'. That was his answer in 1968 to the intellectual and social challenge of the world as he knew it. To most people, it is a common need, but one that is met through establishing a career, a family, a home, and for some by amassing personal wealth and other forms of 'success'. In a sense Martin has kept that need alive, taking on the role of the artist in society as someone who does not 'mind the gap' between impression and understanding, but draws on the insecurity of awareness in order to fuel his art.

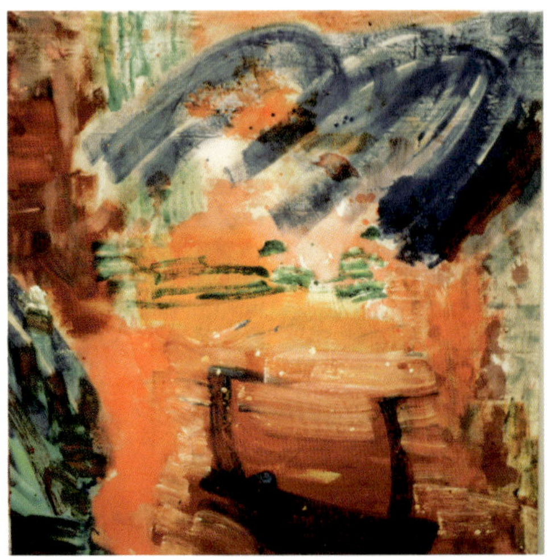

1983

*Movement Types No. 4*

oil on canvas

190 x 190 cm

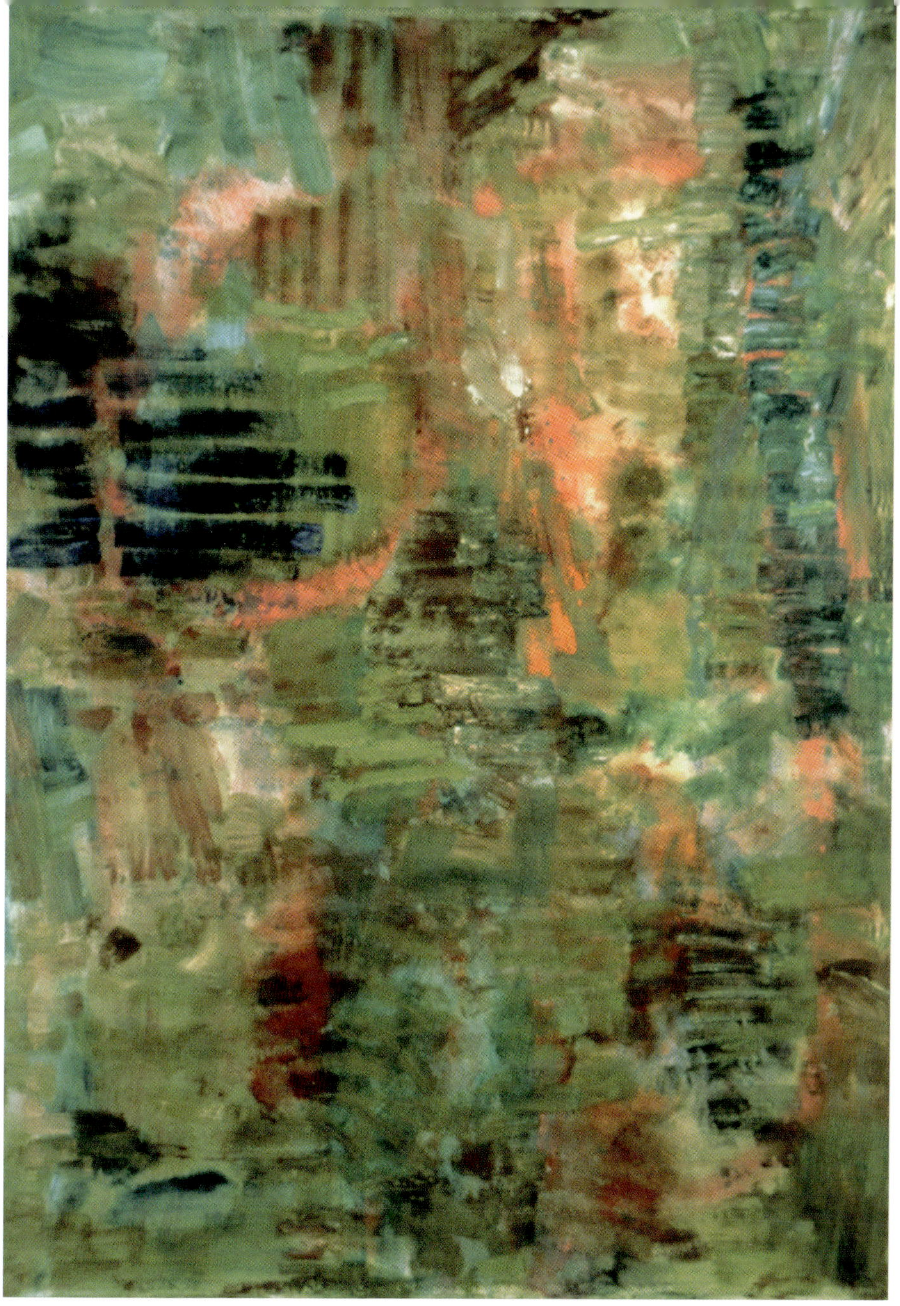

1982-3

*Movement Types No. 3*

oil on canvas

378 x 184 cm

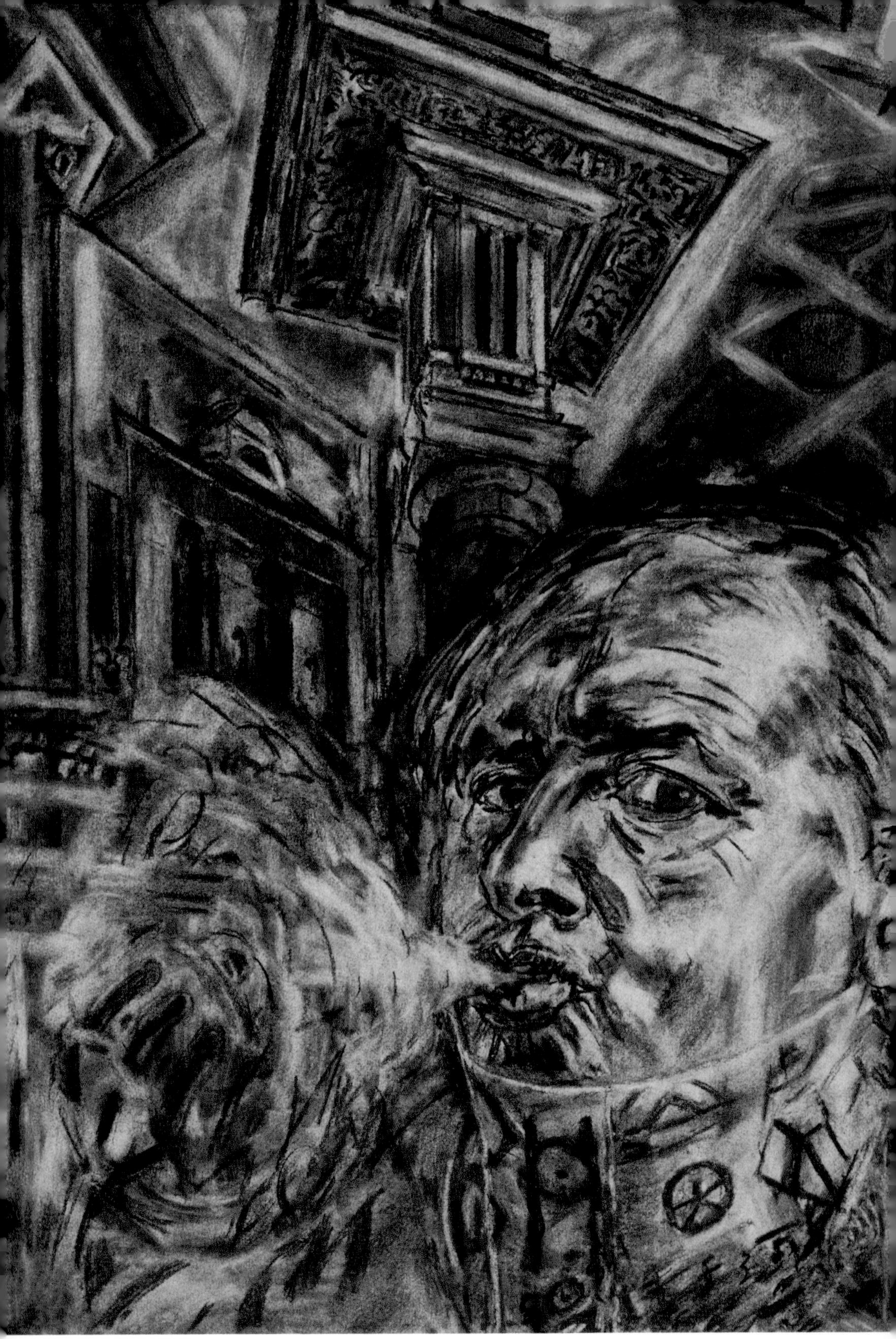

*Signs of Power*

# 5 the Drawings



In 2006 the Victoria & Albert Museum acquired seven drawings spanning the career of Barry Martin. They included two from a series of eight large, intense, charcoal drawings that are, quite simply, almost frightening. Recognisably of the artist, they seem not to be self-portraits so much as portraits of the artist, the universal artist as architect, designer, mathematician, inventor, for they seem to be filled with archaic symbolism, both in the settings and on the bizarre cloak in which he is shrouded.

*1995*

*Self porttrait at Chiswick House*

125 x 82 cm

Charcoal on paper

(Collection: Victoria & Albert Museum)

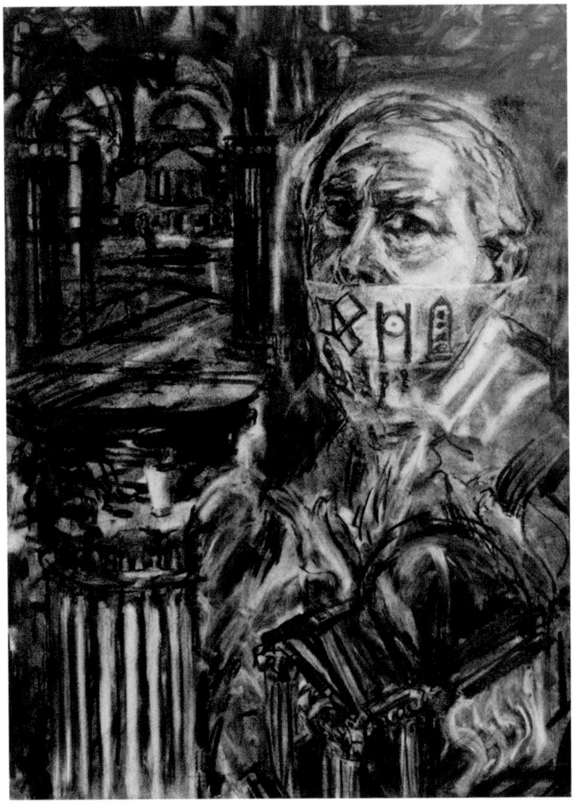

*1995*
*Reflections on Chiswick House*
Charcoal on paper
125 x 70 cm
(Collection: English Heritage, Chiswick House)



From the history of art they call to mind Rembrandt's *tronies*, the fantasy portraits in which the artist posed not as himself but in costume in character. The insistent urgency of Martin's gaze, however, inevitably makes one think of Van Gogh. The universal artist is shown as a solitary wanderer at night among obelisks and temples, his wide-eyed gaze made all the more arresting by the fact that in some his mouth is masked. The cloak's collar is embroidered with obscure cabalistic symbols, suggesting some dreadful secret that he dare not utter, that only the signs may betray to the fellow initiated. Executed in charcoal, each work has the tonal range and luxuriantly soft textures of a mezzotint, with all the subtleties and ambiguities of suggestion that the medium brings to the evocation of full moonlight.

## Martin spotted the Duke of Devonshire's gate-lodge when it was close to death

This is no imaginary setting. The universal artist is depicted wandering alone among the mysteries of Chiswick House, the precious English neo-Palladian villa that survives today set within walled Italianate gardens in West London. Richard Boyle, 3rd Earl of Burlington (1694-1753), known from Horace Walpole's epithet as the 'Apollo of the arts', completed his suburban dream at Chiswick in 1729. Four years later he moved his great art collection there from Burlington House, Piccadilly (today the home of the Royal Academy of Arts). The house is now owned and opened to the public by English Heritage. Since 1989 Martin has been artist-in-residence with his own studio and study in the gate-lodge. This compact hideaway was built in 1835 to the designs of the architect Decimus Burton, who is best known today as the architect of Wellington Arch at Hyde Park Corner. Martin's lodge was built for Chiswick's later owner, the 6th Duke of Devonshire. With his studio in the park, Martin is free to roam after closing time, with 40 acres to himself, drawing and reflecting on his creative forbears. Martin recalls how 'these black self-portraits attempted to reflect my saturation point into this rich and powerful vocabulary'.





1995

*The Communication, Chiswick House*

Charcoal on paper

60 x 135 cm

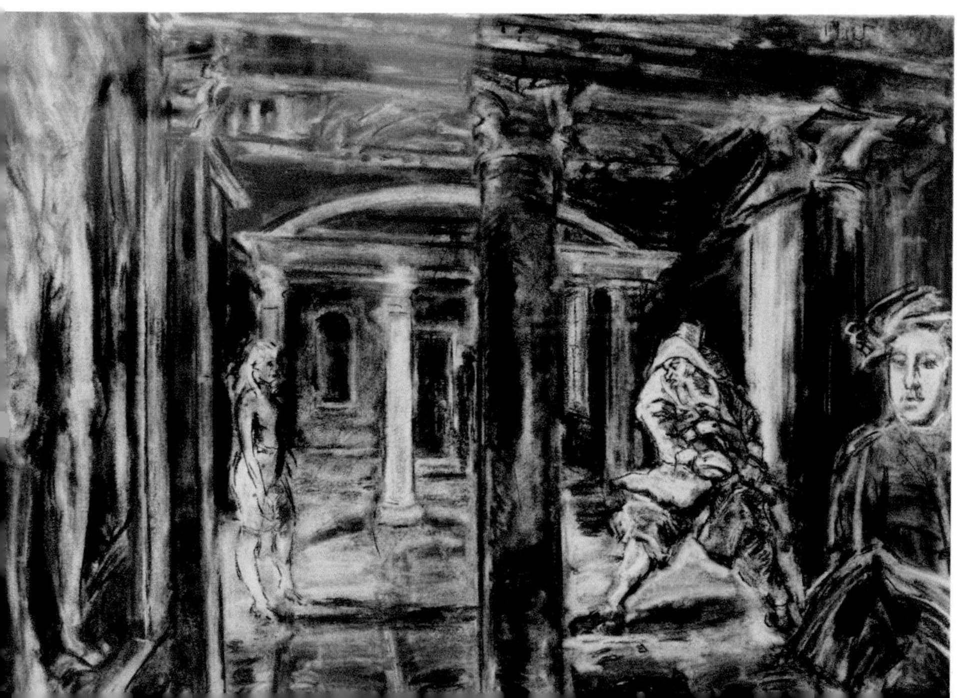

Martin spotted the Duke of Devonshire's gate-lodge when it was close to death. The sad hulk had been abandoned for 25 years, except by vandals and tramps who had stripped out all the floors, joists and lathes to make fires. The gatekeeper's walled garden and outbuildings were indistinguishable, strewn with rubbish and filled with wind-sown sycamore trees stretching over 30 feet tall. After securing a long lease on the ruin he enlisted the expertise of an architect friend, Theo Crosby of the Pentagram group, who designed a new interior worthy of the grade 2 listed building. Preliminary archaeology revealed an Elizabethan well and trough that must have served thirsty travellers and their steeds on the old west road out of London en route to Bath. It felt like a promising find for a new artist's studio, perhaps, even, a sign.

Restoration was completed in 1990. Since then, on Saturday mornings, beneath the strategically-sited single roof-light, successive models have disrobed and been posed by Martin for his art or his private pupils. Below, on the ground floor, as in Burlington's own villa nearby, he keeps his library.





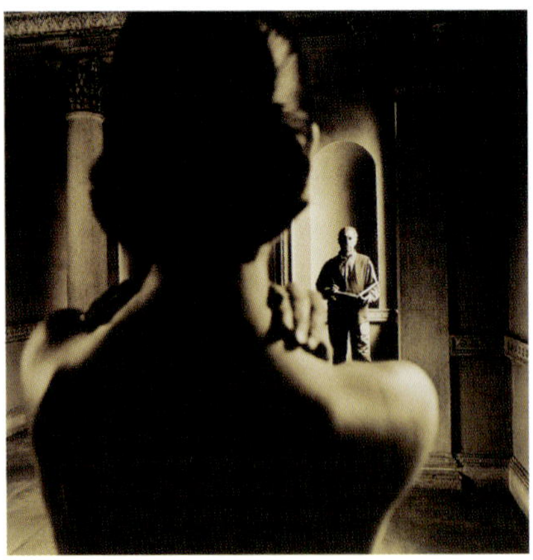

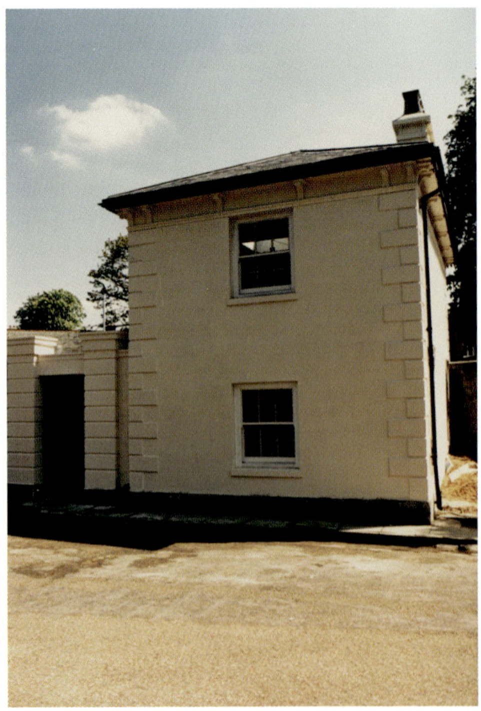

1997
*The artist at Chiswick in the Link room*, Chiswick House, London
Photograph by Bob Miller

The artist's studio,
Chiswick House, London

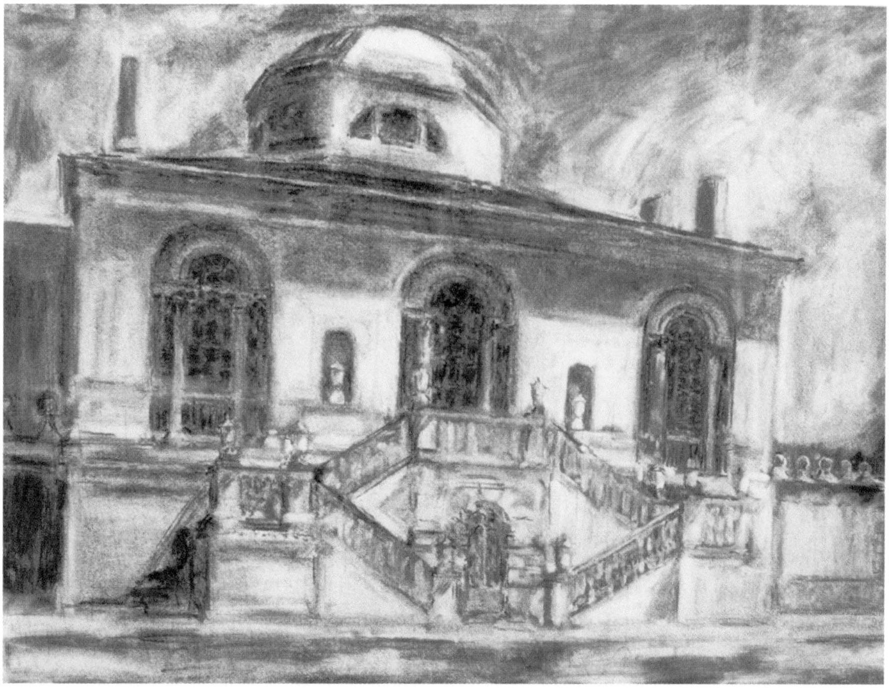

1994

*Chiswick House*,

Charcoal on paper

75 x 105 cm

(Private Collection ,USA)



At first, the inspiration of this unique location culminated in the series of self-portraits. These were first shown in an exhibition at Chiswick House, A *New View*, in 1994, along with drawings by Martin's local friends Peter Blake and Ben Johnson. The show was curated by the present writer (who was then director of English Heritage's museums and collections) as the house's contribution to mark the 300th anniversary of the birth of Lord Burlington. In demonstrating the enduring inspirational qualities of Chiswick House and its gardens the show provided a response by living artists to the major exhibition at the Royal Academy, *Palladian Revival: Lord Burlington, His Villa and Garden at Chiswick*. Disappointed by the limited scope of the show at Burlington House, Martin turned his hand to art history, and set to work researching his own answer to the perennial mystery: how were Chiswick House and its gardens really used by Burlington- as an art gallery, dining pavilion or as something else?

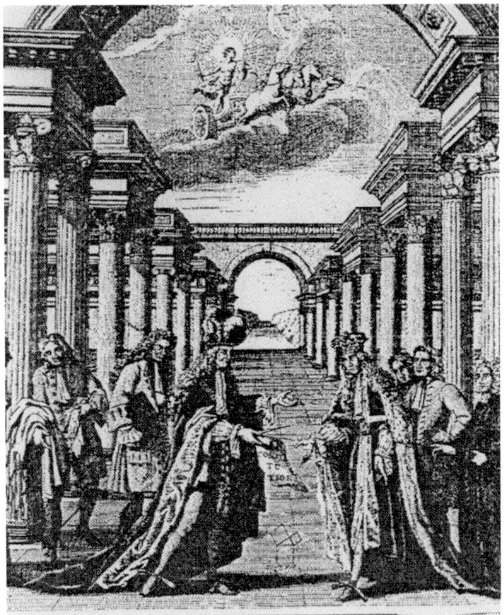

1723
*The Constitution of Freemasonry*
Showing the square on the Hypotemeuse theorem between the two central figures.





With his understanding of mathematics, habitual breadth of reading and interest since the 1960s in ancient Egyptian cosmological symbolism, Martin looked long and hard at the building and gardens. He finally made his breakthrough with the evidence to prove that Chiswick House, with its gardens, must have been conceived as a Masonic temple. The fact that Burlington and his own artist-in-residence, William Kent, were Freemasons had long been assumed but no one had spent time thinking through the symbolism in the decoration beyond the quotations and adaptations from Palladio and other Italian architects of the Renaissance. Nor had architectural historians analysed fully the mathematical ratios of all the building's elevations and plans. The door was open since the classic study *Palladio and English Palladianism* (London, 1974) by Rudolf Wittkower had explained the use of harmonic proportions in Renaissance architecture in terms of the Neo-Platonic theory of the harmony of the universe and of the soul, as united through the design of ecclesiastical buildings. Martin measured and plotted, finding ample evidence of the application of Euclid's 47th theorem ('the square on the hypotenuse of a triangle is equal to the sum of the squares on the other two sides'). This he linked to the frontispiece of The *Constitution of Freemasonry* (1727) and to the symbolism within ceiling paintings by William Kent. Exploring the layout of the gardens, with its sculptures, columns, obelisks and temples, Martin thought through the steps by which a Masonic lodge meeting could have been conducted in a way that linked these landmarks and avenues to the villa's interiors. He first published his thoughts and findings in the

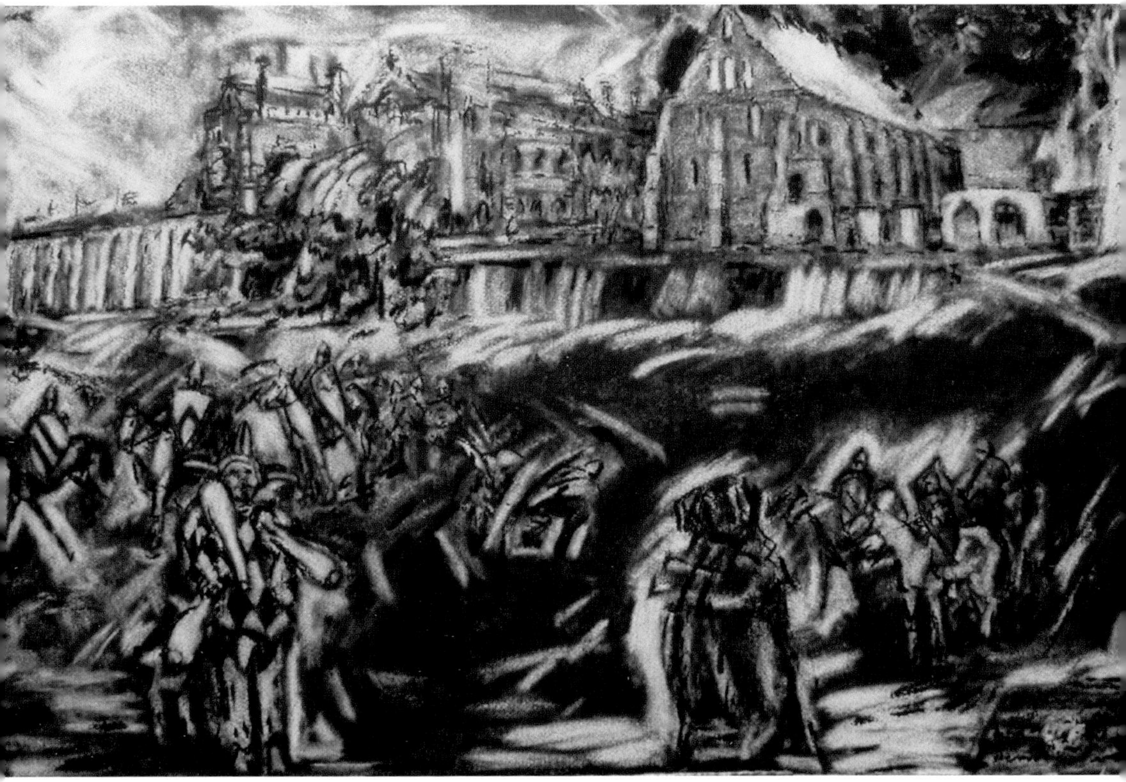

2003

*Battle Abbey*

Charcoal on paper

60 x 130 cm

(private collection)

magazine Chess in 1994 and then in more detail four years later in a book of essays arising from a conference (*Lord Burlington, the Man and his Politics*, edited by Edward Corp, 1998).

The relationship of this research to Martin's art was not a one-way influence. Accustomed to using shapes and symbols enigmatically in his abstract works, he had a natural curiosity about finding them in the art of Burlington and Kent. He wanted to see if they had spoken to self-selecting viewers in the same way, challenging them as he does to see, search, perceive and so understand. In the self-portrait drawings, the mask-like collar is not only covered with signs for the viewer, like some unintelligible speech bubble, for they can also be seen as signals and codes that have been received by the artist as researcher, like fish enmeshed in his net. As his eyes search the twilight Italianate gardens of Chiswick House they also ask us, the viewer, what questions we bring.

From reading the works of Carl Jung and studies on the use of psychology in advertising, Martin has shown his art students over the decades how 'codes, signs and symbols powerfully control and underpin much that happens in the real world. They inhabit a nether world that allows us to interact with it'. In the series of drawings he sought to convey the relevance of the archaic symbolism of Chiswick House to the visitor today, 'with all the dread that incurs'.

In 2005, to mark the 21st anniversary of its formation, English Heritage decided to publish a book that would show how artists and visitors have valued for centuries the historic houses, castles, abbeys and ancient monuments now in its care. Chiswick House featured among the 60 sites selected for *The English Grand Tour: Artists and Admirers of England's Historic Sites*. Barry Martin was invited to produce a new work of a site of his choice for illustration in the book. He spent the summer at *Battle Abbey* in East Sussex (now a public school, but open to visitors in the summer holidays) where the battlefield from 1066 inspired him to sketch. Martin's visits coincided with rehearsals for and the performance of a vast costumed re-enactment. In the final drawing, wielding charcoal with his characteristic stabbing-gesture strokes, Martin evokes a surreal scene that seems to be lit by flashes of lightening. On the battlefield, overlooked by the rambling ruins and restored buildings of the Abbey, soldiers mix with monks and jesters as if thrown up by some vortex in time. Space and shadows turn into

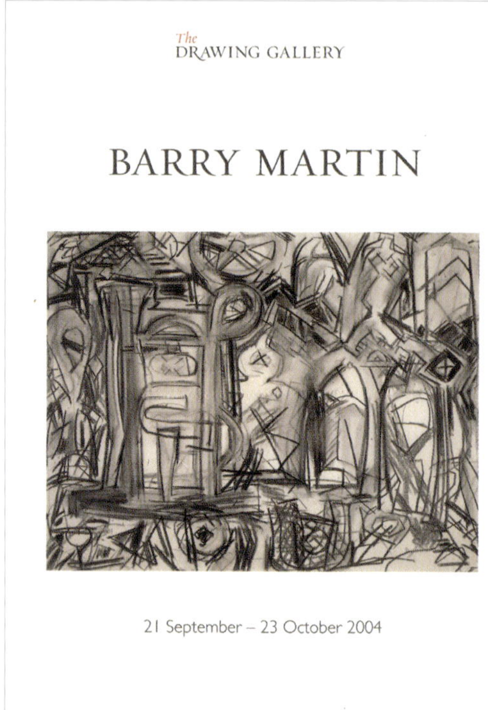
The Drawing Gallery

BARRY MARTIN

21 September – 23 October 2004

2004
*The Drawing gallery*
Statement by the artist in the catalogue the exhibition at the Drawing Gallery, London

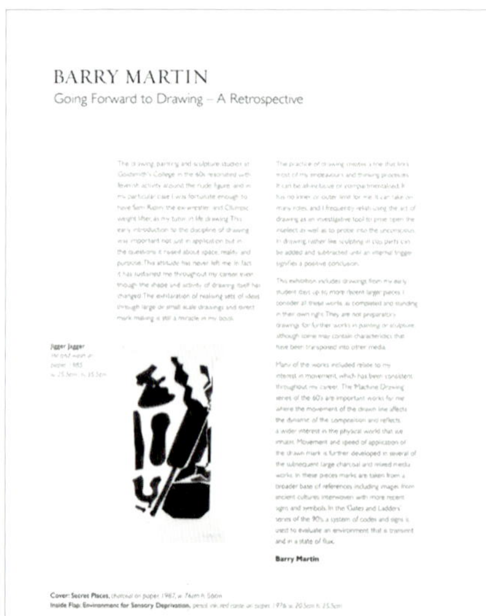
BARRY MARTIN
Going Forward to Drawing – A Retrospective

Barry Martin

**Cover: Secret Places,**
**Inside Flap: Environment for Sensory Deprivation,**

silhouettes of beasts, foliage has faces, teasing the conscious mind, all in a swirl of movement that conveys the clash and mêlée of battle. Like the Chiswick series, it is not only the charcoal but the weight and richness of the paper itself that draws our eyes. Martin compares paper to electrical cable: 'you have to choose it carefully, gauging it the appropriate charge it is expected to carry'.

The same summer saw the opening of a new private commercial gallery, the first ever in central London dedicated to contemporary drawing. At the aptly-named Drawing Gallery (37 Duke Street, St. James's, SW1) the founding director, Yvonne Crossley, chose to launch her ambitious endeavour with a one-man show: *Barry Martin: Going Forward to Drawing-A Retrospective*. Here could be seen how, over 45 years, drawings had been made neither as studies for sculptures or paintings, nor as ends in themselves. As Martin explained in the catalogue, he relishes 'the act of drawing as an investigative tool to prise open the intellect as well as to probe into the unconscious.



1985
*Jigger Jagger*
Ink and wash on paper
25,5 x 35,5 cm
(Collection: Victoria & Albert Museum)

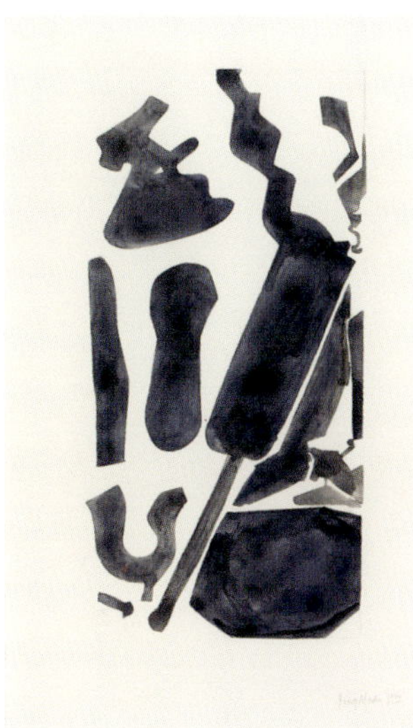

1963
*Machine Drawing No. 1*
Charcoal on paper
76 x 56 cm

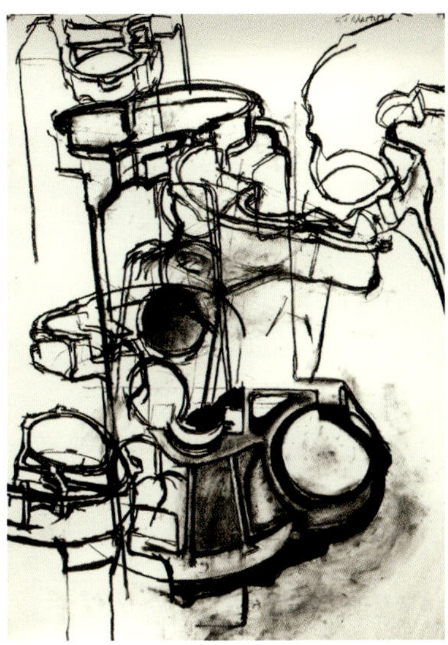

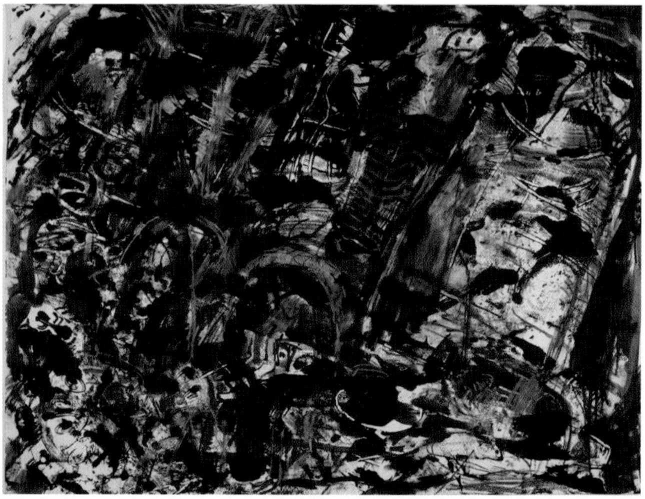

1987
*Environment with Signs*
Ink and wash on paper
59 x 150 cm
(Collection: Victoria & Albert Museum)

The influence of his first teacher in the life-class, Sam Rabin, could be seen in *Life Study* (1961) where the sharp pencil defines form with insistent parallel hatching and extreme tonal variation. The potential of charcoal and of a more free, open approach that suited Martin's fascination with movement is clear in *Machine Drawing No. 1*. Here the anatomy of living mechanical components seem sliced open and inverted for analysis as the artist records them, sketching with an urgent precision that suggests the flow from frustration to the excitement of discovery. Mysterious machine parts again provide the vocabulary of *Jigger Jagger* (1985) but in clean, soft silhouettes that recall the impressions left by the painted naked models of Yves Klein. In *Environment with Signs* (1990) the allusive qualities of understated forms are animated by restless, scratching lines that wriggle uncomfortably.

The most powerful and characteristic works in the exhibition were Martin's large charcoal drawings *Secret Places* (1987) and *Gates and Ladders No. 2* (1995) which are exhausting just to behold. This is drawing beyond the speed limit. They read like frenzied, exuberant explanations of the way some kinetic sculpture still in the artist's mind is meant to operate and so dominate all its viewers. Looking at them, you can't help but sense the artist is there next to you, talking at his usual break-neck speed, firing off a succession of ideas and abstruse allusions before the very air we share turns them stale. This is where drawing beats all other media, languages, alphabets and signs, as the fastest way to get ideas out in the open and then down on paper.

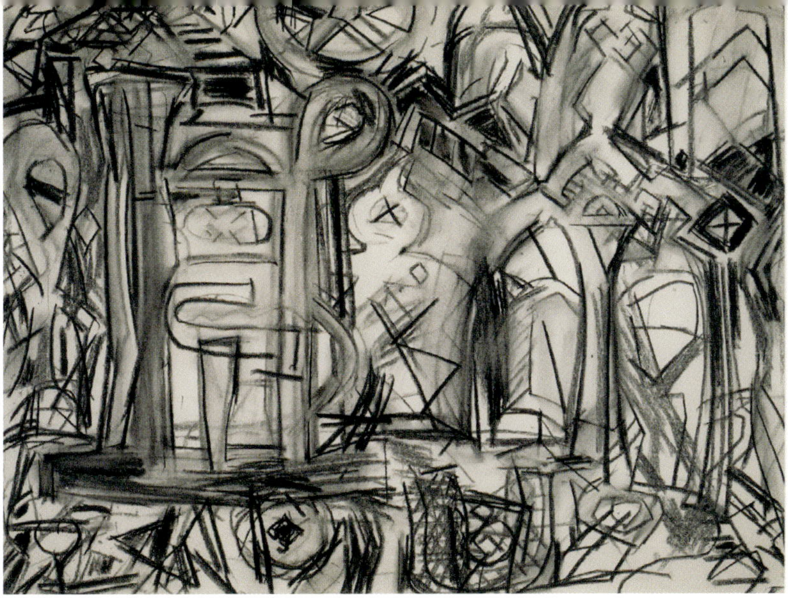

1987

*Secret Places*

Charcoal on paper

56 x 76 cm

Among the diversity of Martin's approach to drawing, a number of portraits amount to a distinct body of work. Most date from 1983-84, are drawn in pastels and came about through the artist's membership of the Hogarth Health Club in Chiswick. This urban country club in West London had become a favourite watering hole for 'resting' actors and dancers, conveniently close to BBC Television Centre at Shepherd's Bush and to Twickenham Film Studios. Regular guests at its smart restaurant included familiar faces from the stage, cinema and smaller screen, such as Vanessa Redgrave, Joan Collins Pauline Collins, John Alderton, Timothy Dalton, Ian Holm and Peter Egan. To the latter Martin owed his introduction to the Club, through Peter's wife (before Myra found her calling as a match for Dr Who).

Martin became, in effect, artist to the stars for a couple of years in London. Through their long restaurant afternoons, as taller tales were told, he would quietly observe how their faces went through their rich

1995

*Gates and Ladders No. 2*

Charcoal on paper

76 x 56 cm

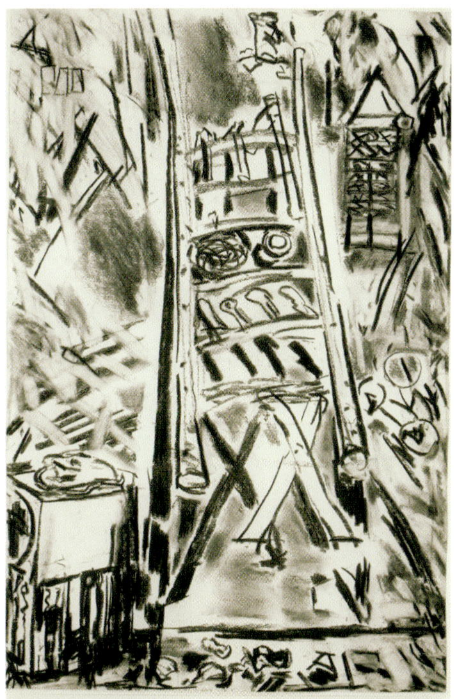

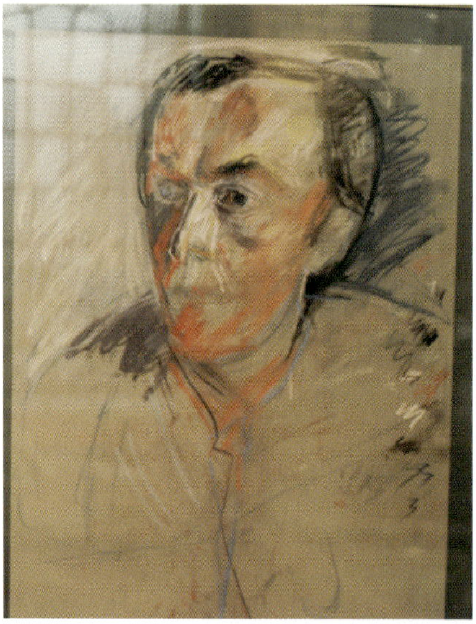

1985

*Portrait of the actor Peter Egan*

Pastel on tinted paper

110 x 76 cm

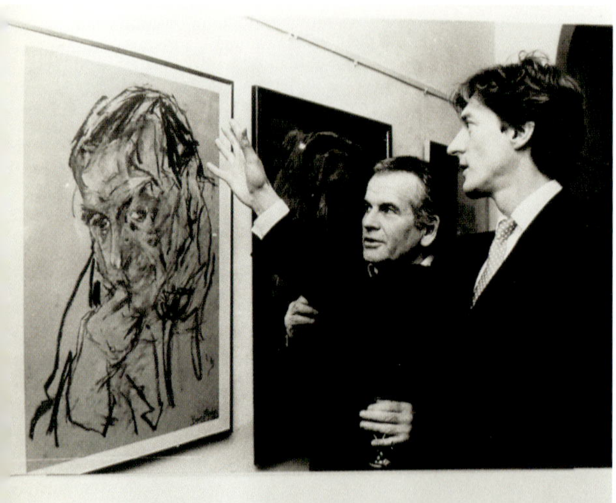

1985

The actor Ian Holm studies his portrait with Nigel Havers at the artist's portrait exhibition

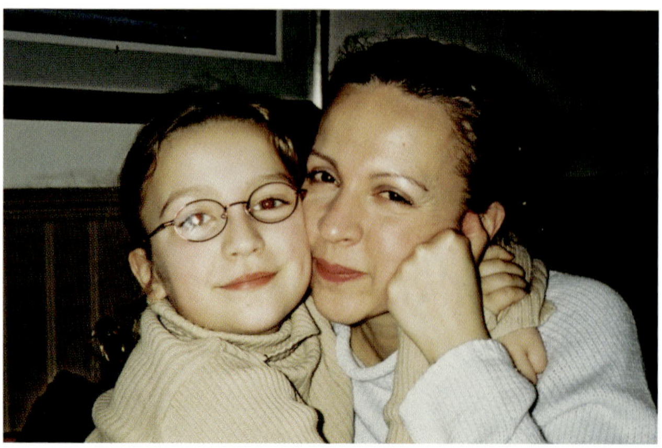

Daughter Jess and Sarah, the artist's wife, Menorca, Spain

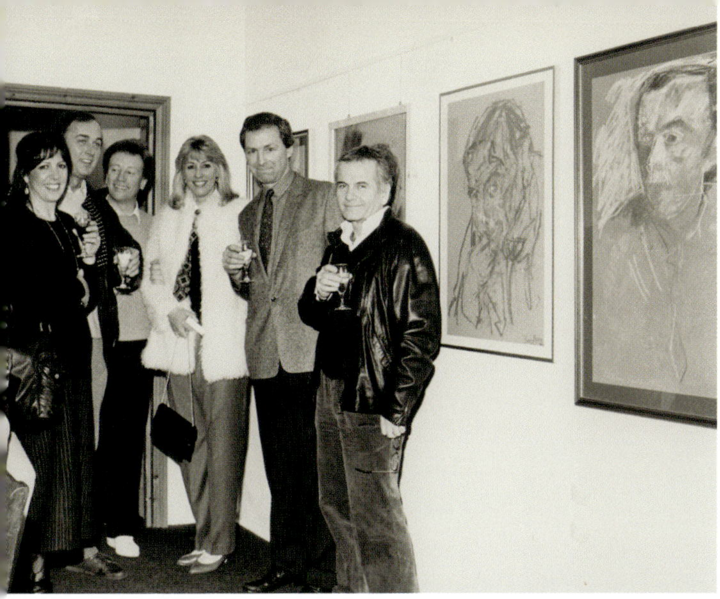

1985
Actors and actresses attending the opening of the artist's exhibition of portraits, London

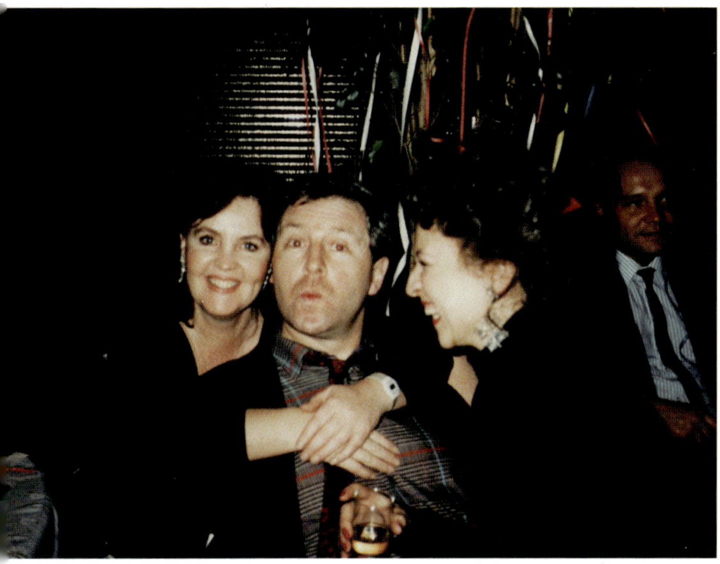

1985
The actress Pauline Collins (left) accosts the artist while Sarah (his wife) looks on.





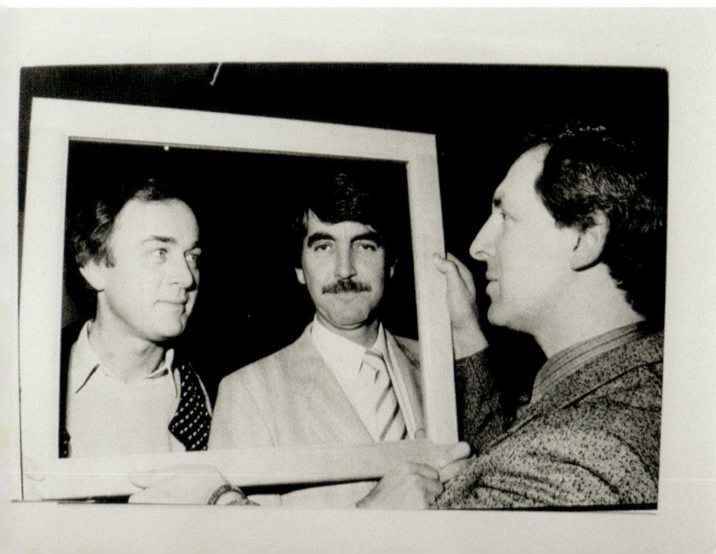

2004
Peter Egan, John Alderton and the artist (right) at the opening of the Drawing Gallery, St James.

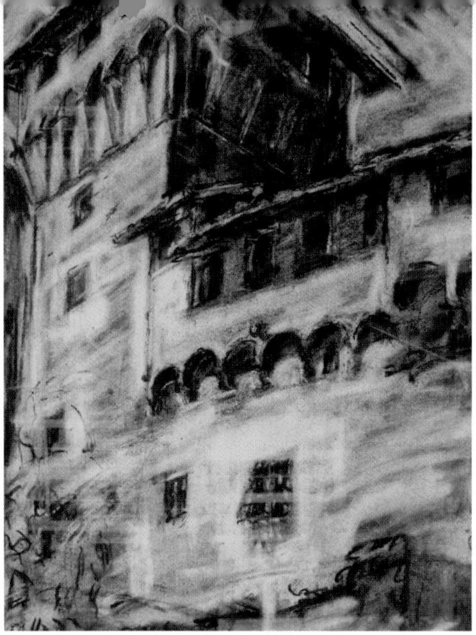

1998

*The Medici Hunting Fortress*

*Upstate Florance Italy*

Charcoal on Arches paper

96 x 66 cm





repertoires of responses, from competitive actors to sincere friends via off-guard celebrities. He recalls how their facial features occasionally seemed at odds, sometimes combining, for example, a theatrically raised eyebrow with a frank sullen pout. The expressive physical terrain of their faces, as flesh and muscle, colour structures and linear rhythms, fascinated him. He was then teaching life drawing at the Royal College of Art. To pass the time, actors agreed to sit, or to come to the studio to polish up their own artistic talents as private pupils. The resulting portraits were not flattering likenesses drawn to convey personality, as a society portraitist must deliver, but rather attempts to capture the tools of their trade, the expressions actors have at their disposal. In his portrait of Peter Egan, for example, the passer-by is grabbed by a single eye, like a burning coal in the night, or a sinister whisper in a dark alley.

Landscape drawing can provide a release from such relentless scrutiny. As with his haunting evocation of *Battle Abbey*, Martin's view of *The Medici Hunting Fortress*, *Upstate Florence, Italy*, combines the best of his fluent attacking style of execution with his more patient, analytical eye for structure. It was drawn in 1998 while Martin spent the summer teaching landscape painting and drawing to twelve mature artists as the guest of Lorenzo Scaratti in the medieval Castello di Trebbio, Italy. He recalls, fondly, standing in the tower surveying the view of the Tuscan hills at sunset. Standing there alongside him, he heard his host comparing the respect shown to his ancestral home by each of the occupying forces during the Second World War. The Nazi commanding officer kept up the owners'

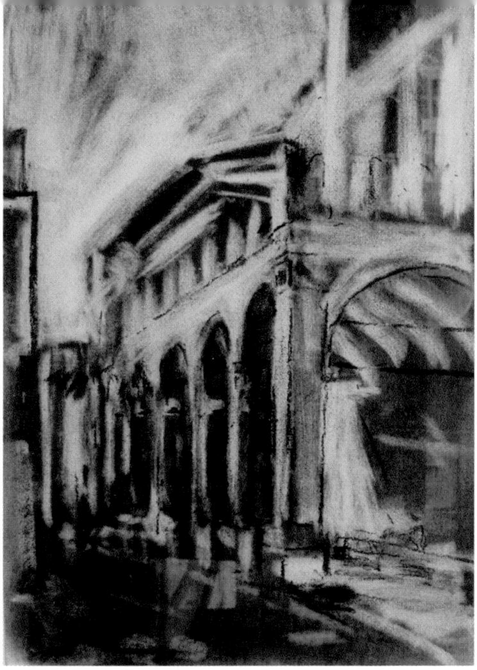

1998

*The Roman Market, Ascoli,*

*Marche Regions,* Italy

Charcoal on Arches paper

66 x 44 cm

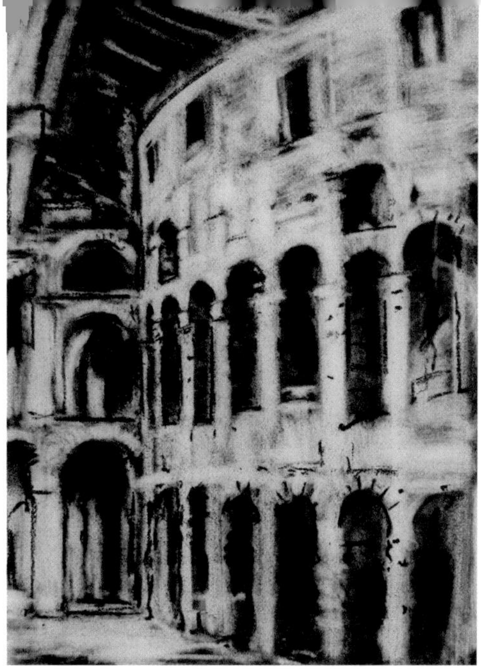

1998

*The Colosseum, Rome*

Charcoal on paper

66 x 44 cm

standards and somehow failed to comply with the command to blow the fortress up when it came time to retreat, whereas the American troops ruined the place, using antique furniture, even the family's grand piano, as firewood (hence the American-style location given in the title of this drawing). Ironically, the invading allies had been part of the same campaign that landed at Anzio, where Martin's father was killed. From Chiswick to Trebbio, Martin has been inspired by the legacy of Italy, by the land and culture of his Italian grandparents. Drawing is his most immediate way of dealing with his need to respond to this, and the rest.

Throughout his career in many media Martin keeps coming back to drawing, as his means to observe, record, explore, analyse and experiment. His natural instinct as an artist is to think first on paper, his anchor medium, using chalks, pastels, pencil or ink, visualising his thoughts as signs and symbols amid the gestures that provide both a release for, and record of, his instinctive creative energy. The variety of his drawings reflects his range and versatility as an artist and affirms the enduring potential of this most fundamental art form.  Somehow, one feels sure that the best drawings are still to come.

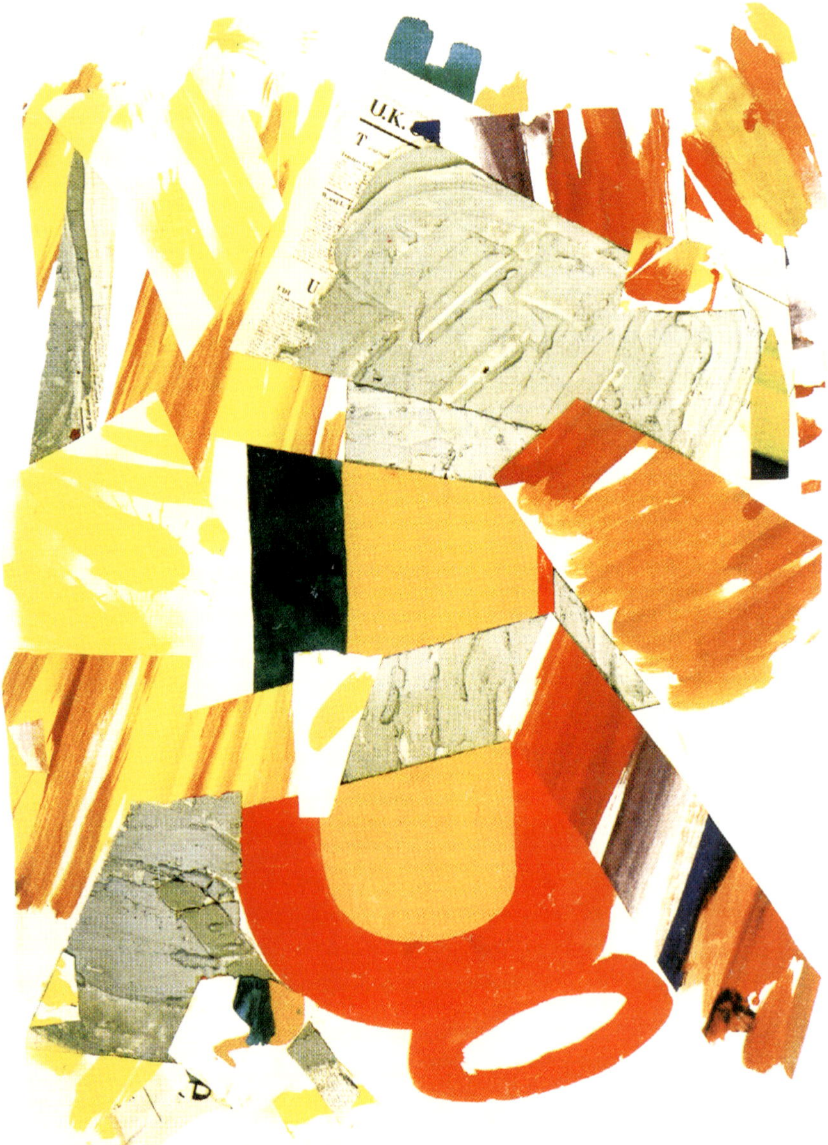

*Surface Movements*

# 6 Collages and Art Criticism



Queuing up for coffee in the spacious Senior Staff Common Room of central London's City University, you cannot help noticing three rich splashes of colour framed on the far wall. Red, orange, ochre, yellow, these fresh slices of painted paper, pasted together as collages, directly echo across the room the culinary palette of the Polish serving girl's less tempting fare, of ciabatta, baked beans, tomato, sweet corn and chips. Pulling up a deep leather armchair, closer inspection reveals the collages are a series, quietly inviting you to play along and see how they unfold. Forms that you might have mistaken from afar for some colour-coded ground plan of a complex campus now shape up.

1977
*The Clails series*
Paint, mixed media, glue,
aggregates on card
63 x 45 cm
(Collection City University, London)

Barry Martin brings over the coffee and stands before his old friends, works he has not seen for years. He is silently satisfied that they are still up and still standing up to scrutiny, thirty years after they were made; he feels they are like 'old diaries of actions', still buzzing with the energy of the inner city in which they were born. In all, the university bought fourteen of the series of thirty-five from 1977 but they were nearly lost in a fire here several years ago; four were destroyed, others were smoke-damaged and had to be reframed. The rest hang downstairs, just off the main entrance hall.

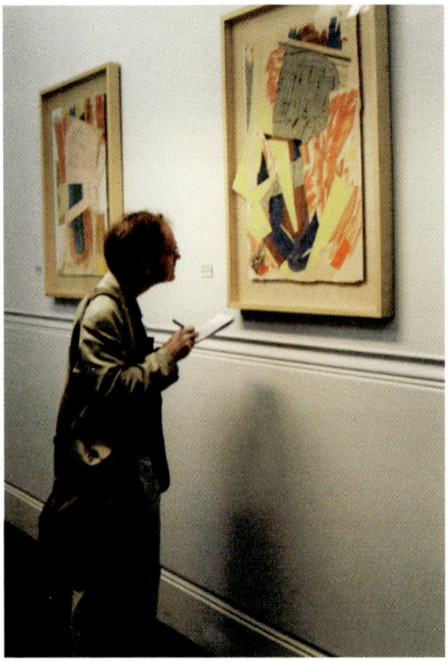

2007
The artist's collages at the City University, London
122 x 92 cm
(Collection: City University, London)



Having escaped the crowded corridors of side-stepping students among urgent notice-boards, signposts, posters and fly-postings you suddenly feel able to stop, to focus on something that visually matters, in this quiet common room where academics read and feed. Slowly but surely these three framed collages reveal their common themes. Reading through the layers of flying slices of painted colour you find a powerful image beneath. Evidently the artist began each one with a painted red oval, about two feet tall, in-filled with ochre, leaning slightly to the right and spanning a smaller, horizontal oval. The basic form is like a new letter in the alphabet, somewhere between the symbol for infinity and a Q with a looping tail. Somehow, this tall red shape calls to mind the kind of meaningless but effective corporate logo you can't avoid recognising when travelling in Europe, like the repetitive badge of some Belgian supermarket chain or brand of petrol that has an irritating habit of popping up as an illuminated plastic blot in the landscape and most picturesque village. Having created this punchy new sign, the artist has trashed it. In each image, in the same way, the smart new corporate brand logo has been tipped to the right, had its central segment sliced out and shoved to the left and then overloaded at the top with a nasty dollop of dead grey that is crudely scraped to resemble rutted cement. Close inspection of the series of three has revealed that each apparently appetising dance of colour is not so joyful but contains within it a system, the emotional associations of which are more challenging, as a cheery tall elegant red symmetrical form is collapsing under a splatter of grey matter.

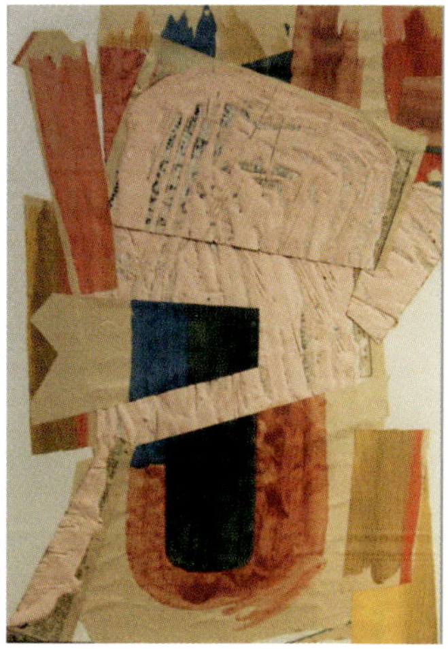

2007
*Clail No. 14*
Mixed media
138 x 90 cm

Within each of the series, this formal dilemma has been splashed with assorted slices of his own paintings. At first, its just wild; there's a sense of free energy that triumphs over the broken badge. And then you notice that things are not so random, that the swirling quotes from lost paintings each have a job to do, are hard at work propping, swimming upward, restoring balance, leading the eye in and around what began as a hopelessly unstable toppling motif. The movement is not only planar, across the surface, but seems to push and

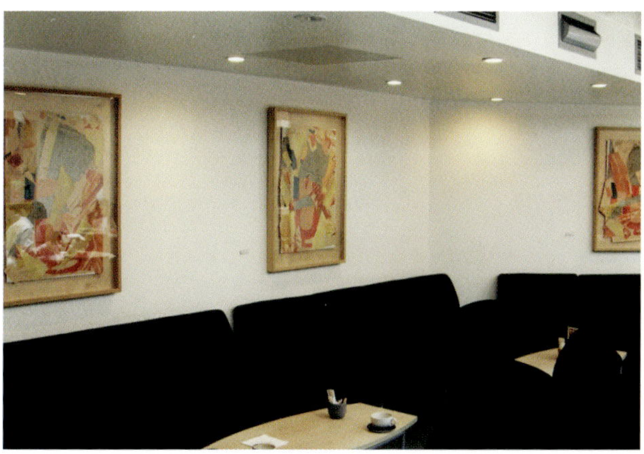

pull in depth as colours assert and withdraw, and paper overlaps like the slats of a Venetian blind caught by the breeze of an open window. In each collage a strip of newsprint assert the flatness of the surface, straining to maintain the lateral tension like the horizontal strut of a twisting kite. Within the series, each collage tackles the same challenge of salvaging the stability of the decimated red motif without restoring its strangely familiar unfamiliar form. As a series, in effect they present the same image at different moments in time, as different stages in a shared endeavour. Each one could be read as a document of the performance life of a kinetic sculpture made only of colour and brushwork. The combination of earlier fragmented paintings and mark-making further lifts them outside the traditional notion of a work of art as a product of a specific time and place.

**Each one could be read as a document of the performance life of a kinetic sculpture made only of colour and brushwork**

As the university common room begins to fill up for lunch, Barry Martin explains how the collage series came about, thirty years ago in a very different London and life. Just a mile or two across town he had two studios, in Shaftesbury Avenue, in the former Hopital et Dispensaire Francais (today the Covent Garden Hotel), upstairs above the AIR Gallery, close to St Martin's and the Charing Cross Road community of artists. He had just given up the role of editor of the art journal *One*, which he had founded in 1974 with the sculptor William Tucker in an ambitious attempt to raise the general standard of art criticism in England. Writing had become an increasingly important part of Martin's output as an artist. Things did not get off to an auspicious start as his first article appeared in *Ink*, the sister underground magazine to Oz that went down with the Oz obscenity trial.

Between 1972 and 1979 Martin wrote regularly on modern painting and sculpture for *Studio International, Art Monthly* and *Artscribe*. Two articles in Studio International in particular caused a stir: a review of the Royal Academy's survey exhibition *British Sculpture* '72 and one in 1974 on the Dutch Artists' Unions that had grown from the 'BBK', the Second World War resistance fighters. More significantly for Martin's own position was his series of articles for *Studio International* on his contemporaries, including Anthony Caro, John Hoyland, Philip King, Jeremy Moon and William Tucker.

While visiting artists in New York in 1976 Martin had been struck by their frankness of debate, by the open dialogue that stimulated their work. The London scene, by contrast, he felt seemed 'buttoned up' and protective, an attitude he blames on a lack of confidence among those artists who saw themselves working in the shadow of their American contemporaries.

In crossing the line between artist and critic, Martin risked losing the friendship of fellow painters and sculptors alike. But he felt it had to be done, for few newspaper critics really understood what artists were about, in his view. One leading critic-turned -magazine editor declared that painting and sculpture were dead, and that henceforth only Conceptual Art mattered. The galleries and dealers responded promptly by withdrawing their advertising; the magazine then folded. As an artist, Martin brought informed debate from the studio to the printed page. As a critic, his aim was not to be independent and judgmental, but to give honest feedback, 'to create a platform for professional debate', in the way that leading playwrights were writing theatre reviews in London at that time. The risk was worth it; while some artists drifted away others invited him to write introductions to their exhibition catalogues and books. But the open debate did not take off, and it was all a lot of work.



1977 was the busy year of the Queen's Silver Jubilee, when Martin served as a guest curator of the Jubilee Exhibition of British Sculpture in Battersea Park, for which he wrote a catalogue essay (as discussed in the chapter on Word Art). Martin was also included in the Jubilee Exhibition of British Painting at the Royal Academy. Meanwhile he taught in the Fine Art Department at Croydon College of Art, part-time, sharing students with John Bellamy and Bruce McLean. 1977 was also the year that he finally

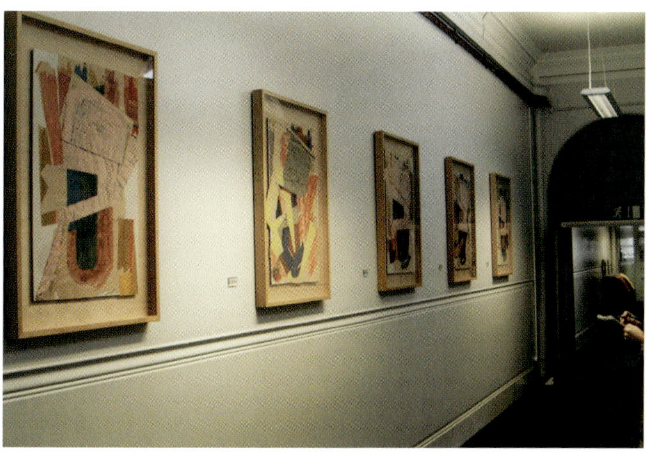

1982

Installation view of Collages at the City University, London

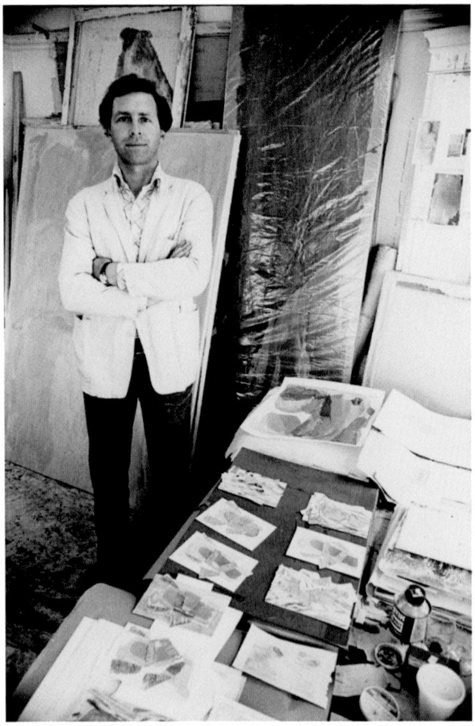

1976
The artist standing in his studio, Shaftesbury Avenue



renounced his adventurous bachelor lifestyle, thanks to the most beautiful nineteen-year-old Arts Foundation Course student that year at Croydon College of Art. Sarah had only arrived in Britain from the West Indies when she was seventeen. Martin married her within months of their first meeting. Gone for good was the international fashion model from the Bond Street agency with her catwalk shows in Park Lane hotels, and a lifestyle that Martin could do without.

Above Shaftesbury Avenue, one studio was kept clear and clean for drawing. Upstairs, in his painting studio, one day he found himself sitting on the floor, quietly cutting up still-wet paintings. All around him emerged an expanding nest of dislocated recycled brushwork, the chaos of autumn leaves, the psychedelic stripes of confetti, sitting like a King Cnut of painting in a rising sea of colour. Composing on the floor in 360 degrees, Martin surveyed the waves of art extracts; some asked to be shuffled like playing cards, others pulled and pushed like bed clothes, stirring his imagination through fresh collisions and random compositions in-the-round. As he ran out of paintings so newspapers got caught up in the beach-combing.

The series that emerged was over thirty-five-strong and first filled a room as a dazzling installation at the Art Net Gallery off New Oxford Street, sandwiched between the antiquarian bookshops that huddle in the shadows of the British Museum. Martin dubbed the collages 'CLAILS', his acronym for 'Communicable and Lively Advents Interfused with Light and Symbolised'. In November 1978 a selection along with new paintings became a one-man show at the Patrick Seale Gallery in Motcomb Street, Belgravia; in January 1980 collages and paintings featured in his first one-man show in Spain, at the Galeria de Arte Goya, near Goya's home town in Zaragoza. In his essay for the catalogue to the Belgravia exhibition Martin described how 'these collages are simply one method I've devised to break time and sequence' and reasserted his commitment (first quoted in *Studio International* in 1966) to witnessing the 'construction of the/a Space-Time era'. He explained how the central motif of the collages, 'an archetypal form, led me to read authors such as Jung who consciously laid bare much of what I had instinctively felt'.

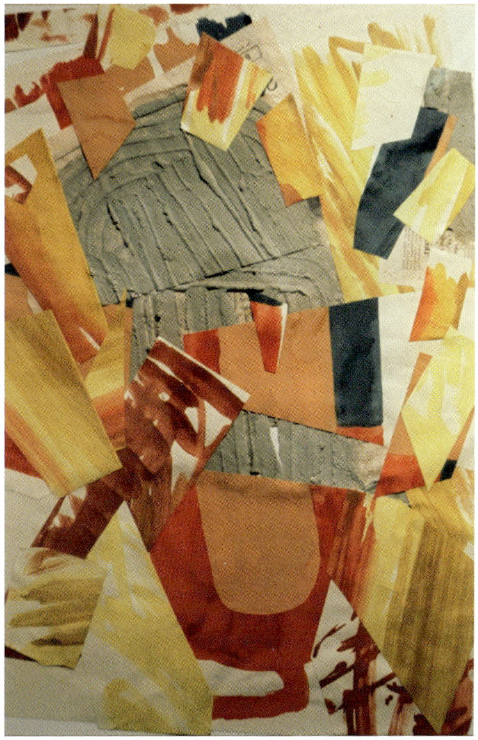

1977
*Clail No. 17*
Mixed media, paper, card, paint, fillers
138 x 90 cm





The most substantial of the exhibition reviews came from Bryan Robertson, the former director of the Whitechapel Art Gallery (1952-1968) who had retired to London in 1975 after five years as director of the State University of New York's museum. Robertson's review filled three pages of *Art Monthly* with a general assessment of Martin's contribution to contemporary British art. Alongside an illustration of *Clail 17* Robertson described the London art scene of the 1970s, as he found it on his return from New York. After 'the excessive promotion of style' in the 1960s, the 1970s was, he felt, the decade that saw 'the convergence of creative doubt and fatigue', for the 'fresh authority' that art had acquired in the 1960s was gone. Since the mid-1960s, he felt that art 'was no longer necessarily a vocation...but often a business conducted in terms of stylistic enterprise' where student shows had ceased to serve as 'student occasions but provided a hunting ground for dealers and critics in search of new talent'. The 1970s had made things worse: 'the economic decline of the 70s has aggravated the situation. In lean times, collectors want gilt-edged investments'. Martin, however, 'has tackled everything with vigorous intelligence' and the work of the past four years, in painting and collage 'seem to be the most concentrated works that he's produced so far'. Robertson concluded his review on a sonorous note, with great expectations:

> Martin has been very much part of the context of the 60s and 70s with all their positive achievements and negative digressions. At thirty-five he has retained the vitality that he's always given to aesthetic research and enquiry, but gradually the vitality is being channelled into more contemplative areas in painting. The strands are coming together.

The City University purchased their fourteen *Clails* as part of the project to furnish their new buildings. Originally they were hung with loans from the Arts Council's collection but today Martin's work seem to stand alone as the only art still on display. Martin could not have known how appropriate it would be that his Jungian archetypal form now resembles a corporate logo, or that his torn fragments of newsprint, chosen for its pink paper, came from the *Financial Times*, for the Clails series now hangs in an intense business-breeding campus. Close inspection of one cutting reveals a private joke, a pocket-size cartoon of a school careers master interviewing a tramp. This detail might now seem like an ironic comment in an inner-city institution that has as its slogan 'the university for business and the professions'. Martin casually recalls that another buyer of a work from the series was Unilever.

As an artist who first came to prominence in the 1960s, Martin had played with collage more than a decade before, when the medium absorbed so much of the market imagery of Pop Art. The best example of his earlier experiments with the medium is *Movement Collage* (1965, Tate). In the note Martin provided on the work for the Tate he explained how he took the familiar imagery of mass consumerism, so beloved of the Pop Art generation, and denied its currency as contemporary subject matter by attempting to use motifs for their formal values alone. Taking everyday images from magazine advertisements he 'tried to use the colour, tone, shape and linear movement of each image and place it into a new composition where a dynamic force could be released through its juxtaposition, independent of its subject matter. In a sense I was trying to turn on its head the cult of personality that pervaded London and its streets at that time by turning well-known images into formal considerations'. The energy of Tottenham Hotspur's celebrity footballer Danny Blanchflower is represented by his legs alone; International Rescue's emergency jet Thunderbird 1 has been cropped of its identifying number and Thunderbird 2 is pivoting on its nose; the interior of a cosy cabin on a yacht slides out of the picture on its side and a passenger jet just sticks its nose in. A splash of blank blue paper at the heart of the image reminds us that this is all only paper arranged in a formal composition, but is torn in a way that adds to the varieties of movement reconciled through composition.

The only unbroken image presents the jolly smiles of a well bed -and -breakfasted father and children as they wave farewell in their office and



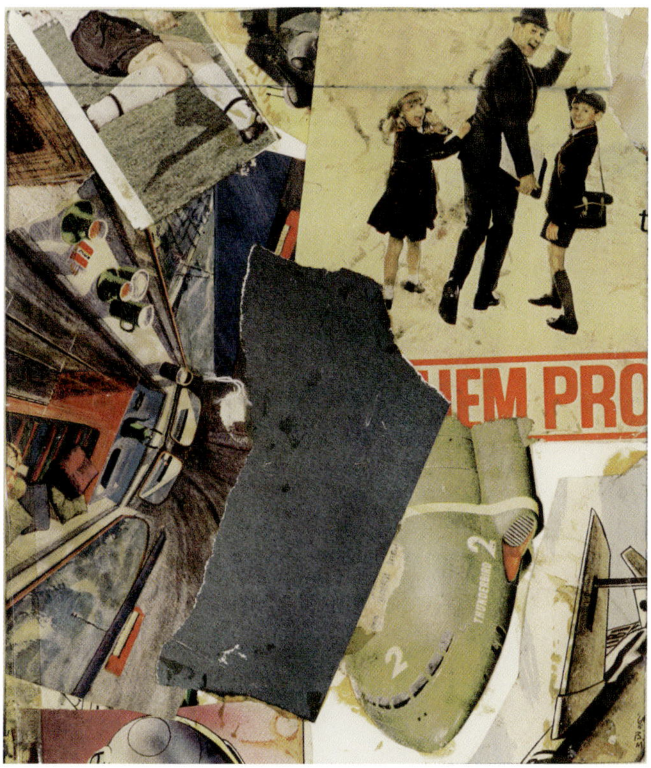

1965
*Movement Collage*
Collage images from magazines glued to card
34 x 20 cm
(Tate collection)

2000/2001

*Rim or Imager*

Laser ink print, edition of 100.

107 x 183cm

(Collection: Slade School of Fine Art, University of London)

The artist was invited to The Slade School of Fine Art, University of London, in 2000 to create a print with their assistance and facilities. The right half of the print has its origins in a collage created along with others in 1965 that explored the theme of movement personified in every day objects.

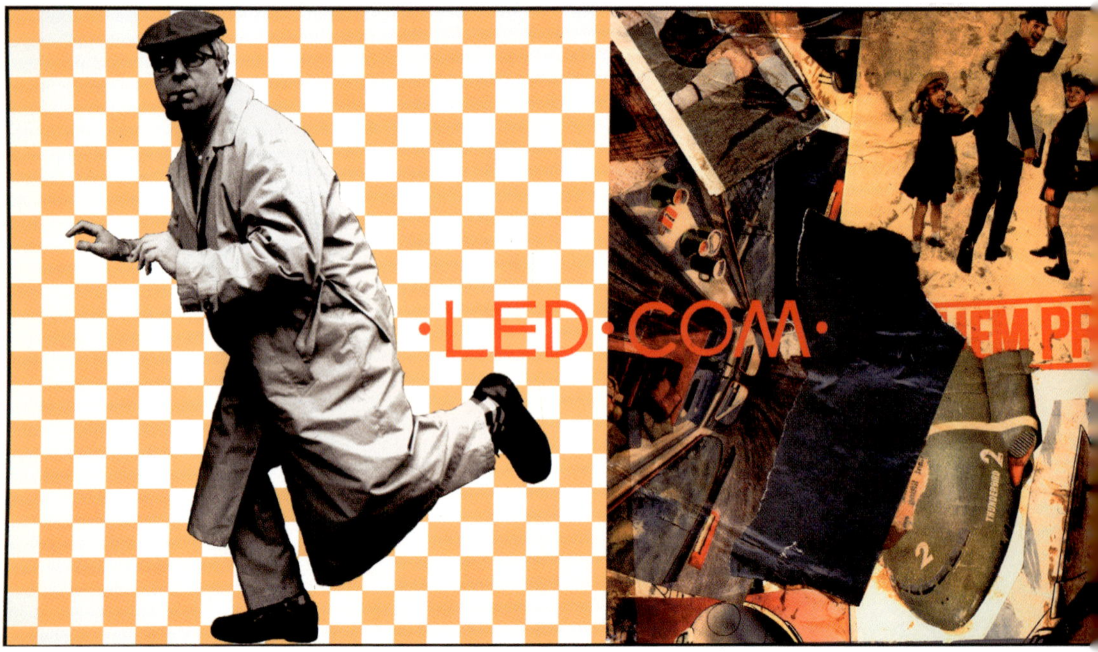

school uniforms. They wave above the name of the product they are advertising but only six red letters remain. Setting the viewer in the role of mother on the doorstep the image may play an ironical note, reminding

**Setting the viewer in the role of mother on the doorstep the image may play an ironical note, reminding the viewer of life as a lonely consumer**

the viewer of life as a lonely consumer. Or it may just be a mistake, for the artist drew a thin blue line across, 'like the editor's blue pencil' in order 'to register my conceptual concern'. In the same corrective way the red printed lettering 'is meant as an enigma to the conscious reading of the collage in any semantic way, whilst occupying an important structural construct in the mechanics and movement of the composition'. According to the Tate's catalogue entry on its website, '*Movement Collage* reveals the influence of British Pop Art and particularly collages by Richard Hamilton' whose most illustrated work, *Just What Is It That Makes Today's Home so Different, So Appealing*? (1956, Tubingen, Kunsthalle) gave the movement its name. Martin, however, feels he was trying to use Pop Art's imagery without celebration or social comment, to see if images of everyday objects that present movement could serve formal artistic ends.

More recently, Martin returned to *Movement Collage* in 2000 when the Slade School of Art invited him to produce a print using their studio resources. The laser ink print now in the Slade's collection reproduces the collage alongside an image of the artist in disguise running across a chessboard (as discussed by Raymond Keene in his chapter on Art and Chess).The two images are linked by six superimposed letters that appear to be an internet address (led.com) or simply flat formal stitching. In fact they allude to a new departure at this time, when Martin experimented with word art and mirror writing. In the same way as the *Clails* recycled paintings, and so embedded in each work different points in time, the printed collage is paired with another previous work to play on the idea of collages of collages, of time turning in on itself, moving simultaneously both backward and forward, as past and future in the present. Its cryptic title, *Rim or Imager*, is an anagram for Mirror Image.

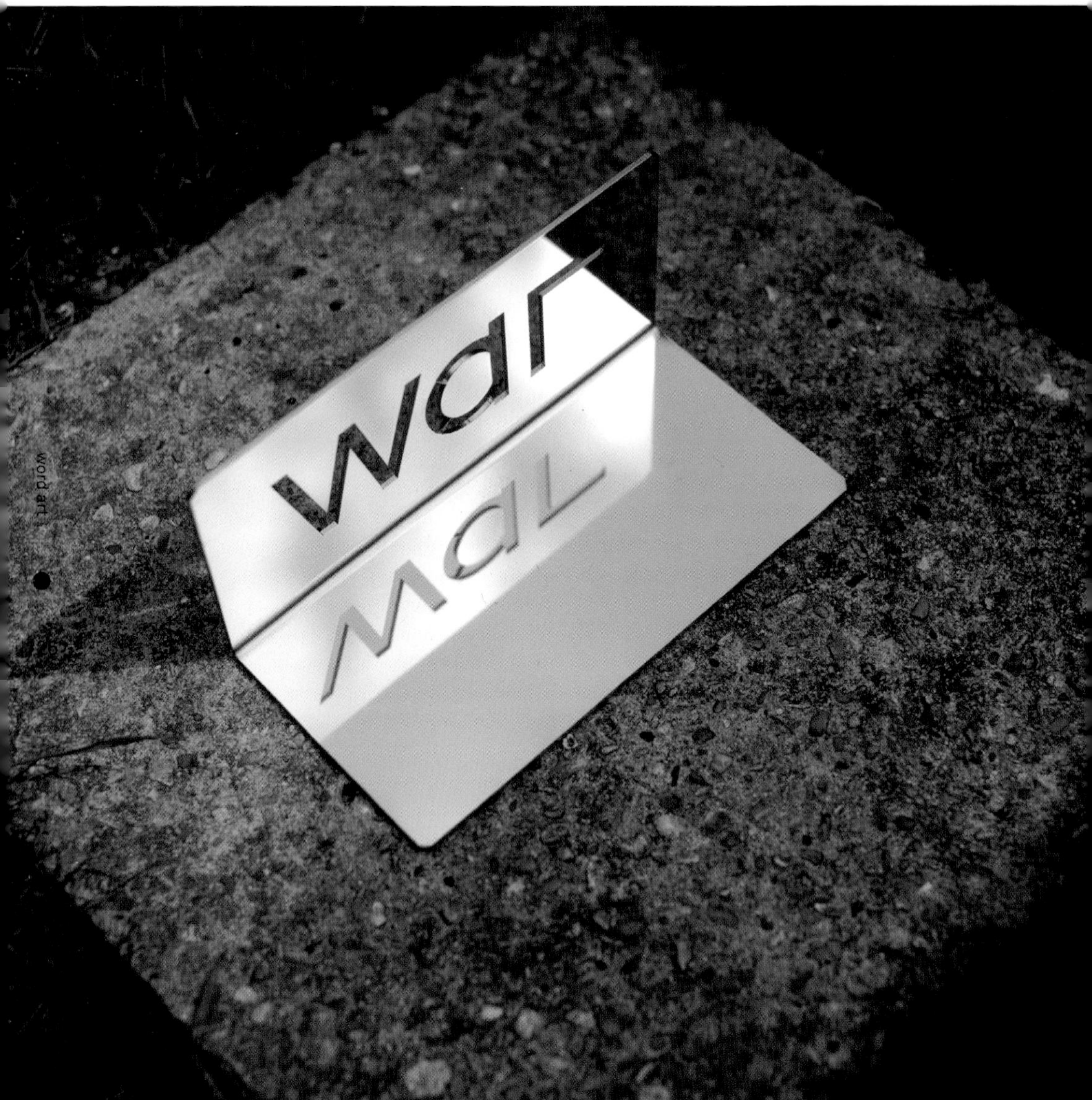
war

# 7 Word Art

On 6th November 1999 The Times carried the following story in its Diary column, under the headline 'Peace Piece':

> The war with the French over British beef took an unusual twist the other evening when a sculpture belonging to Jacques Chirac was stolen from a London art gallery. The sculpture was removed at a private view at the 291 Gallery's Arthinking exhibition, which is showing the work of a number of former Turner prize nominees, among them Cornelia Parker. The thief, I understand, had apparently been told that the sculpture, a work in steel that carried



1998
*War is Bad*
10 x 18 cm
Stainless steel
Made in an edition of 20

This small size work was intended to be sent to World Political Leaders and positioned on their desks as an aide memoire. There are a number of works in this series and in part are intended to enable the viewer, 'to observe and reflect on the process of change itself', and, 'Crossing thresholds of meaning at a glance creates mystery,' as well as bringing self-questioning and self-examination to the fore

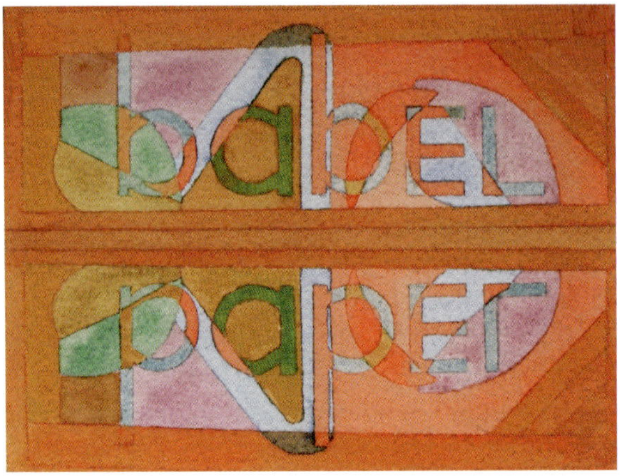


1999
*The painted Word Babel-Paper*
Watercolour on Arches paper
45 x 30 cm

> an anti-war statement, was destined for the French President's office. In a spirit of anti-French feeling, he or she slipped it in his pocket and vanished into the night. Barry Martin, the artist, is outraged at the theft, especially as the sculpture's inscription 'War' and 'Mal' was aimed at promoting harmony between our two great nations. 'I thought I was doing a great moral deed, because the piece is a statement about war, and someone has done a great immoral deed in stealing it'





According to the 291 Gallery's press release, the group exhibition had 'been selected to further a critical dialogue between the visual field of art and the textual domain of philosophy.' It described the show as 'a site of paradoxes, brain teasers and philosophical conundrums' and challenged the press: 'Philosophy is too important to be left to specialists. In Voltaire's words: 'It's up to you to learn to think!''. Martin's work, *War is Bad*, is brilliant in its simplicity. A single sheet of stainless steel is bent at right angles with the word WAR cut through the upright. Thanks to a Modernist typeface designed by Martin, the mirror image of the word that appears in the horizontal half of the sheet reads as MAL. Made in an edition of twenty in 1998, this punchy sculpture was intended to be sent to the world's political leaders to sit on their desks as an ironic executive toy and aide memoir.

*War is Bad* evolved from a series of word sculptures that Martin had shown at the Mind Sports Olympiad, at the Olympia Conference Centre in London in August 1999, under the collective title: *Look- Reflections on Structure and Meaning*. There he mounted on the wall in a single row a series of six small reliefs of words, hewn from Welsh slate (taken from the broken water trough he found in the garden of the gatekeeper's lodge that is his studio at

Chiswick). Each word carved in slate was reflected in its own stainless steel plate. Thanks to Martin's new typeface, words presented their reflected meanings with surprising results.

The pairings began when he first reflected WORD and found it answered with MOLD, the phonetic spelling of mould. As Biblical associations rushed to mind ('in the beginning was the Word...') he realised the potential of his discovery. There followed, for example, LOOK/ROOK, and the matching CHECK/CHECK. Suddenly it seemed as though Martin had uncovered a language hidden within language all along, as if he had opened the door to a parallel 'Through the Looking Glass' world and released alternative meanings that no one had spotted before in English. When Lewis Carroll's

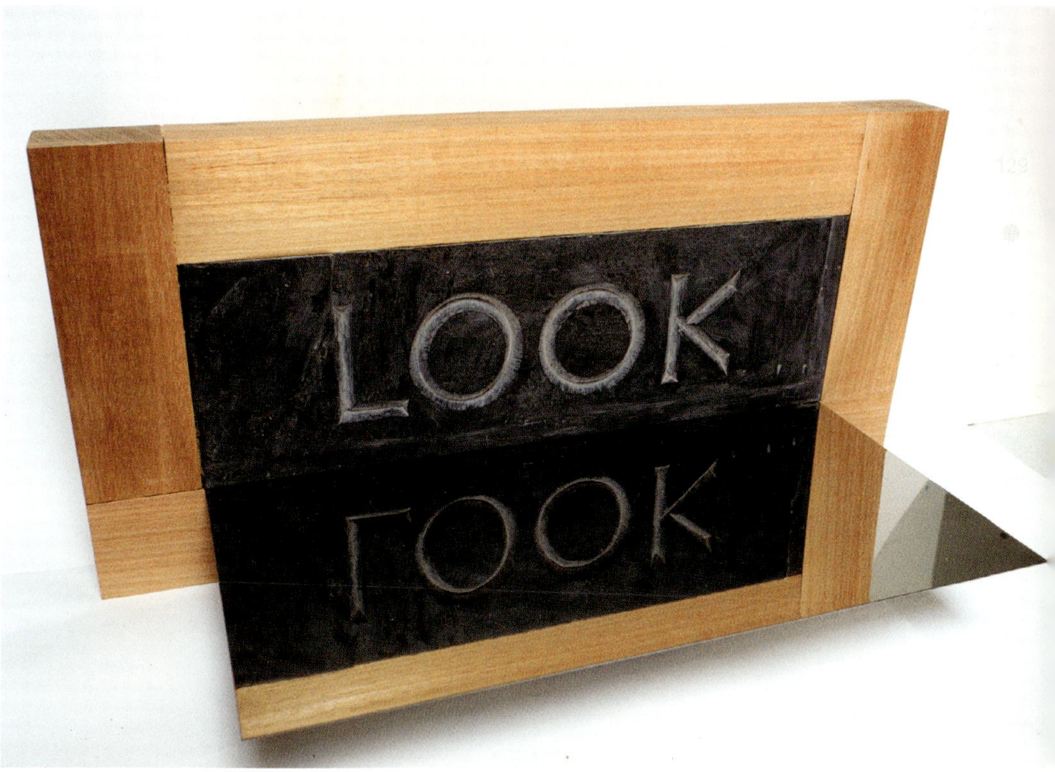


1998

Look/Rook

Welsh slate, stainless, wood

26 x 51 cm

(Collection: Mr. & Mrs. Hurst-Brown)

Alice first finds the poem *Jabberwocky* it is meaningless, being printed in reverse in a 'Looking-glass book' that she must hold up to a mirror to read. Martin's mirror language is not reversed and unintelligible but inverted. His random word pairings immediately puzzle the viewer, as the mind swiftly provides a reason for the association, when none was (we assume) ever

**We try to see a story no matter how abstract the sculpture can be**

there. Whilst celebrating the power of words, the sculptures also challenge the status of words as carriers of intrinsic significance, by showing how readily their associated meanings can be inverted.

In this graphic exposition of the rivalry between the languages of art and literature Martin returned to a dilemma he had addressed in his introduction to the catalogue of the Silver Jubilee Exhibition of Contemporary British Sculpture, held at Battersea Park in 1977. Martin wrote of the difficulty of communicating through abstract art in Britain, where the culture is predominantly literary, where audiences are relatively unfamiliar with ways of appreciating art in terms of its own formal values, as in music and dance. He described how 'standards taken from this country's literary convention have dominated and largely formed the way most of us look at the arts; we try to see a story no matter how abstract the sculpture can be. In the play and novel, form and content are contained within the work. They have a beginning, middle and an end. Recent sculptural thinking, for some, has been to do with 'un-containment' allowing the total idea to spread across numbers of works'. He found an 'immense chasm between the public's understanding of contemporary sculpture and the sculptor's real intentions' which he felt was 'precipitated by a hostile press steeped in a literary tradition and not conversant with the language of sculpture. A result of the ascendancy of the written word over the visual arts has been that it is now possible to substitute the one for the other'. The result, in 1977, was a situation worthy of Joseph Heller's novel Catch 22 (New York, 1961): 'Since much sculpture has been stripped of any literary or figurative connotations the artist has come more and more to rely on the critic to explain his sculpture to the public. Most contemporary British critics have failed the artist in this respect and are neither willing to create nor capable of encouraging creative debate about the subject'.

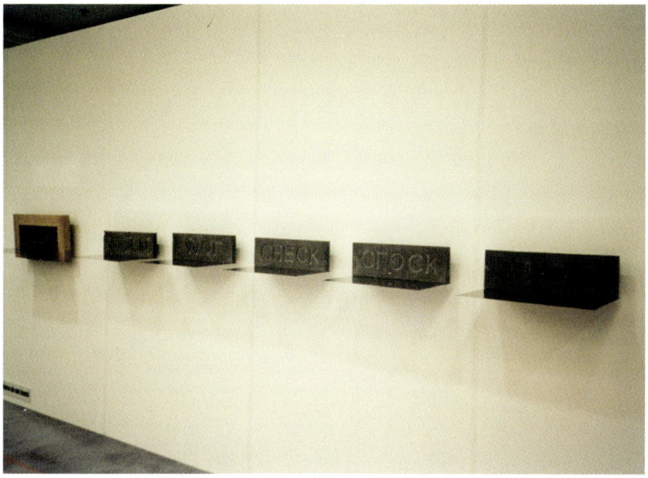


1998

*Olympia*

Welsh slate and stainless steel

*26 x 51 cm*

Installation view of the exhibition

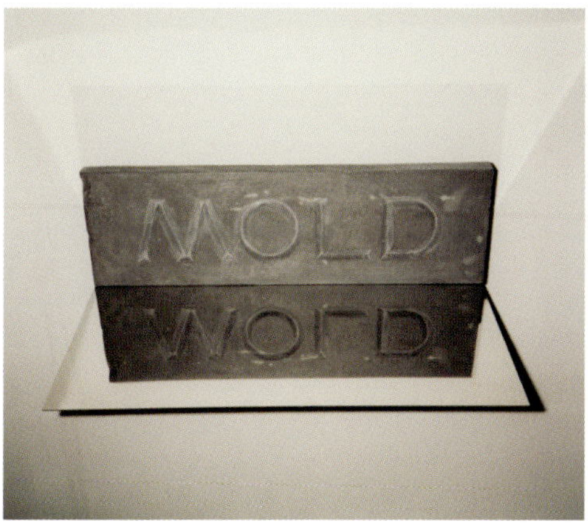


1998

*Mold - Word*

Welsh slate and stainless steel

26 x 51 cm

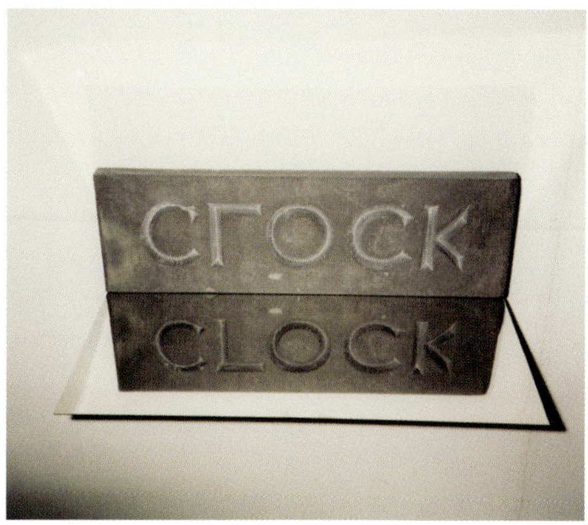


1998

*Crock - Clock*

Welsh slate and stainless steel

26 x 51 cm

*War is Bad* is much more than a convenient vehicle for social comment. As both sculpture and words, form and content, it breaks the closed circular argument that Martin felt prevented public understanding of abstract art. It seemed absurd that this anti-verbal art could only be explained by writers, when writers are preconditioned to use literary formula as their method of evaluation. *War is Bad* teases the literary viewer by offering a word and then, through reflection, shows how the word is only a shape, or another word. Shorn of supporting sentences and grammar, single words look new, both vulnerable to reinterpretation and rich in formal qualities as blocks of graphic design and as signs. Punning on how reflections prompt reflection, and playing with the mind's immediate need to reconcile two juxtaposed words, Martin's word art can undermine our own confidence in the way we think, in the vocabulary we have learnt to use in our heads. This concern for the integrity of the cognitive process, of the ambiguous relationship between observation and understanding, the gap in perception, is at the heart of Martin's abstract art.



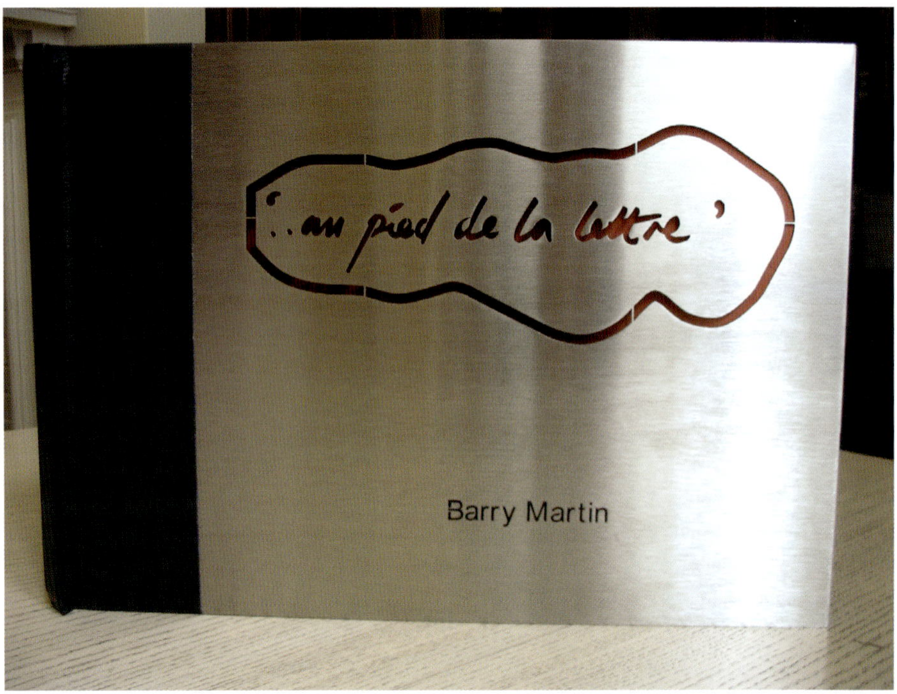


1999

*The artist's book: au pied de la lettre*

Stainless Steel

21 x 30 cm

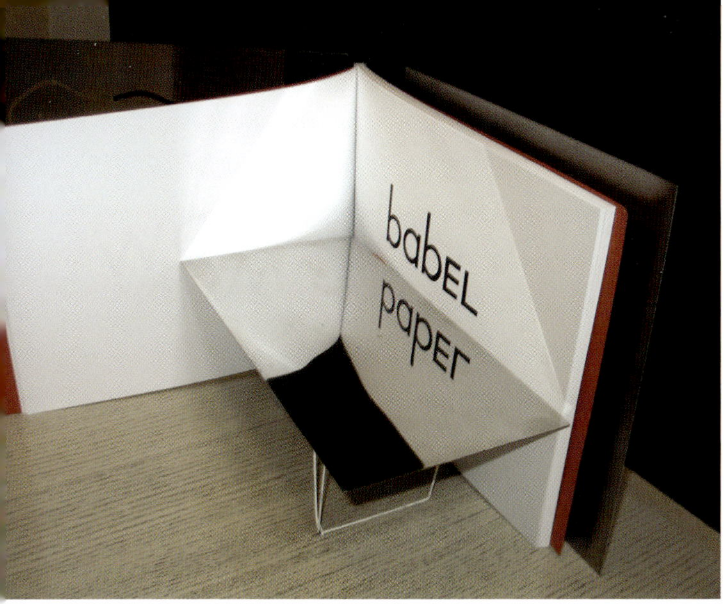


1999

*Au pied de la lettre,* open at *'Babel'*

Stainless Steel, Paper, Print

21 x 30 cm

Concrete Poetry had become popular in Europe around 1965 and historians have attempted to link it to the re-emergence of Kinetic Art, as another aspect of the revival of the Modern Movement. On the printed page Concrete Poetry is kinetic in the simplest sense of there being interplay between arranged typography and space as detected by moving eyes. In the 1920s Dada artists had explored the ways sheets of words could be read as pictures, and how typography could create visual puns or give a word and its image interchangeable meanings. In the lyrical Concrete Poetry of Ian Hamilton Finlay (1925-2006) economy and simplicity are key. Most of his poems invite contemplation as a whole, as shapes and meaning, seemingly independent of any poet. A delicate sense of beauty and his own quiet sense of humour are the themes that unite his poems on the page, wall texts, as neon signs or as inscriptions cut in stone. Martin sees Finlay as belonging to the great tradition of British Romantic landscape painting and poetry, whereas his own word art is more urban and questioning, exposing the processes of cognition in daily life as a cause for concern, rather than composing with their mysteries.

Running with the potential of his mirror-language, Martin produced a book, *au pied de la lettre*, in 2001. The title refers to the potential of the footnote to upstage the main text. Through thirty-two pages he presented as many new pairings. Within the sharp-edged, stainless-steel covers with their laser-cut lettering, the shiny reflective paper and polished steel mirror form a free-standing sculpture, one with an assertive, mechanistic feel, as if we are back within one of Martin's metal machines from thirty years earlier, where meaning flowed from movement. Indeed, as the 'reader' turns the pages and reassembles the integral mirror as a tiny trestle table on which each new word will appear, so the process is a kinetic one. Inevitably, one tries to guess before the hidden word is delivered, but the mind tends to read the printed words in reverse, as mirror writing, rather than inverted, as they will appear. Strangely poignant pairings presented by the book include, for example, PAPER/BABEL, LAW/RAM, MOOR/WOOL, and ROI/LOI. Each pair, left alone together on the white spread, act like grit inside an oyster, and evoke associated images from the reader's imagination.

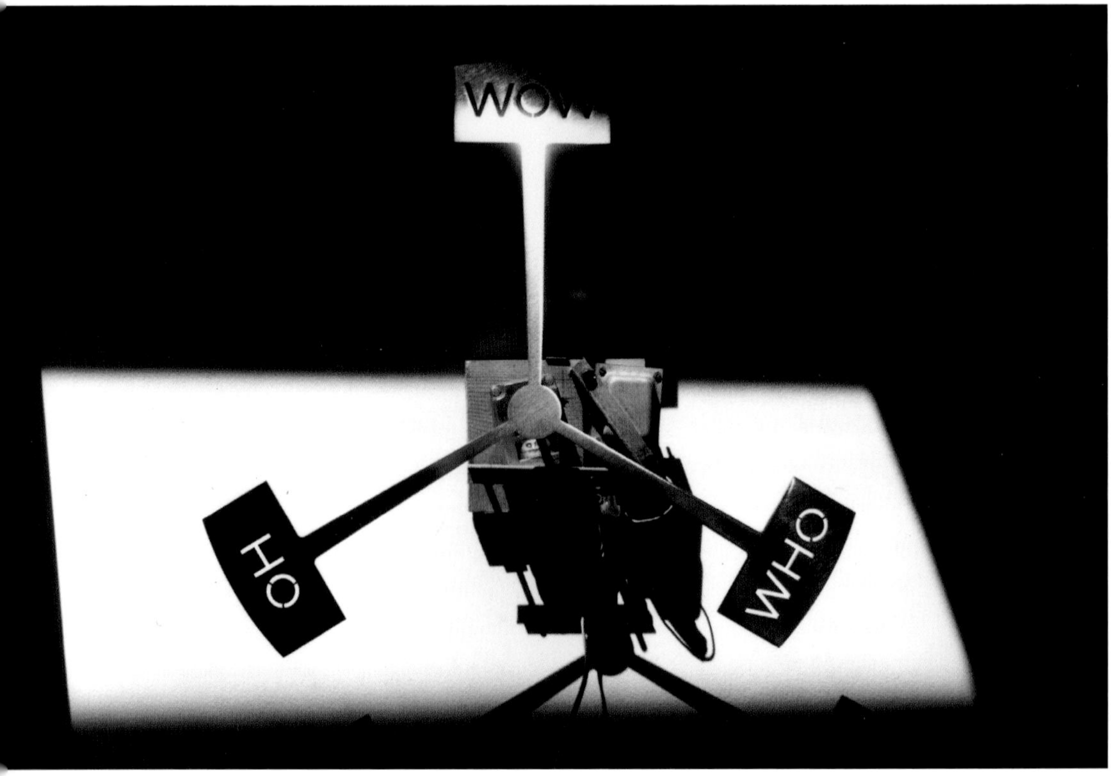


1999

*The Wow Factor*

Stainless steel, electric motor

50 x 15 cm

As the work slowly revolves clockwise the words change their meaning.

In his introduction to Martin's book the British Museum's expert in Mesopotamian cuneiform inscriptions, Irving Finkel, describes the sense of mystery, as if encountering a familiar language for the first time: 'one looks again at his lettered installations and looks again, peering down into his mirror sheet of water, where unguessed secrets lie'. The effect may be like Narcissus at the Pool, but fortunately the mirror is not actually of water, and the copy acquired by the Tate for its archives does not spill, at least, not literally.

At the annual exhibition of the Royal Society of British Sculptors in 2000 Martin showed *The Wow Factor*. In a return to Kinetic sculpture, and the mischievous humour of Dada, he mounted three perforated metal placards at the end of three spokes that rotated before a window. The perforated placards spelt out three words: WOW, WHO and OH. As they slowly turned viewers smiled as they became MOM, OHM and OH. The *Spectator* concluded its review of the exhibition: 'the piece could provide a slogan for the show- from Wow to Oh in one easy revolution. Let it not be the RBS's epitaph'.



The most dramatic example of Martin's adventures in word art is his earliest. *TRUST* (1969, Private Collection) is certainly his biggest, and most costly, work in words to date. It sprung from almost tragic circumstances. In 1969 a mutual friend took Martin to visit an American supermodel in a private London hospital. There could be few more pitiful and poignant sights in Chelsea's high society 'swinging Sixties' scene, than this tall beauty, her face so familiar from countless fashion magazines and catwalks, lying in a clinically-cold bed, her spirits broken by a failed romance, trying to recover from her attempt at suicide. Even at that she felt she had failed. Through the lens of a photographer such as David Bailey in her present state this broken swan could have symbolised the end of the decade. But that was not why Barry Martin was here, not to add to the art of her admirers but to help their mutual friend think of some way to restore her spirits. Rejected by her lover, she suffered the further indignity of being told, in his spiteful parting words, 'You'll never be able to repay that loan'. He had lent her £3,500 (a sum equivalent at that time to several months' earnings) and her career did indeed appear to be at an end. Martin was asked to come up with something special.

*TRUST* was commissioned as a parting gift from the supermodel to her former lover, through the patronage of a friend who still prefers to remain anonymous. It consists of a six-foot long Perspex case, divided diagonally into two across the central letter U. Each letter was over a foot tall, made of coloured Perspex, the left side in blue, the right side in red. Framing the word, wads of genuine banknotes were arranged, totalling in value £3,500, each one silk-screened with the word TRUST to match the blue or red side of the case.

On New Year's Eve, as the 1960s began to melt into the 1970s, Martin and their mutual friend loaded the loaded message into a London taxi and sent it on its way, to a party hosted by the estranged lover. When it eventually arrived at its destination, a country house in Cornwall, and was unwrapped among bemused guests, *TRUST* made quite an awkward impression. The supermodel's loan had been repaid, with interest. Unfortunately the celebrities' story leaked out, into the national press, and Martin was falsely accused of cooking up a publicity stunt at others' expense. Insulted and incensed, he has never asked what became of the work. But he learnt from the commission never to underestimate the power of a single word.

## A simple pun that transforms a broad imperative into a personal question



As with all of Martin's art, *TRUST* operated on several levels, and would repay close inspection of the details, if it still exists. Paper currency is, of course, of no intrinsic value. Every British banknote carries a printed promise signed by the Chief Cashier on behalf of the Bank of England: 'I promise to pay the bearer on demand the sum of...'. In theory, anyone could turn up at the Bank of England, hand over paper money, and receive in return its equivalent value in sterling silver or gold. Money is only a system of promissory notes, their value based on trust, and yet it holds society together and tears it apart. By overprinting actual banknotes, Martin raised the work from a personal exchange at the very end of a relationship to one addressing the mechanism that connects the modern world, indeed, the only internationally-shared belief system, the faith in money. The actual value of the global economy depends upon a fragile human quality, of trust. The message is writ large in industrial Perspex, like a commercial road sign, but it is broken into two diagonally across the U, a simple pun that transforms a broad imperative into a personal question.

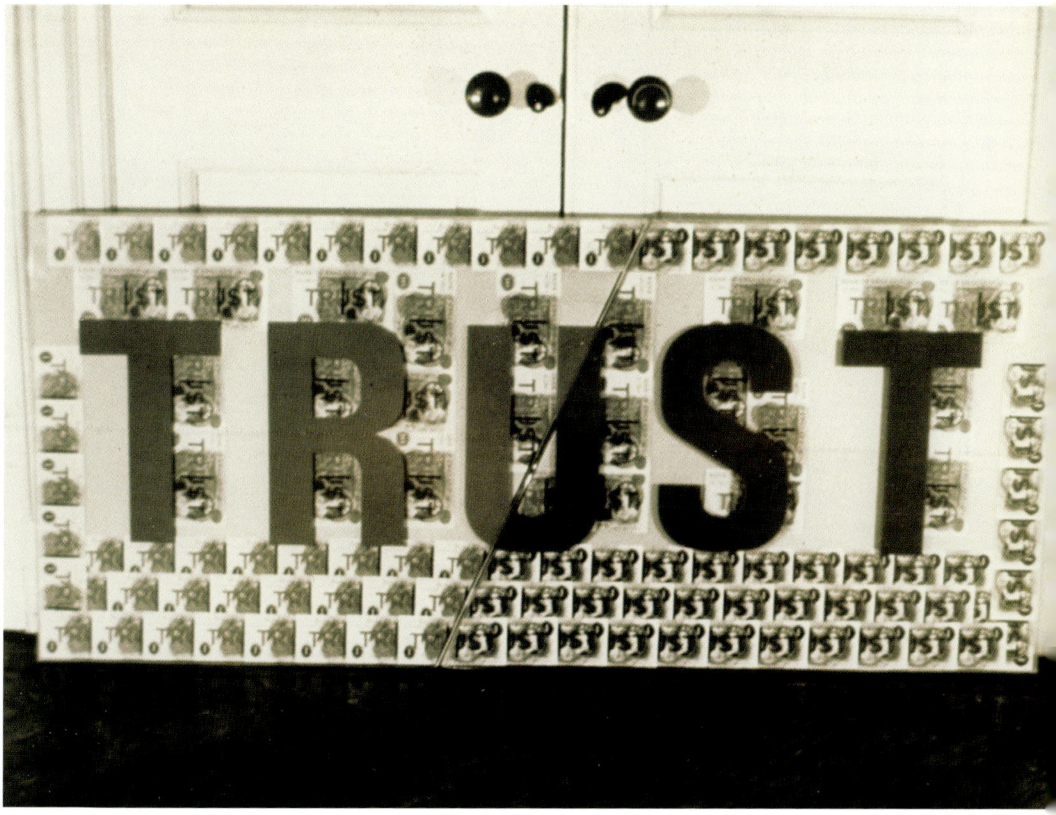


1969

*TRUST*

Perspex, coloured perspex letters, with £ 3,500

in Banknotes, silkscreenprinting

92 x 183 cm

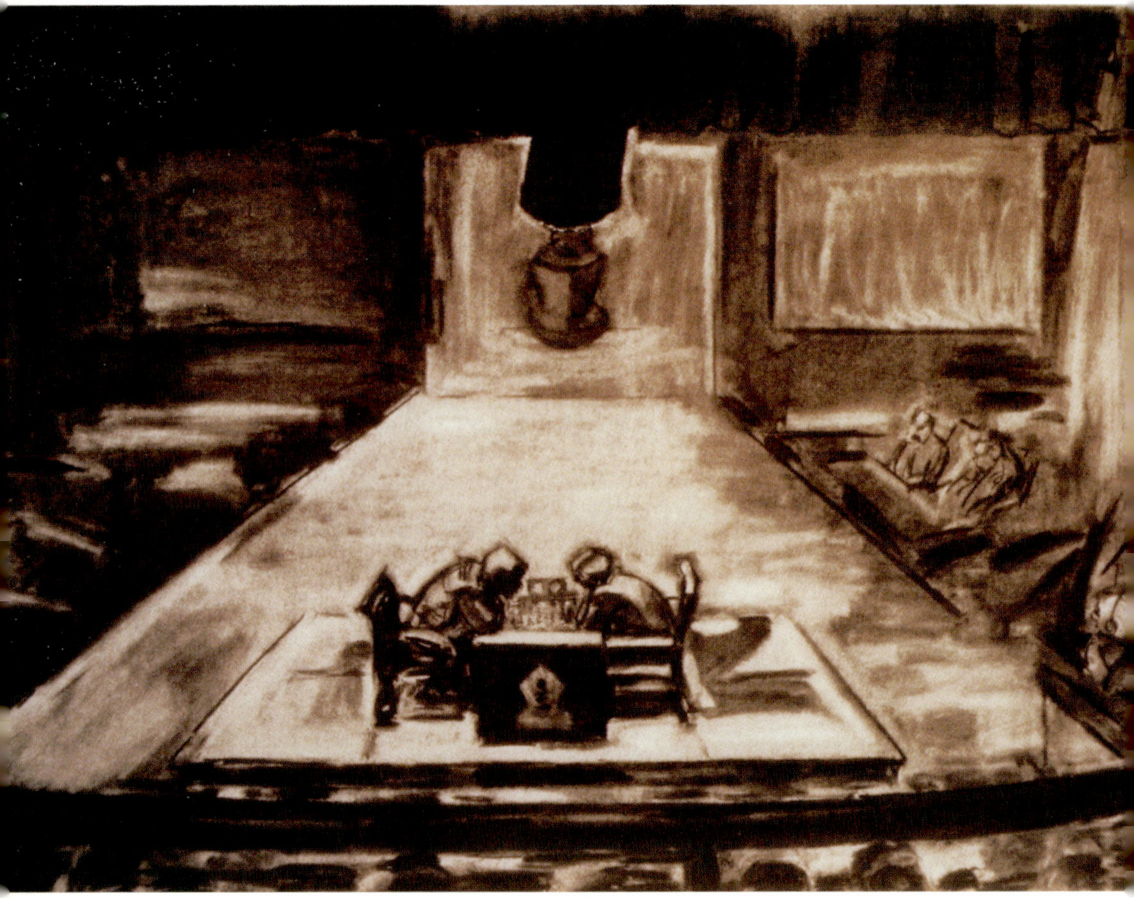

# 8 The Artist as Chess Player



Raymond Keene IGM OBE

Many artists have explored chess since its inception around two thousand years ago, but of these Barry Martin has been the most consistent, the most dedicated, the most inventive and, pace Marcel Duchamp, perhaps the most important.

1993
*The Wold Chess Championship, between Garry Kasparov and Nigel Short*
with Princess Diana looking on from the RoyalBox (far right), Savoy Theatre
Charcoal
100 x 126 cm

Chess, with its assorted emblematic military and hierarchical forces and the endless complexity and profundity of its variations, offers a symbol of the universe and its infinite powers, extent and laws. The symbolism emerges on many levels; that of destruction, creation, termination, rebirth and resurrection. In the venerable canon of chessboard-related symbolic richness there is balance, harmony, the evident tension between black and white, the opposites of night and day as well as perpetual conflict, tempered by the ever present possibility of reconciliation in the outcome of a drawn game. In chess one detects an imperative towards meditation, yet also a yearning for risk and mystery.

In Martin's portrait of former world champion Garry Kasparov, commissioned by *The Times* in 1993, the player at the board about to execute his move becomes a rough beast, full of violence and hatred, an icon of will, a ruthless mafia boss (Kasparov's favourite opening is the Sicilian defence) indeed - on many levels - a killer. This image, was chosen for the front cover of the present writers, book on Kasparov's use of the Sicilian defence.





1993

*Garry Kasparov*

Pastel on paper

90 x 60 cm

These original drawings were turned into a limited edition silkscreen print sponsored by *The Times*, newspaper. The Nigel Short pastel is in the National Portrait Gallery, London.

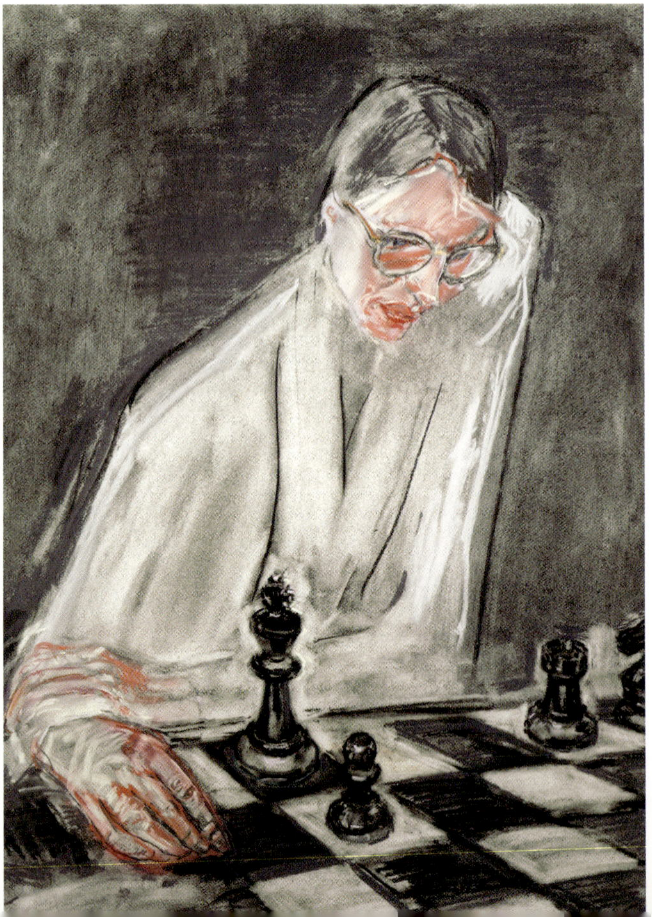

Faith and courage are required for any belief system. In Martin's *Sanctuary for Heroes*, chess-like forms inhabit and protect a sacred fortress - Jerusalem of the Crusaders, Valhalla, Camelot - we cannot be sure, but the entities on the battlements are just as surely inspired by chessic forms as are the 'Moules Maliques' in Duchamp's *Large Glass*.

Conversely, faith and courage are also demanded if the decision is not to believe. You can be absolutely certain, one way or another in your own mind, yet there always remains that element... that frisson of doubt. It used to be that way with chess analysis as well. Now, along come Deep Blue, Hydra or the Fritz computer program and all doubt is banished. There can be no room for faith, no allowance for intuition and no leap of belief where certainty is mathematically programmable. After consulting computer analysis one now knows for sure whether a particular variation functions perfectly or is unsound.

Fortunately, chess is not confined to mere analysis. That would be a reductionist point of view. Mystery and art remain as a function of human



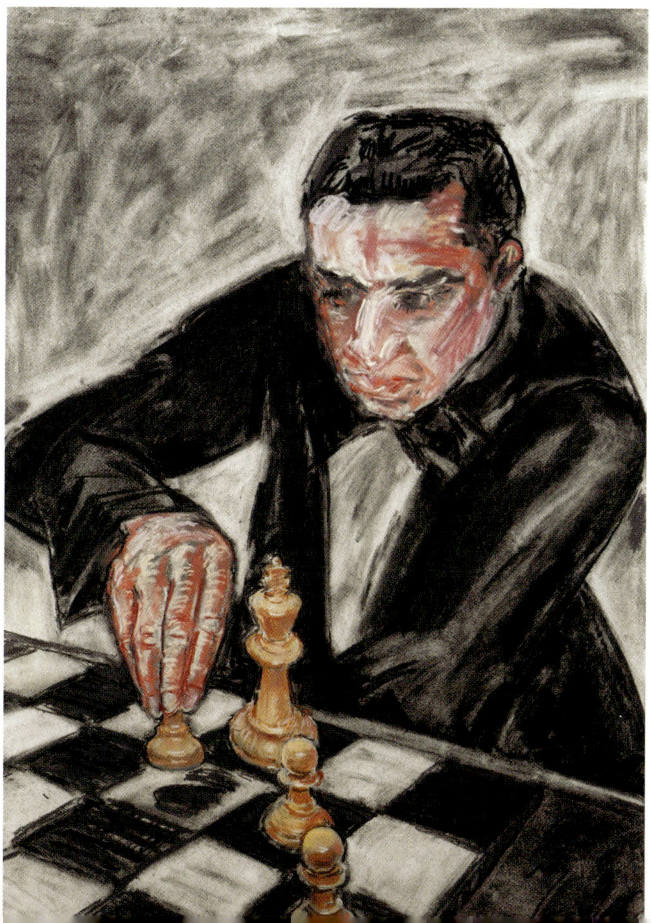

1993

*Nigel Short*

Pastel on paper

90 x 60 cm

imagination. Nietzsche's Superman functions in the knowledge that God is dead and that the universe is ultimately meaningless because it recurs cyclically. Yet the Superman has the courage to act as if this knowledge were not crippling. To carry on loving chess, playing it, analysing it and depicting its cerebral and fantastical operations in the knowledge of the existence of God-like analysis from Fritz and its silicon confreres is an act of Nietzschean moral affirmation. Intuition can master depth, as we see for example in Martin's bejewelled, near miniature creation: *Power and Transfiguration of the Queen*.

The Queen is central to any full understanding of the development of chess and to the symbolism of infinite and universal regeneration which underpins the game. Martin's oeuvre has expressed this so cogently, even perhaps in his more jocular productions, such as the ever metamorphosing potato chess set.
The history of chess iconography , with its roots in many ancient societies, such as Egypt; India; Greece and Persia has been investigated by Martin





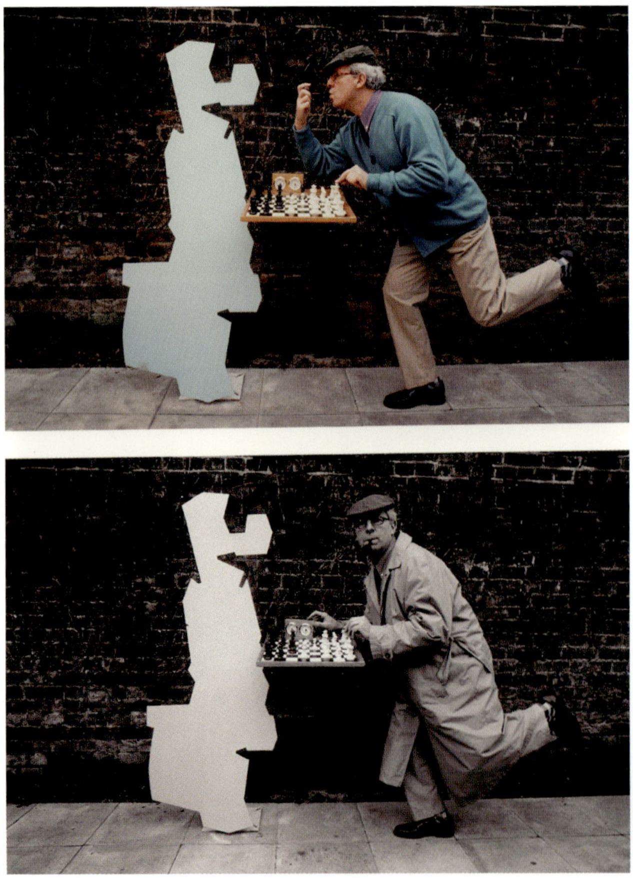

1999
*Self-portrait with chess-playing Hollywood Star*
(from the 'Poise' series)
Laser Ink print

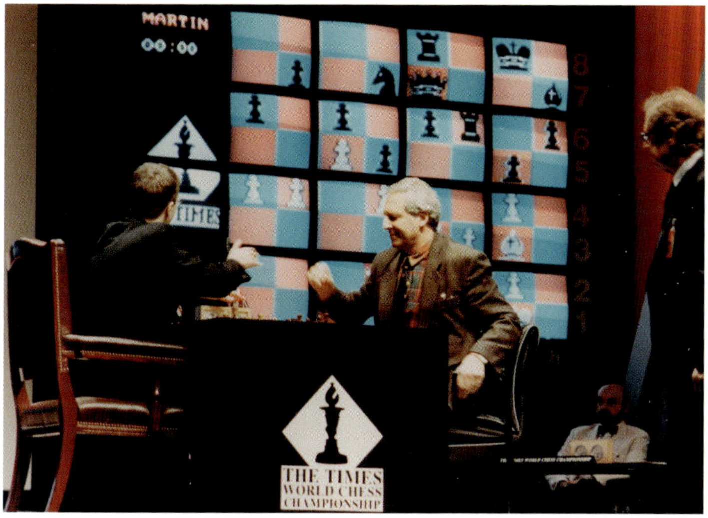


1993
The artist (right), plays Nigel Short on stage at the Savory Theatre. In front of a live audience and television coverage. Yuri Averbakh (far right)

and used in sereral of his paintings and sculptures. This interest has also led to various articles and lectures. Perhaps the best known of these is "Men of Staunton or Are They?" (*Chess Monthly* 1993) which created a large amount of discussion worldwide. Martin argues persuasively that the Staunton pattern chess pieces, now in universal use for tournaments and official matches of all kinds, find their roots in ancient Egyptian and Greek symbolism, going back to the horses' heads of the Elgin Marbles and even further back into antiquity.





## The older version of chess, with its chariots, elephants and viziers, was by no means unsubtle

Chess, as we now play it, was introduced in the mid to late 15th century, and swept away the older Arabic/Indian/Persian version of the game known as Shatranj, with mysterious ease. The chief difference in the modern game, as Martin has consistently emphasised, is the massively enhanced power of the Queen; and modern chess is certainly a more complicated game than Shatranj, offering a greater mental stimulus and challenge. Nevertheless, the older version of chess, with its chariots, elephants and viziers, was by no means unsubtle, and an impressive Shatranj culture had built up in Arabic lands over the centuries. Baghdad, in particular, was a thriving centre of Shatranj expertise, with a fervent population of gamesters led by Aliyat, or grandmasters, who numbered such illustrious names as the 10th century AD as Suli and Al Laj Laj amongst their adepts. These were men who not only played with great success, but also wrote down their most profound thoughts on the game, as we know from surviving scraps of records found in Constantinople, and other outposts , refuges and sanctuaries of learning.

Shatranj differed principally from modern chess in the following ways: pawns could only move one square at a time, even on their first turn; bishops (elephants) leapt two squares forwards or backwards diagonally, while the queen (then known as the vizier and to which pawns had to promote) could only move diagonally one square at a time. Victory was achieved by checkmate, stalemate or capturing all opposing pieces apart from the king.

The golden age of Islamic chess lasted around 150 years and began during the rule of the 4th Caliph of the Abbasid dynasty Harun ar Rashid (786-809 AD). During this time, the classic games were played , puzzles devised and the openings catalogued, with such wonderful names as 'torrent', 'sword' and 'goat peg'. Both basic and advanced principles were adumbrated





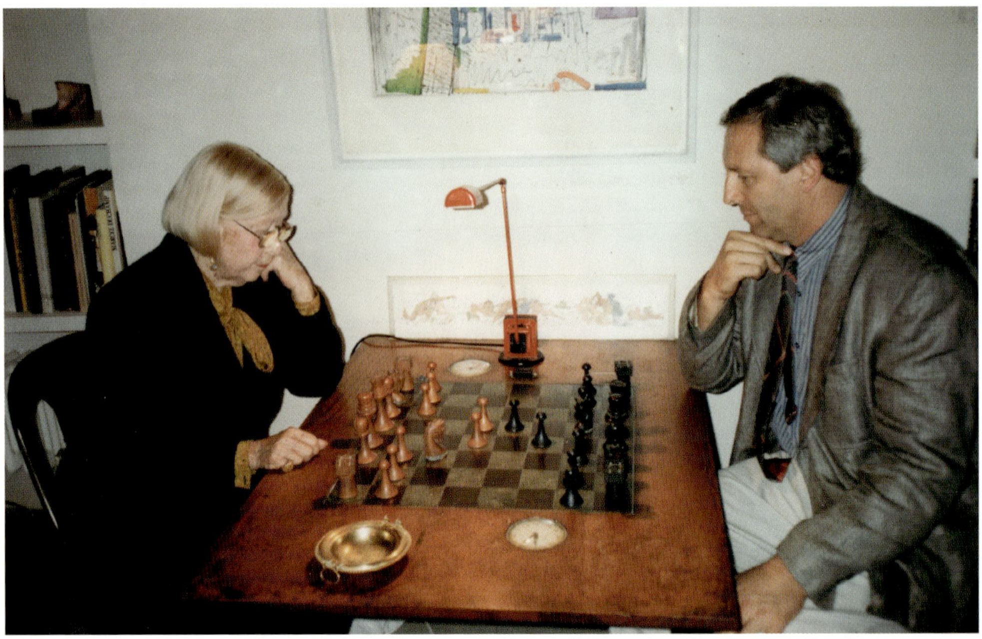

1991

Teeny Duchamp and the artist playing with Marcel Duchamp's original designed chess set and board, France

and recorded by an elite group of aliyat, many of whom found favour at the Caliph's court. Shatranj was, somewhat later, honoured in mediaeval Christian art by the chess book of the Spanish king, Alfonso the Wise, and the elements of Moorish or Islamic influence are quite unmistakeable.

The rapid disappearance of Shatranj is a puzzle. True, the new Renaissance-inspired form of chess which we still play now, was better suited to the times. Chess is a game of war, the pieces representing a military hierarchy. The introduction of a long range piece, such as the modern Queen, may well have been a parallel to the 15th century deployment of distance weapons, such as the artillery, which in 1453 reduced the hitherto impregnable walls of Byzantium. Modern chess is more complex than Shatranj, but that would scarcely account for the almost complete obliteration of Shatranj in favour of the new matrix. It is arguable that Wei Chi (also known as Go) is a more difficult and richer game than draughts, or that Shogi and Xiangqi, respectively the Japanese and Chinese forms of chess, have advantages over the western game of chess. That does not, however, prevent all versions from co-existing in amicable fashion.



If Jerusalem of the crusaders, Valhalla or Arthurian Camelot, then why not also Constantinople? From their final "Sanctuary" in Martin's translucent depiction, we can imagine the Palaeologian heroes looking down on the massed ranks of the new weapons, the giant cannon of the Hungarian engineer Urban - the military equivalent of the chess queens - which will destroy them. In spite of this, they refuse to renounce their faith. Furthermore, in Martin's *Queen*, may we detect the billowing smoke and confusion of the cannon, the swirling emblematic purple of the doomed Byzantine emperors, amounting to the infinite complexity of a turning point in history, the death throes of the vestigial and anachronistic Roman Empire, as history enters a new age? The changes in the game of chess reflect this epochal advance. Martin's inspired work was chosen to illustrate the front jacket of Sir Arthur Conan Doyle's spiritualist novel, *The Land of Mist*.

To resolve one further mystery we may return to an even earlier vision - Baghdad - the very home of the original version of chess; not the debased 21st century Baghdad, but the glittering Baghdad of the Arabian Nights as it faced the might of the Mongols almost a millennium ago.

The principal difference between the modern and old forms of chess is to do with the Queen. The reason for the easy triumph of chess over Shatranj can be traced to the Mongol warlord Hulagu, brother to Kublai Khan , of 'stately pleasure dome' fame, grandson to the world conqueror Ghengis Khan. In 1258, Hulagu utterly destroyed Baghdad, the centre of Shatranj, its players and its writings . Glubb Pasha, the noted Arabist who once opened the Hastings Chess Congress, reports as follows in his book *Lost Centuries* :

> The 37th Abbasid Caliph, Mustasim, and his sons were sewn up in sacks and trampled to death by Mongol horses. From the death of the Prophet in 632 AD, the Arab Caliphate had lasted 626 years. For five centuries, Baghdad had been the heart of the Muslim world, a city of palaces, libraries, mosques and of colleges, mathematicians, philosophers, poets, historians and theologians. After the destruction wrought by Hulagu, mounds of smoking rubble, from which rose an unbearable stench of decaying flesh, now alone marked the site of so much wealth, glory art science and learning.





And chess, one might add, in the form of Shatranj! Here we have the solution to our mystery: why chess with the new Queen so rapidly swept aside the old game. In Martin's picture, we can see the irresistible force of the new idea; we can touch its all conquering power and attraction. The accumulated knowledge of centuries of commentary, games and patient explanation about Shatranj by the first grandmasters in history had all gone up in smoke. When modern chess emerged, there was simply no surviving corpus of intellectual opposition: the history, literature and culture of Shatranj had been systematically annihilated by the Mongols. It is as if all knowledge and wisdom concerning modern chess were suddenly to be lost. Under such circumstances, a vigorous new game, similar but with a bigger board and exciting new pieces, such as stealth bombers, nuclear submarines and tanks armed with uranium-enriched shells, might well replace the older, poorly documented version overnight.

As we know, chess already competes, with surprising success, against computer simulations. Without its rich literature, games by the greats and an accumulated treasury of brilliant combinations and checkmates to entice the neophyte, chess itself, as we know the game, might well succumb with extraordinary rapidity to the advent of a rival with more blatant popular appeal. Martin's efforts in the field of art help, as with his *Sanctuary*, to man the intellectual bulwarks against such dangers of dumbing down, and with a 'piece' such as his *Queen*, he mines, facets and burnishes the history and critical Hegelian "Wendepunkt" which brought us the modern game.

Martin's strong interest in chess led to his selection as the official artist for the world championship match between Nigel Short and Garry Kasparov in 1993, and also for Kasparov and Vladimir Kramnik in 2000. Among his commissions was the Howard Staunton Memorial at Kensal Green Cemetery, 1997; Martin also unveiled an English Heritage blue plaque to Staunton at 2/117 Lansdowne Road, W11, in 1999. He was artistic consultant on Raymond Keene's *Chess for Absolute Beginners*, 1993.

The full story is, however, considerably more detailed. In 1989 Martin won the Chelsea Arts Club Open Chess Championship, overcoming 20 other contestants. World Champion Garry Kasparov presented him with the C.A.C. Chess Championship prize at the Grandmasters' Dinner (1989). In attendance were numerous other Grandmasters including Jon Speelman, Julian Hodgson and the author of this piece. The following year (1990) Martin formed the C.A.C. chess team and saw it accepted into the London Clubs' Hamilton-Russell Cup League. He captained the C.A.C. chess team for the next 16 years until 2006 – playing against clubs such as the RAC; Athenaeum; Oxford and Cambridge; East India; MCC, himself competing on either board one or two. In a variety of chess displays during the 1990s, Martin took on several Grandmasters and Masters,achieving draws in Simuls against David Norwood GM; Julian Hodgson GM; Bob Wade IM, Bill Hartston IM, the present writer and others. David Bronstein, the former world championship challenger, sat watching Martin's game against David Norwood. At the end Bronstein immediately shook Martin's hand and congratulated him since, he was the only one to draw in an endgame of four centralised pawns, a white bishop each and no spare squares.

The early 1990s saw Martin raising money at Longleat fort the World Wildlife Fund against Ray Keene GM, with other players such as Dominic Lawson and Cathy Forbes (England's woman chess champion), all of whom lost. Martin was the only person to draw after a very hard game; even the host at Longleat, Alexander Thynn, then Viscount Weymouth, lost. Martin achieved an officially recognised International Elo rating of 2010 by winning and drawing in the first Staunton Memorial Chess match in 1995 held in Chiswick House grounds. He went on to play and captain the Simpson's-in-the-Strand team in the 4 NCL Division 1 chess tournament. He also won the prize for drawing his game at the Christie's simultaneous display in Chelsea.

In 1991 Martin and I went to meet 'Teeny' Duchamp at her family home near Fontainebleau. We were allowed to explore the house which was full of Marcel Duchamp's works, sketches and notebooks. Martin played Teeny a game of chess on Marcel's own designed chess set and board (the Buenos Aires Set). Marcel Duchamp of course was an artist of prime importance for his influence on the 20th century but also a master strength chess player who represented France in the Chess Olympiads of the 1920s. From his notebooks it became clear that Duchamp was a follower of the hypermodern grandmaster Aron Nimzowitsch, who preached the doctrine that a move is less beautiful than the thought behind it- a view clearly echoed in Duchamp's own artistic production. We went on to see the *Échec* exhibition in Paris at the Bibliotheque , with a view to borrowing some sets for a possible event at the Tate Gallery.

The principal event in the first half of 1991 was Martin's co-organisation with myself and Richard Humphreys, Senior Curator, Tate Britain, of the 'Art and Chess' symposium at the Tate Gallery. This assembled many experts in the field of chess interpretation such as Richard Eales, the noted chess historian from the University of Kent at Canterbury, and Prof George Steiner





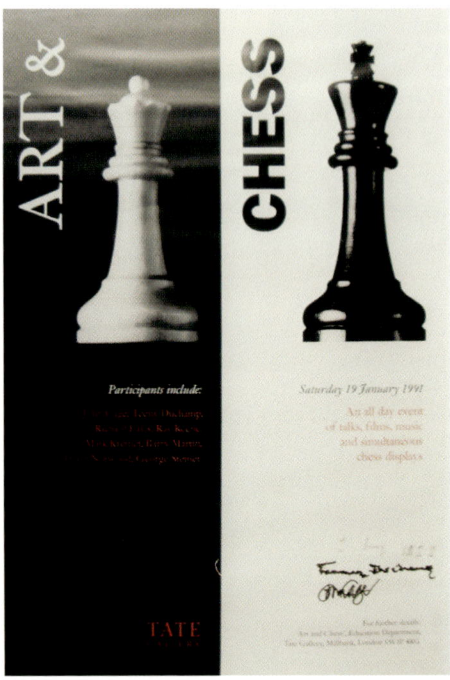


1991
*Poster for Chess Symposium at Tate Britain.* Dedicated to the artist and signed by John Cage and Teeny Duchamp.

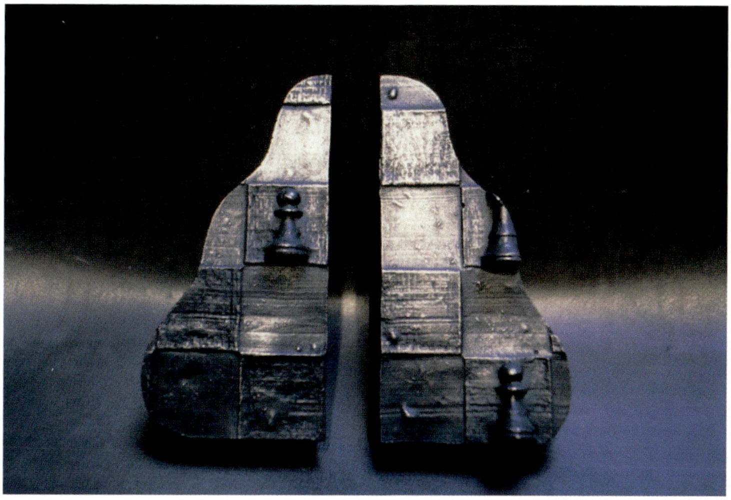

1995-2000

*Two Piece Chess Monument*

Bronze

Cast by the Royal Collage of Art



from Cambridge. Martin's personal contribution was a paper, 'Y to shoot the King...' a further oblique reference to the all pervading influence of the power and nature of the Queen which underlies so much of his work. John Cage, Duchamp's chessplaying disciple, and Teeny Duchamp were guests of honour, while critic David Sylvester and Duchamp acolyte Richard Hamilton attended, as did many artists, including Anthony Hill. As the finale of the Tate's Chess and Art day Martin had arranged for four young ladies to perform an early Cage string quartet. Just as the piece reached its climax, the cellist dropped her instrument and fell to the floor-written in by Cage as a coup de theatre, we all wondered? No! It was an epileptic seizure , from which she soon recovered, but Cage relished the random nature of the happening, even though he had not orchestrated it!

Martin crowned the day at the Tate by organising a dinner at the Chelsea Arts Club to conclude the symposium. It also celebrated John Cage's birthday and Martin designed a birthday cake for the composer in the shape of Duchamps' infamous urinal, *The Fountain*. John Cage enjoyed the event immensely and inscribed one of the Tate's chess posters, along with Teeny Duchamp, to the artist.

To celebrate Nigel Short's World Chess Championship match against Garry Kasparov at the Savoy Theatre, London, Martin was appointed the official artist for the match by *The Times and* commissioned him to produce two limited edition silkscreen prints – of Short and Kasparov. *The Times* presented the Nigel Short representation to the National Portrait Gallery for their collection. Much of the artwork produced was in colour, exhibited in numerous exhibitions with some now in museum collections, including the Hastings Art Museum. A large charcoal drawing of the match was used as the final television image for each of the Channel 4 daily live

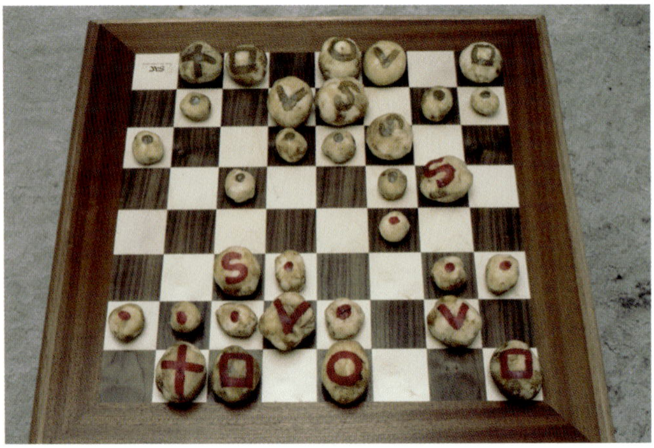

1992

*Organic Chess Set with King Edward Potatoes*

Potato and acrylic paint

60 x60 cm



transmissions of the championship. It was the most widely reported and important chess event to have been held in the UK for over a century - probably since the de facto World Championship match between Steinitz and Zukertort in London 1872.

As part of the 1993 Kasparov versus Short world championship, Martin played Nigel Short in a 3-minutes blitz game, on stage at The Savoy, watched by a large live audience and also televised. The time-based nature of chess, as in other games, has been of great interest to the artist and relates to his interest in time and movement as expressed in many of his other works. Martin lost on time, but still ended in a good position in terms of placings on the board. Yuri Averbakh, the arbiter, later wrote to the artist and congratulated him. Martin presented some drawings of Short and Kasparov to the Moscow Chess Museum of which Yuri Averbakh was the Director.

The 1993 world championship was preceded earlier that year by a second 'Art & Chess' symposium at the Tate Gallery where Martin delivered a paper on the historical development of the Queen in chess. Martin forged a connection with the town of Hastings, host since 1895 to the world's longest running traditional chess tournament. In 1995 he exhibited 16 drawings at the Hastings Museum of Art's "Bad Bishops and Red Rooks" exhibition.

Martin made enquiries about the grave site of England's greatest player, Victorian polymath Howard Staunton, who in 1843 won the unofficial world chess title by defeating Saint Amant in Paris. This win resulted in the world's chess fraternity focusing on London as the global centre for chess. However, the man who started all this, not to mention lending his name to the design of the chess pieces we now use, seemed to have been forgotten. Martin discovered Staunton's grave site in Kensal Green Cemetery, London, but the great man's last resting place had been reduced to just a patch of mud. Accordingly Martin resolved to form the Howard Staunton Society to raise money to replace and rectify this national disgrace. He masterminded a letter to *The Times* signed by himself along with numerous grandmasters including Jonathan Speelman, Julian Hodgson, Bob Wade and others. This *cri de coeur* raised national awareness. The outcry resulted in a blue plaque for Staunton, and the creation of a splendid tombstone for him at Kensal Green.

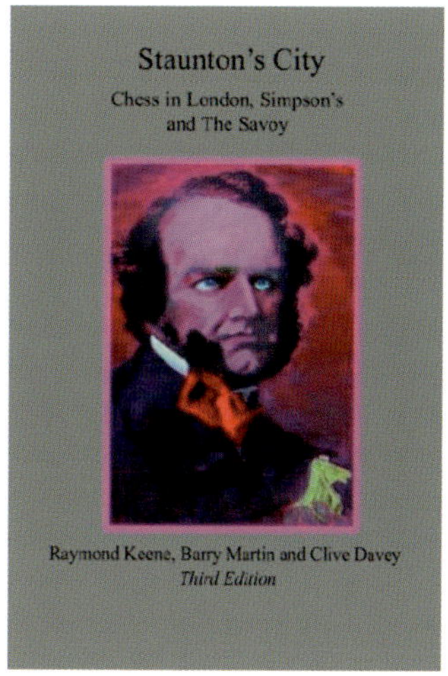


2005

*Howard Staunton*

An original oil painting by the artist seen here on the cover of the book *Staunton's City* third edition

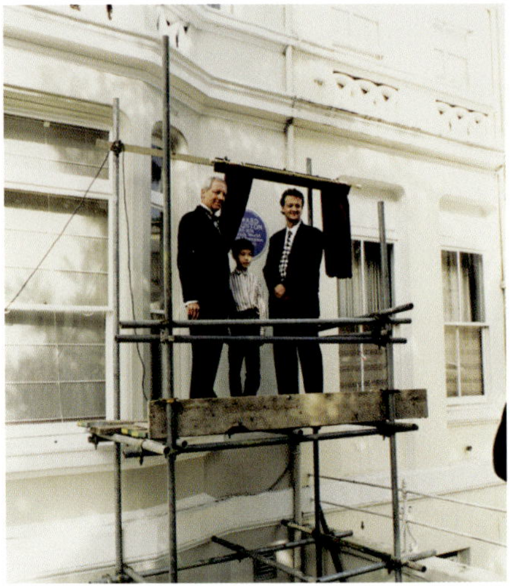

1998
Barry Martin Unveils the Slaunton Blue Plaque in Notting Hill. He is joined by Julian Hodgeson, GM, and a young David Howell.

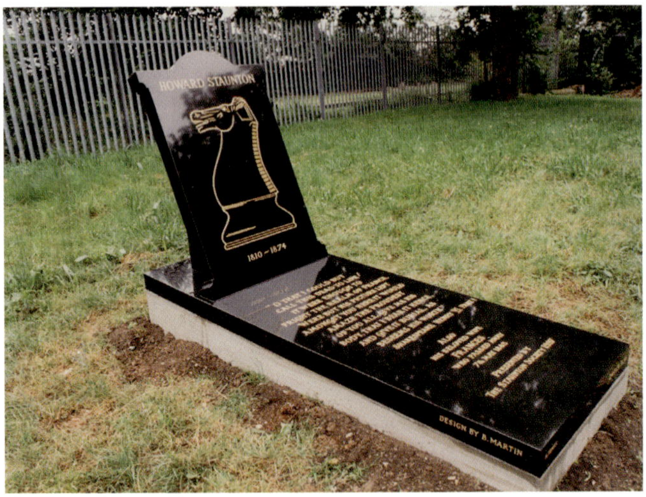


1997
*Headstone for Howard Staunton,* presented by the Staunton Society design by Barry Martin.
Kensal Green Cemetery, London

Martin is noted for his art performances at chess events, which are often designed to determine the colours of play. An exception, was a featured performance to conclude the Kramnik versus Kasparov world chess championship in 2000 , at London's Riverside Studios. This was called *Led Com*. A film of the performance was taken by the Yugoslav journalist Dmitri Bjelica. One offshoot was a very large print, 8 feet wide (2003), depicting the artist standing on one foot with one hand formed in the position to make a chess move, against a chequered background. This was created from the experience of the performance of the same name at Riverside and was produced when Martin was invited to work in the Slade School of Art, London.

The raison d'etre of the event was to demonstrate the counterpoint in chess as reflected in art between the muse of classicism and the muse of modernity, more than hinted at in the title. The performance took place in the cleared public cafe of the Riverside Studios during the dramatic fifteenth and final game of the championship itself which, appropriately enough, created Kramnik as the new world champion, sensationally deposing his great predecessor Kasparov.

In Kasparov's chessboard oeuvre there had been until that time a blend of the classic and the romantic, a subtle mixture of the teachings of Staunton, Philidor, Morphy, Alekhine but also the hard-nosed science of a Botvinnik and his Soviet research school and of Kasparov's perenial rival Karpov,

2003

*Drawing of Lots, Simpson's in The Strand*, London 1st Staunton International Chess Tournament.

(from left: Jan Timman, John Emms, Jon Speelman, David Howell, right)

Players had to fish for a coloured chess piece in Simpson's world famous crab soup.





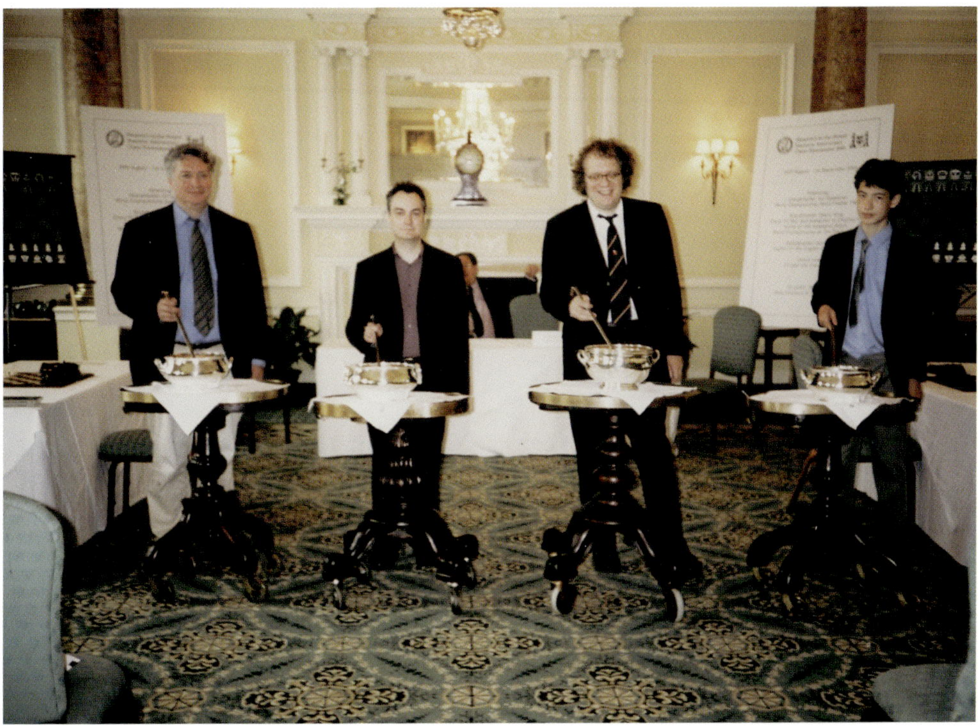

from whom he had, by contesting well over 100 games, learnt a variety of invaluable tactical and strategic lessons.

On that selfsame afternoon- the baton passed on-and it passed on as Martin's *Led Com* was in progress as the intellectual and artistic backdrop. A new age dawned-an age of computer based research and analysis stretching to the endgame from the very opening. Kasparov himself, somewhat embittered by defeat, would come to decry the new directions as overly pragmatic, accountant's chess, but the spirit cannot be tamed or annihilated by information alone. Information, the superhighway of the internet, communications and raw data are all fuel for the human imagination. This we see in *Led Com* the alchemical transformation of the opposites and parallels of the classic and the ruthlessly modern into a human dimension.





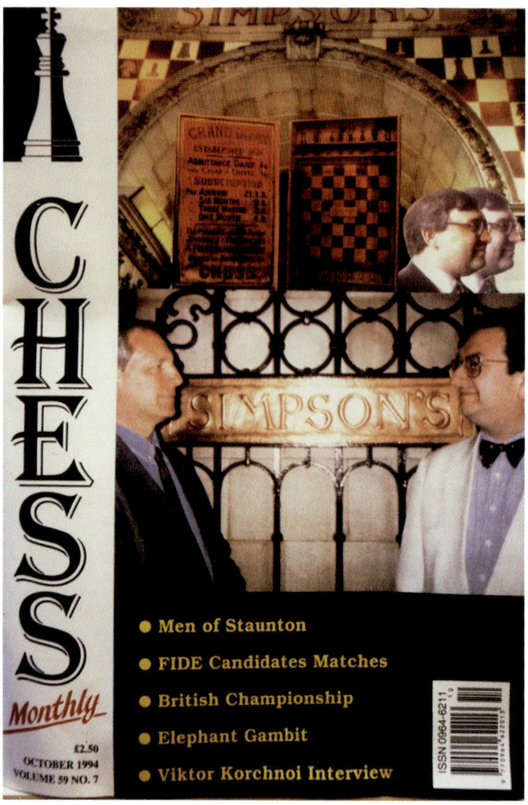


1993

*Chess Monthly*, front cover

The artist (left) R. Keene O.B.E. GM

(right) Celebrating the inauguration

of the Staunton society

Amongst Martin's other chess activities around this time was a visit to Jordan, where he was invited by Prince Mohammed bin Talal, King Hussein's brother, to give a lecture to Bedouins, entitled "Staunton at Petra." Martin also sponsored the Oxford v. Cambridge Varsity match for three years. The Varsity match ('the boat race of the brain') dates back to 1873 and is the world's longest running chess tournament.

In 1997 he organised the Mind Sports and Art exhibition at the Royal Festival Hall to mark the first Mind Sports Olympiad. From 1999-2004 he made a number of bronze and plaster chess-related sculptures, cast by the Royal College of Art, London. In 2003, he was accorded the honour of a retrospective of his art/chess pieces at Somerset House in the Gilbert Collection, running alongside the Exhibition "The Art of Chess". This event included several of the White Cube Gallery artists, such as Damien Hirst; the Chapman Brothers and also Yoko Ono, all exhibiting their chess set designs with a historical context, which included chess works by Marcel Duchamp, Man Ray and Max Ernst. Martin was official artist for the simultaneous matches held to open the Exhibition.

In 2007 Martin co-organised the fifth Staunton Memorial Tournament , sponsored by the Dutch art and chess lover, Jan Mol, founder of the Serious Fun Club. As the strongest UK tournament for twenty one years this proved to be a Sanctuary for Heroes of the chessboard, including Jan Timman, Jon Speelman and Michael Adams, and one chess Queen, Jovanka Houska.
In this way, throughout his career as a artist, Martin has maintained his international reputation as a chess player and drawn inspiration from the game for his art.

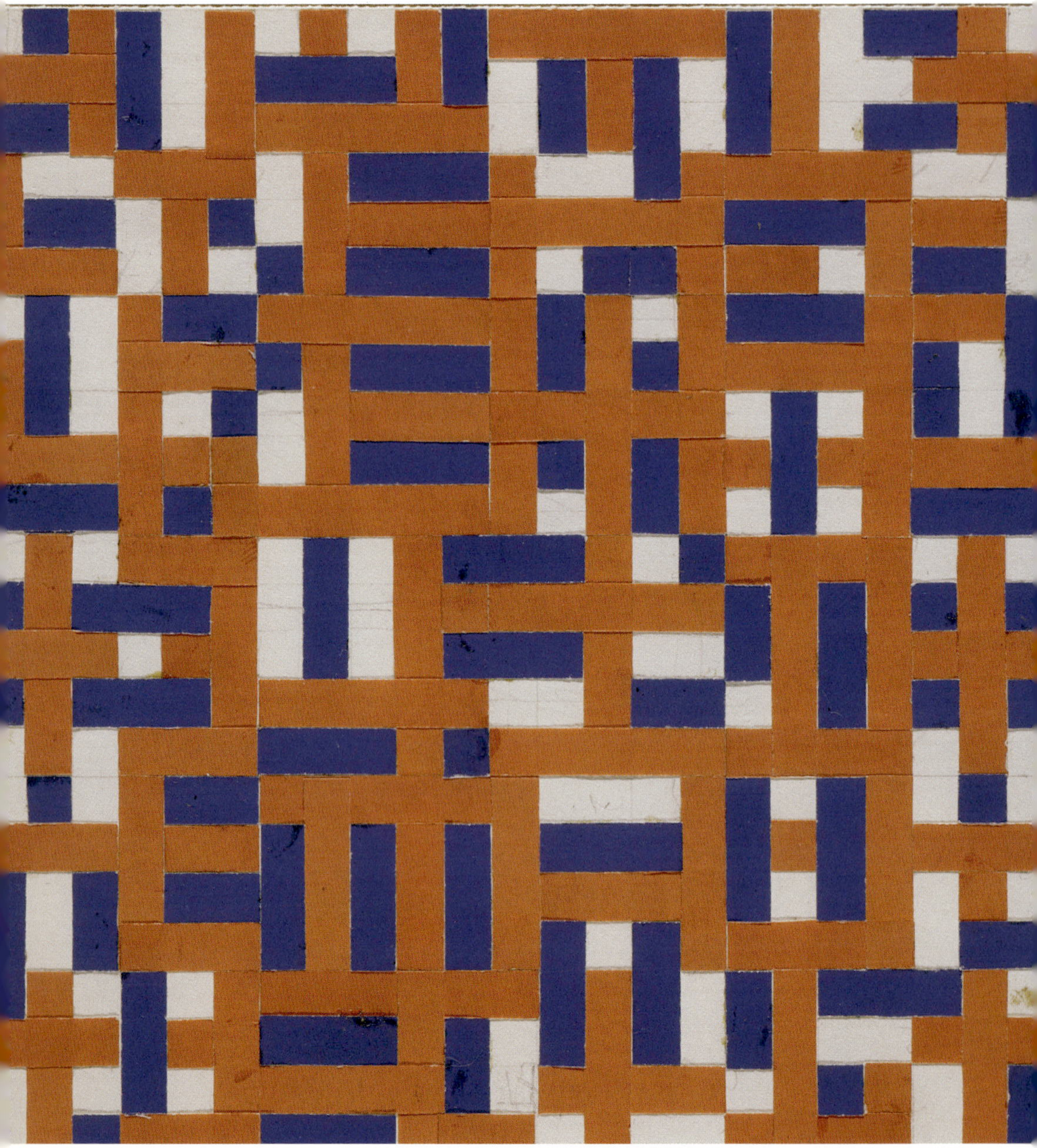

# *Sketchbooks and Films* 9 in the Tate Archive



Adrian Glew

*... good art won't be denied in the long run – as long as whoever it is that produces it keeps on producing it & doesn't get in his own way...*[1]

(Clement Greenberg to Barry Martin, 1977)

1963

*Coloured collage, Blue, Orange, White*

Collage paper onto white card

14 x 14 cm

You may be reading this sentence, this page, this essay for the very first time. Or perhaps, you have returned to it a month or two later, a year or decade hence. You may have arrived with no pre-conceived notion or you may be returning to re-visit something important or essential to you. This is how an artist, like Barry Martin, uses their notes, their drawings, their sketchbooks. They represent physical manifestations of highly creative moments, synaptic connections that fire for an instance, yet important enough to note down for posterity. Definitely non-linear, artists' notebooks and sketchbooks become lodestones carefully kept in studios or close to their artistic hearts; protected and treasured like Fabergé eggs.

Barry Martin, whose papers are now housed in the Tate Archive[2], has used such books ever since his student days both to inform his present and presciently to prepare for a future when an idea might suddenly resurrect itself with a converse slant for a different age. As Martin himself has remarked:

> Concentration on 'action' revealed that actions have to be made at the 'right' time and in their own context to have meaning and yet be capable of physical transference to another context, in order to create as meaningful a statement as is possible within the aesthetic framework.[3]



As a child of the Second World War, Martin became aware of the fine dividing line between one moment or action and the next, of a potential future or infinite oblivion, when a V2[4] rocket landed close to his parents' home in south-east London, near Bromley, killing eighteen neighbours.[5] Covered in plaster by the falling ceiling Martin, though only four years old,

[1] Clement Greenberg in a letter to Barry Martin, 2nd August 1977 (TGA 9911)

[2] Presented by the artist in 1999 (TGA 9911).

[3] Introduction by Barry Martin to a solo exhibition, *Collages & Paintings*, Patrick Seale Gallery, London, 15 Nov – 5 Dec 1978.

[4] Derived from the German name, Vergeltungswaffe, or in English, Vengeance Weapon, powered by ethanol ironically derived from thirty tons of potatoes.

[5] One of over 1350 (or 40% of the total number) to hit London from Summer 1944 to Spring 1945. It has been estimated that 2,754 were killed and 6,523 injured by these attacks in London with south-east London particularly vulnerable. One explosion at a Woolworth's department store in New Cross, for instance, killed over 150 civilians.

remembers being frightened yet fascinated by the noise and mayhem.[6] This significant incident – with particles, that once constituted a metallic whole, flying off in differing directions - can be seen as a metaphor for Martin's life-long interest in movement over time and a fascination with new and evolving shapes and forms. The pages of a sketchbook or the papers forming an artist's archive could equally be viewed as 'particles' forming a whole that has a past yet, conversely, a potential future.

These nascent interests were reinforced in the immediate aftermath of the war with the re-appraisal of all the certainties that existed within Britain beforehand: what was once expensive health care became free at the point of delivery; all forms of movement were propelled into the jet age, landscape artists became abstractionists overnight. This was a world of future possibilities, yet, with such immense changes came paranoia; paranoia reflected in those higher education establishments, such as Goldsmiths' College and Saint Martin's School of Art, that Martin attended and taught in from 1961-67.[7] Some tutors seemed more interested in churning out clones of themselves rather than equipping students to estimate 'themselves in relationship to the environment and capable of growing from it.'[8]

Initially, Martin followed the conventional rote of art schools: drawing from life whilst experimenting with different media and techniques. One of these techniques, that was to have a bearing on his later work, was the pointillist brush-stroke or rather anti-brush-stroke, which appealed to Martin's interest in painting as denoting units of colour, hue and light. Even at this early stage, Martin was moving beyond the objective gaze to an analysis of the separateness of the brush mark and the colour relationships within a painting, pondering on how the very surface of the painted artefact was a three dimensional cornucopia, resulting in a whole series of constructed paintings.



[6] Interview with the author, October 2006.

[7] Student at Goldsmith's, 1961-66 and student/lecturer St. Martin's (1966-67) and Goldsmiths (1967). Martin was also external assessor of the sculpture degree course at St. Martin's from 1974-79.

[8] Barry Martin, *Light & Movement Paintings and Sculpture* 1960-1974, London: Hillstone Press, 1984, p.47.

A key example from this early period is a linocut, now in Tate's Collection, *Three Interlocking Spirals with Differing Rates of Acceleration*, 1961 (illustrated on page 82). Here, one can see Martin successfully combining spirals, interlocking circular forms and serpentine elements to depict the movement of an unidentified machine, reflecting the intense energy, fierce debate and centripetal/fugal forces within society at that time. The mechanical nature of the form is further heightened by the limited use of cool blue, black and white colours, creating an image that almost metaphorically sucks the viewer into the innards of a fast moving pantechnicon. The stripes within the picture only serve to emphasise the speed of the gearing and metallic components depicted, yet at the same time, it is as if a moment in time has been caught, as Martin has enunciated, 'a notion of instance was seized upon in the earlier paintings and sets of circumstances were frozen into them'. This harks back to Futurist, Vorticist and Cubist pre-cursors as well as the seminal work of Marcel Duchamp, *The Bride Stripped Bare by Her Bachelors*, *Even (The Large Glass)*, 1915-23. The result is a work by Martin that transcends the view of speed and mechanisation as new gods by the Futurists and the image of a machine as a never-ending sexual automaton by Duchamp to something



**...this text later formed the basis for a ground-breaking film, which incidentally became Malcolm LeGrice's first foray into film-making**



that is hard to achieve, a work that with its detached coolness is both terrifying and alluring at the same time. This synthesis reflects Martin's view of himself and the outside world at this time and, in particular, his interest in 'a finite structure centering inwards'.

Thus followed a sustained interest in making manifest these inner feelings in sketchbooks resulting in a cornucopia of ideas for new work in two and three dimensions. In a blue/grey sketchbook, dated 1964-66[9] movement is explored in various ways and media connected to an interest in how man controls the environment. It is perhaps not surprising that much of this book is devoted to a text based on a joint project with Basil Beattie that Martin finally undertook in 1967 to explore the interaction of groups and individuals. Illustrating the potent power of the notated idea, this text later formed the basis for a ground-breaking film, which incidentally became Malcolm LeGrice's first

[9] TGA 9911

foray into film-making, of an environmental piece using blind-folded students at St. Martins in 1966. But more of that later. Also noted in this sketchbook are texts and wiring diagrams of photoelectric cells for a proposed environmental piece, which the visitor could walk through to emphasise again the connection between the individual and space, the rational and the aleatory. Again this idea was later used in Martin's contribution to the exhibition, Electric Theatre, held at the ICA, London in 1971.

It was only a matter of time before Martin's greater interest in tactility would lead him towards constructing machines that could 'have an existence of their own and stand in space' But there was another more intriguing psychological element that was instrumental in Martin moving to the more tangible 'object' within an environment. This stemmed from Martin's own observations of his interactions with people within society, which seemed transitory, ethereal, ephemeral and mis-interpreted. An object in space,[10] however, made an unequivocal statement, something that could not be ignored and that had to be negotiated. So, in 1964, Martin created his first machine out of brass, metal, and wood, *Metal Surface*. For Martin, steel with its hardness and greyness 'would seem to place it in the middle of things' and 'Its tactile coldness seemed to be very important. It seems to stand up for one's efforts'.[11] Harking back to Martin's war-time experiences, when metallic bombs smashed objects to smithereens, here they are rendered impotent by individual components being utilised to make a whole that is durable and immutable. Part of the movement discloses other parts of the machine building a picture of the whole as if one is entering a city where everything is visible and where everything is integral to everything else. Interestingly, Martin had already made a number of important charcoal drawings by 1963, titled, *Machine Drawing No.1 and 2*, which pre-figured his move into this three-dimensional work. *Tret*, 1965 (Arts Council Collection) was another key piece from this period. The working drawing for this work[12] illustrates Martin's analysis of correcting a totality of forms that were in themselves shifting their positions in relation to each other and to the overall form: a conceptual act that enlarged his awareness about the infinity of space and its possibilities.

[10] Ibid, p.7.

[11] Ibid., p.21.

[12] TGA 9911. This is a working drawing from the original (now in the Art Council) interestingly drawn onto engineer's waterproof paper chosen as a medium as Martin's studio at this time was so damp.

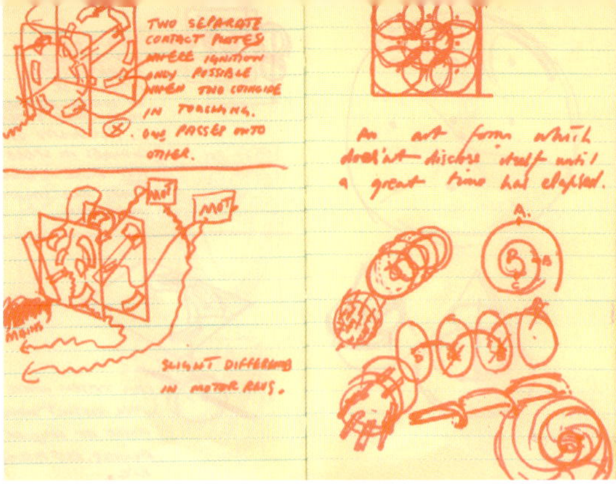


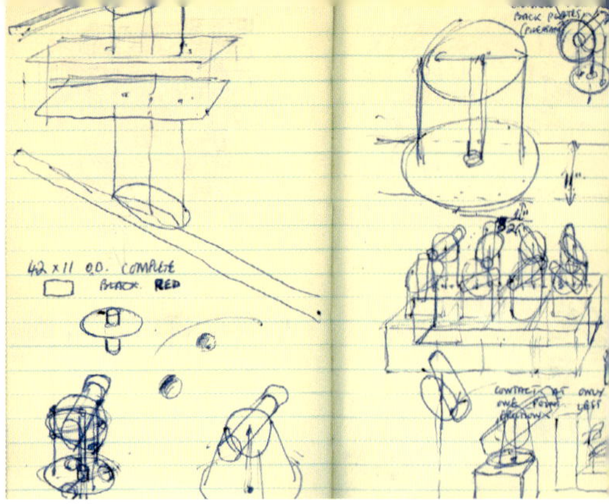


1965-6

*Interoir and Exterior Environment*

Ink on paper

16 x 19 cm

Tate Archive sketch book

1964-5

*Orchestration of Light, Movement, Space*

Ink on paper

16 x 19 cm

Tate Archive sketch book

In a red bound sketchbook in the Tate Archive, dated 1965-66,[13] there are intriguing drawings pre-figuring another key metallic sculpture, *Double Ringed Movement*, 1966. On a double-page spread both the reasoning and totality of the piece are economically delineated. On the left-hand page the engineering aspects of the work are covered whilst the right-hand page illustrates the individual elements that would eventually be made out of perspex. Significantly, Martin also notates, on the same page, an encapsulation of the work as well as his ideas about a new art form, '... which doesn't disclose itself until a great time has elapsed'. This work and Metal Surface were linked to motors so that an additional kinetic frisson was added to the experience of the viewer. In *Double Ringed Movement*, which is wall-mounted, it is as if the war-time wall of Martin's bedroom is exploding in front of the viewer, heightened by the flashes of light picked out by the rotating perspex discs reminiscent of the gyroscope, vanes and rudders of the V2 and the characteristic spiral motion seen when bombs drop vertically ground-wards from a plane.[14] It is as if the supersonic rocket, travelling at four times the speed of sound, is rendered powerless so that viewers watching the rotating Duchampian discs have time to take in the spectacle and make their escape. An out of this worldly feel is referenced

[13] TGA 9911.

[14] In fact, during tests, the V2 rocket was painted in a black-and-white chessboard pattern, which assisted in determining whether the rocket was spinning around its longitudinal axis.

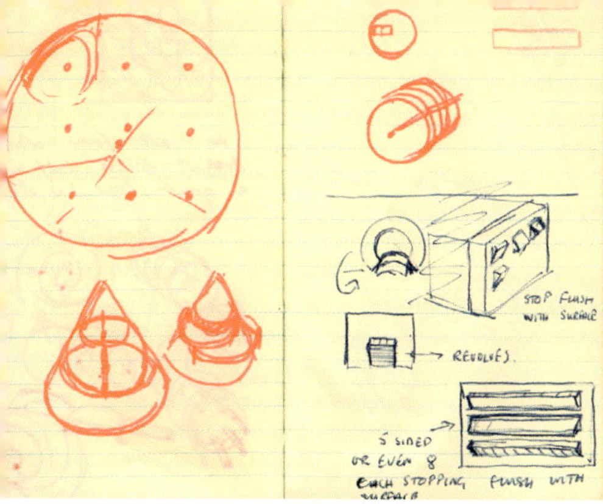


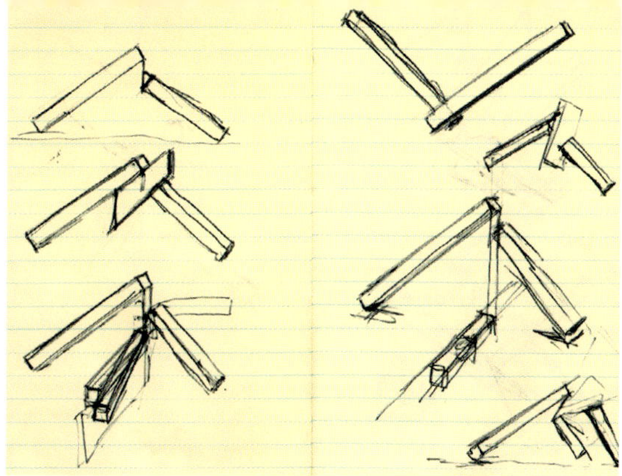

1964-5

*Movements About a Cone*

Ink on paper

16 x 19 cm

Tate Archive sketch book

1964-5

*Art form which Doesn't Disclose Itself until a Great Time Has Elapsed*

Ink on paper

16 x 19 cm

Tate Archive sketch book

in another preparatory drawing from the red bound sketchbook that depicts the rotating discs as if they were moons circling Jupiter. By looking at systems and inter-related sub-structures, machines are liberated from their functionality and are positioned on a level that is far from subservient to the viewer, so much so that a new set of relationships can be established. Martin succinctly summarised the problem as 'one object cannot occupy another's space, but if one moved in relationship to the other – it could now occupy the left space occupied by the former solid.' [15]

Running parallel to these seemingly cold metallic machines that both attracted and rebuffed the viewer, Martin was also experimenting with adding colour to static three-dimensional objects, such as the Vertical Upright and Enclosure series of 1966-7. These were made to:

> ... try to hold up an area of space with colour, which would then relate to other areas. I wanted this to open up the tight structural centre, which was appearing too finite. The actual three-dimensional nature of the sculpture would give many different viewpoints, which of course my paintings wouldn't lend themselves to.[16]

[15] Red bound sketchbook, 1965-66, p.11 (TGA 9911).

[16] Op. cit., p.14.

This statement seems very much related to the work of Hans Reichenbach who in his book, Space and Time,[17] which Martin had read, developed and

**Light now had the power to create an environment that the viewer could enter and experience in all dimensions**

updated notions of the geometry of space and time around the idea of coordinative definition. This, in turn, deals with the reality that as humans we can never directly apprehend length and our inability to decide the equality of length of two distant objects, relying instead on a man-made physical construct such as the cubit or metre. Again in the red bound sketchbook there are intriguing sketches of a structure that creates building blocks in space held in place by its own weight, a work that pre-figures the work in the City of London by Richard Serra not completed until 1987. [18]

Colour also re-entered Martin's two-dimensional work at this time, as exemplified by a fourth work in the Tate Collection, *Movement Collage*, 1965 illustrated on page 123) representing an early engagement with representations of movement in a Reichenbachian universe. Starting from a torn piece of blue paper that dominates the centre of the composition, echoing Martin's exultation to students to 'get hold of the commercial advert and tear it to pieces'[19], the other collaged elements radiate from this focal point. Seemingly pleasant images such as a businessman and children waving to the viewer and the capsuled dwelling, represented by the bright cushions within the interior of a yacht, are contrasted by what appear to be more menacing images of parts of aeroplanes, spacecraft[20] and the aggressive posture of a footballer kicking a ball (or is it a bomb?). There are throw-backs to that distintegrating ceiling again: everything is torn, soft and hard surfaces intermingle, figures are disturbingly too

[17] Hans Reichenbach, The Philosophy of Space and Time, 1928. English translation by Maria Reichenbach in a Dover reprint of the same title, 1957.

[18] Fulcrum, 1987 made from four pieces of Cor-ten steel each standing 55 feet high located near Liverpool Street Station, London.

[19] Transcript from tape three, side two of an interview with William Fitzwater, Summer 1968, p.19.

[20] Martin has had a continual fascination with space and space travel as evidenced by his membership of the British Interplanetary Society and subscription to its magazine, Spaceflight.

close to mechanical objects for comfort. It is as if the aleatory world of a Kurt Schwitters or Max Ernst has met the more orderly collaged elements of a Richard Hamilton or an Eduardo Paolozzi. A merging of Futurism, Surrealism and Pop in two-dimensional space, that mirrors Martin's experiments in three-dimensional forms at this time, as Martin has commented about his works in the early 1960s, 'I already considered the painted surface to be an objective force in itself – a physical factor, already a piece of sculpture, already with its depth away from the wall'[21]

Coupled with this love of colour was an innate fascination with light. Light or rather the lack of it was explored to the full in a ground-breaking interactive environment created by Martin for a filmed perfomative piece, entitled, You Will, You Are, You Have at St. Martin's School of Art in 1966;[22] a film that is now housed in the Tate Archive. Here twenty-five student participants – including Barry Flanagan, Hamish Fulton, Richard Long, Bruce McLean, George Pasmore and Wendy Taylor – met in an ante-chamber constructed outside Barry Martin's basement studio at the college.[23] They brought with them swimming costumes. They were given no information about the event and once dis-robed were soon hooded and led blindfolded into the environment that had been divided into various sections containing tactile materials and forms including a female model who posed absolutely still. o further cause disorientation the floor level was raised in certain areas and spatial sounds such as whale calling, steam trains and static noise were relayed into the space while the participants were asked to explore the area silently. Meanwhile, two hidden cameras recorded the event simultaneously from each end of the studio. After forty minutes the event was stopped when it was observed that participants exhibited a number of effects such as an inability to move, crying, fighting and obsessive activities, before all the participants were led out silently still wearing their blackout hoods. A week later they all returned to watch the film for the first time which was screened on a split-screen format creating a 360º enclosing environment mirroring the environment that they had once occupied. The film worked on a number of levels. Participants were able to compare what they imagined and experienced first-hand



[21] Op. cit., p.7.

[22] Original title, You Will Come, You Are Come, You Have Come. Martin was assisted by Gerard Hemsworth, Malcolm Le Grice and Su Brown (TGA 9911).

[23] The studio was twenty four feet long, fifteen feet wide and fourteen feet high.

to what they could actually see on screen heightened by the sensory deprivation experienced during the event. Martin was using another facet of his time-based works to investigate perceptual psychology and related cognitive states of understanding. This was one of the first Happenings and Environments to be created within an art-school context[24] and as such not only became a catalyst for many of the artists who had taken part but also to other students at St Martin's and Goldsmiths', where the films were later shown. Indeed one could argue that Martin and Richard Long were the first exponents of an evolving artform that would catapult sculpture into new realms of time and space.

Light itself enters other realms by opening up the potentialities of space and time, particularly if allied to kineticism. Martin began to make works that incorporated powered light sources in 1967, although as we have seen some of his earlier mechanical pieces incorporated perspex and plastic to reflect ambient light and reflection. Indeed, in the red bound sketchbook of 1965-66, Martin first made notes about how polythene could be cut to cover a vast area of eight by four feet for students to explore the properties of the material in a group setting. This was later realised as a two-week project with first year fine art and painting degree students in collaboration with Basil Beattie at Goldsmiths' in 1967. Students could analyse in terms of measuring the thickness, distribution and frequency of how their paint marks interacted with others on another painting through and around a light-infused medium. Like machines at that time, light was primarily thought about and used in a utilitarian rather than an aesthetic way. With nothing on the market that Martin could use in a personal way in his art, he decided to invent something of his own. The result was a patent - filed on 25 August 1969 – for a mechanical device for producing simultaneous movement around two axes to create decorative visual phenomena that was first seen in the King's Road, Chelsea that year. Again the germ of the idea lies in one of Martin's sketchbooks where numerous drawings depict the mechanics and dimensions of such a kinetic light piece. This novel means of moving light through space would have profound cross-cultural implications in the presentation of music notably in the new communal



[24]Happenings originated in the USA with the first manifestation cited as Allan Kaprow's, 18 Happenings in 6 Parts of 1959. In the UK, Adrian Henri, Jeff Nuttall and Bob Cobbing were early exponents of the genre.

[25] Located in a semi-derelict space in Oakley Street, Chelsea, London, 1968.

spaces of discotheques and nightclubs of the late 1970s and beyond. Martin's original model now forms part of the Science Museum's collection of key pieces of industrial design.

Light now had the power to create an environment that the viewer could enter and experience in all dimensions; sometimes opening up the space and sometimes shrouding it. One of the first of these environmental pieces, begun in the summer of 1967, served as the large hanging centrepiece for a Buckminster Fuller geodesic-inspired dome designed by the architect, Keith Critchlow for Su Braden's Pavilions in the Park in London.[25] By dressing the dome with coarse sand on the floor and with alternate matt white walls and shiny black PVC-covered doorways, Martin was able to project light in red, blue and green from a central source suspended from the ceiling to create a tactile environment that could be seen yet perversely not touched.This relates back to a small sketch of 1965-66 where Martin delineated a space with multiple light sources: their brilliance affected by somebody approaching them. The inter-relationship between onlooker and work and the subsequent shifts between light and shade culminated in Martin's most ambitiously realised kinetic sculpture, realised for the Hayward Gallery in 1970.

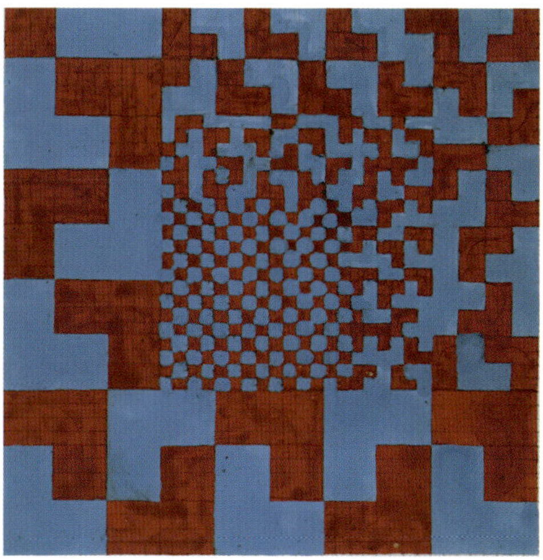

1964

*Red and Blue Spiral*

Watercolour onto white card

12,5 x 12,5 cm

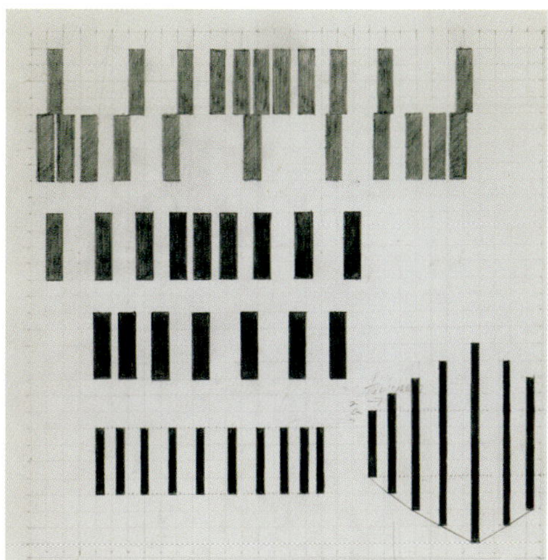

1964

*Sequence - Rhythm and Interval*

Pencil on card

41 x 26 cm

From the 1960s, Martin has tapped into the quotidian energy of time and space to create unique static, kinetic, light and interactive performance pieces that still resonate today. And since the 1970s, Martin has continued to explore the potentialities of time, space, light and movement in his sculptural and two-dimensional work. Writing, lecturing and being involved in the game of chess also provide Martin with forums for such explorations. However, it is from an examination of Barry Martin's sketchbooks and related archival material, that one can see how seemingly peaceful artefacts can illustrate the development of an artist living in and through a frenetic urban environment. As Martin has noted, 'It's almost as if I was damned never to rest, to find a resting point, but always having to move.' [26]

Movement and, in particular, the movement of man or machine seems to be a constant metaphor coursing through Martin's work equating to the artist's perception and participation in the ebb and flow of the city. At one moment, taken along like a passenger on a runaway train, and at other moments its driving force creating new routes for art to take. A note on one of the drawings in a sketchbook manifests this feeling when Martin refers to 'The Ambiguity of the Machine' and 'Coloured lights, which keeps changing colour'. The latter reference alludes to the artist's metaphorical use of colour change as heightened emotions elicited by his relationship to the city and intra-personal relations. It is as though optical colour changes from light projections into defined spaces could, in themselves, be symbolic transformations from the 'real' city itself. The one reality eliciting another newer reality, just as one idea or sketch begets innumerable two and three-dimensional ideas for realisation.



1964-5

*Assymetric Pressures and Support*

16 x 20 cm

Ink on paper

(Collection: Tate Archive)

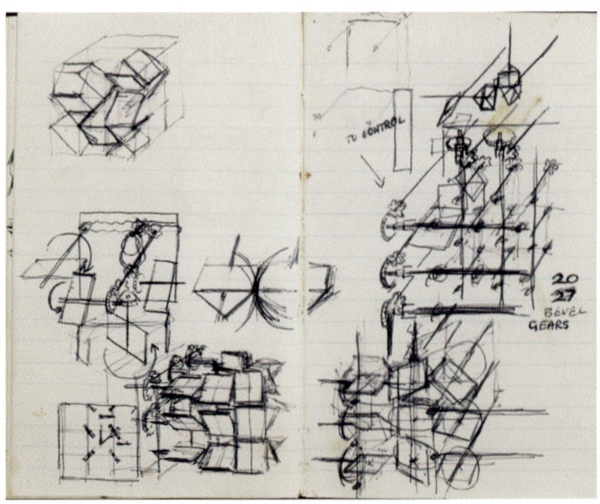


[26] Red bound sketchbook, 1965-66 (TGA 9911).

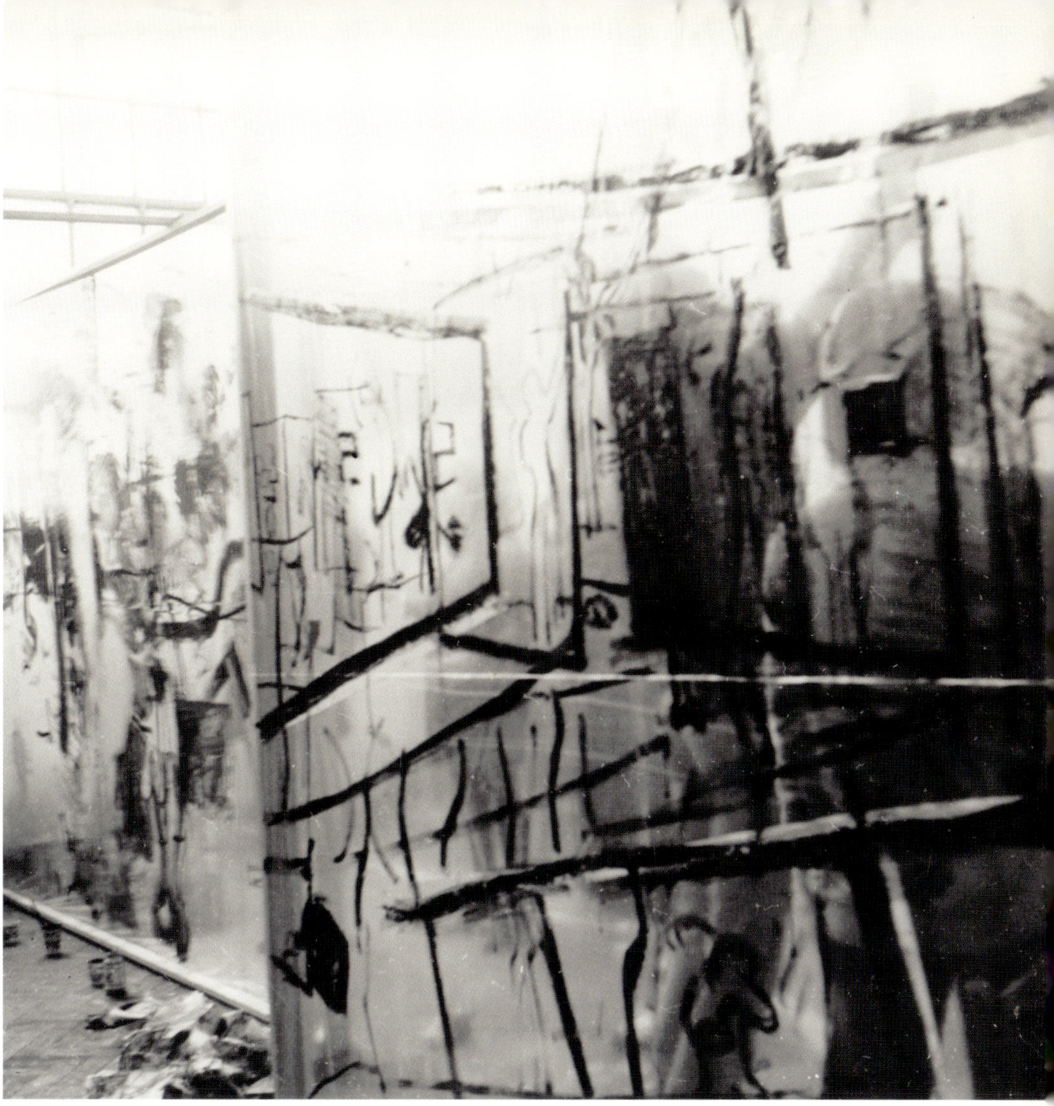

1967

Photograph of the *Large size Polythene Project*

225 x 380 cm

polythene, wood stretchers painted on by Goldsmidths' students

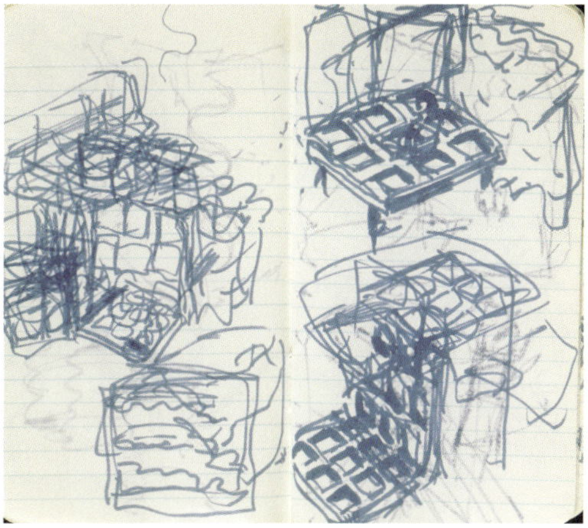

1967

*Plan of the Polytheme Project for Degree Painters,* Goldsmiths College - University of London: Layout plan, Skechbook

18 x 20 cm

Ink on paper

(Collection: Tate Archive)

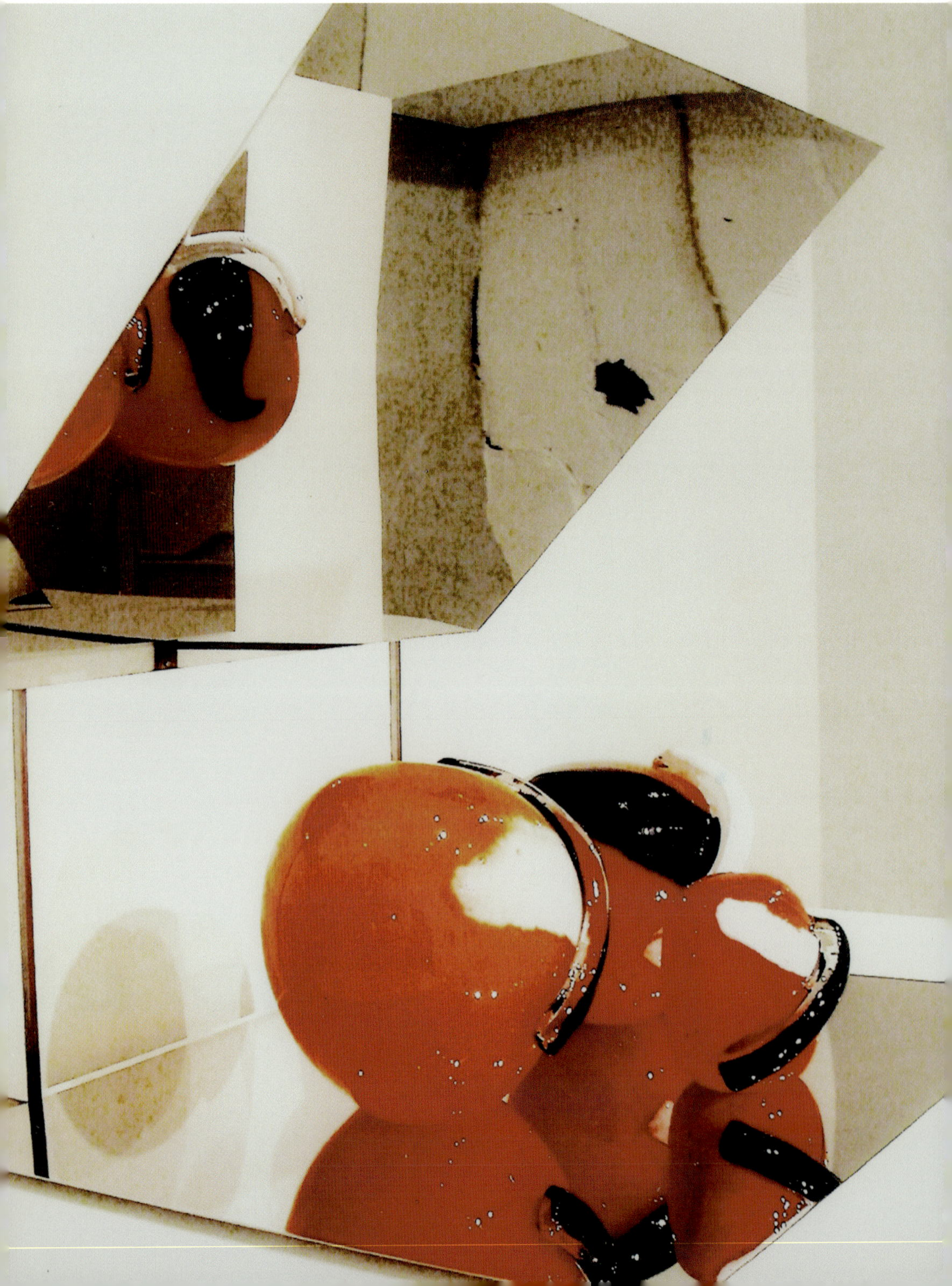

# *Sculptures in*
# 10 Glass and Bronze



When you hold one of Barry Martin's glass sculptures your hands enter a world of their own. The sculpture wants to be held, like a small pet that nuzzles quietly into your palm, arousing your instincts of protection and nurturing. At first, it feels surprisingly heavy for its size, and ice cold, but immediately your fingers find curves, hollows, volumes and edges that they want to follow, that they somehow need to explore by themselves. This sense of touch is so rarely savoured by those who can see, and holding one of Martin's glass sculptures is reward-time for hard-working hands.

2003
*Reflections on a firebird*
Glass and stainless steel
65 x 60 x 60 cm

Exhibited Zest Galley 2004

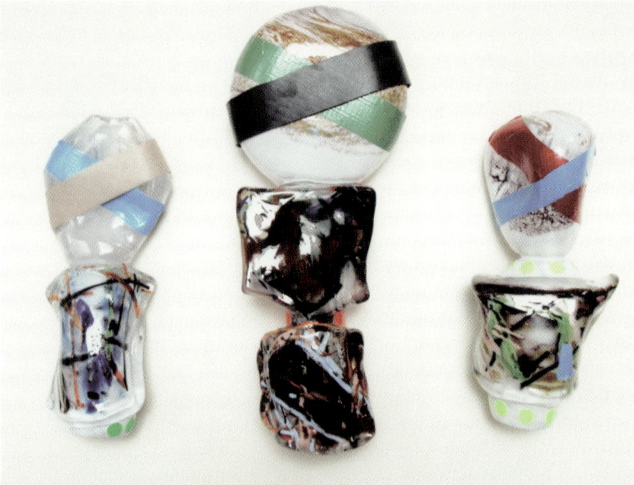

2002

*3 Elementals*

Glass, rubber coloured tape

31 x 48 cm

(Private Collection New Zealand)





In 2004 Martin presented *The Firebird Series* at Zest Gallery, a specialist in contemporary glass art, in London's Earl's Court. The exhibition subtitled 'Votive Movements in Bronze, Glass, Grass and Brass', presented the fruits of Martin's collaboration with the glassmaker Adam Aaronson. The palm-scale glass sculptures made their debut in pairs, with other elongated glass works, mounted on bronze slabs that stood on polished brass plates. By total contrast with the sensuous coloured glass, the blunt slabs are each angular and incised like some Aztec tools of ritual human sacrifice. The contrast sets up an aggressive/vulnerable dichotomy for the viewer. In silhouette, the slabs could be the universal masculine counterpart to the soft abundant forms of the ancient sculptures of the Earth Mother goddess.

**...but immediately your fingers find curves, hollows, volumes and edges that they want to follow**

The sharp tonal contrasts of the opaque bronzes further enhance the mouth-watering translucency and promise of colour within the glass sculptures. It is as if one were a child choosing for the first time from a dazzling array of ice-creams in trays. The sheer joy generated by these glass sculptures brings back what must, for many, be the earliest memory of being asked to exercise the power of personal choice, and the first conscious act of visual preference. That great gamble, of the first chosen ice cream, when the promise of taste must be judged by sight alone, must make or break many a future connoisseur. But the seemingly precarious position of each glass sculpture inevitably evokes another infant memory, of Humpty Dumpty about to fall from the wall, and with it a first awareness of the risks of life, of vanity and hubris. These Easter eggs, left by some exotic bird of paradise, the Firebird, ask to be saved from the sinister, unstable walls that could carry them off as stolen trophies.

So, where did they come from? Martin's imagination has drawn on earlier themes, most clearly his creation of kinetic sculptures using coloured electric light and natural light made to dance through coloured filters and mirrors. These exotic fruits provide some permanence for the temporal effects he created a generation earlier, but on an intimate scale. Like rare insects trapped in amber or botanical specimens set in crystal, these stripes and speckles of colour are frozen in time and space, like the single twisting strokes of an artist's brush caught in mid-air, moments before they crash into the frontier of a two-dimensional canvas.

To art connoisseurs and historians, *The Firebird* series may not seem quite so fresh, burdened as we are by the visual baggage of earlier art. The series may stir memories of the seemingly organic small-scale sculptures of Arp, Brancusi and Hepworth, but none contained colour in this floating, melting way. There is also something of the Surrealist art of Miro in the stirring of lost childhood memories, of something to do with that first seaside holiday...but also of the first sense of insecurity.



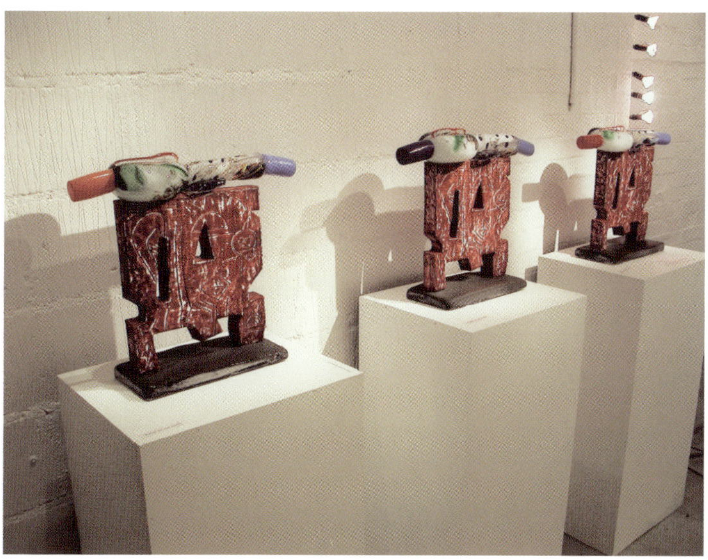

2003

*The Firebird Series* exhibition

Bronze, glass and Brass

21 x 29,5 cm

Installation view

Zest Galley 2003

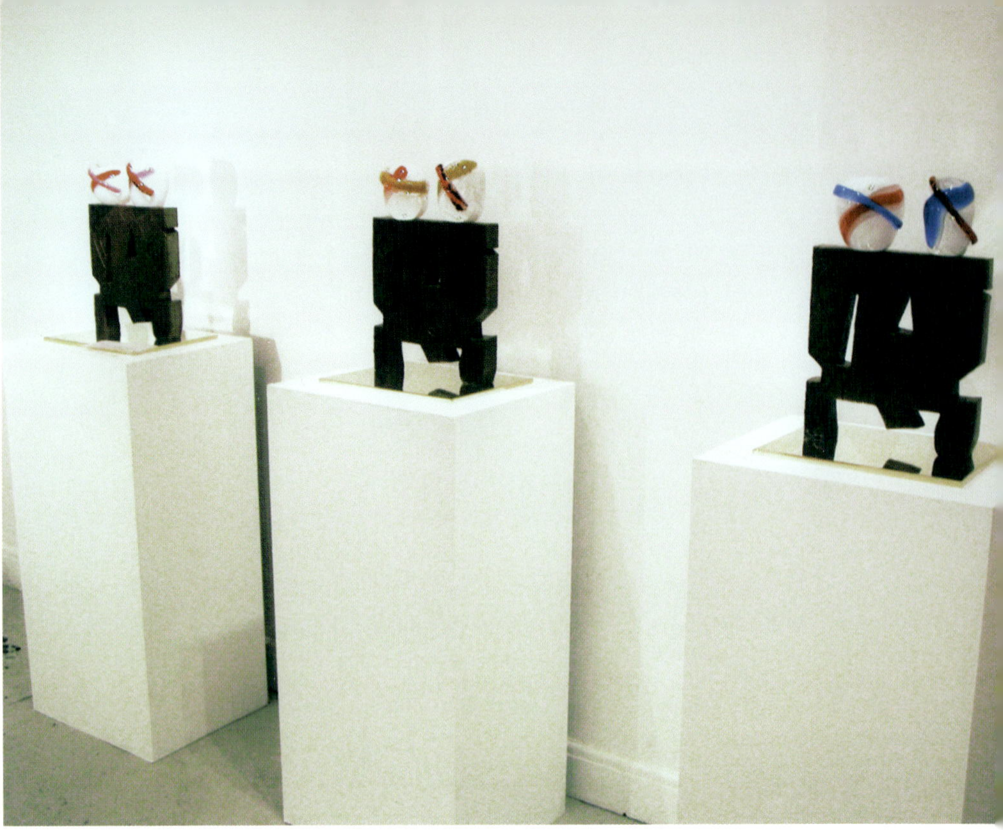





1998-2003

*The Firebird Series* exhibition

Polished stainless steel, acrylic, glass and lettering

245 x 245 x 123 cm

Installation view

Zest Galley 2003

Martin traces his immediate visual inspiration to the Asian galleries of the Victoria & Albert Museum, to the rugged Korean ceramics of the 18th century with their masterful gestural painted decoration of lotus leaves over incomplete glazes. He also saw the potential of the medium for his work in the V&A's gallery devoted to the art of contemporary glass. The title of the exhibition series hints at its source in Stravinsky's ballet, and the subtitle to its fulfilment in a major outdoor sculpture, *The Firebird*, that is still hatching.

In their quiet way, Martin's sculptures in glass and bronze also seem to crystallise his youthful speculations over the biggest questions about Space-Time, as a series of non-verbal, non-mathematical attempts to answer the dilemma of locating our brief lives in an expanding relative universe. Despite our growing knowledge of Outer Space, the dilemma is, of course, as old as time. Martin's glass sculptures could be seen to embody the visionary words of William Blake ('Auguries of Innocence', c.1803):

> To see a world in a grain of sand
> And a heaven in a wild flower
> Hold infinity in the palm of your hand
> And eternity in an hour.

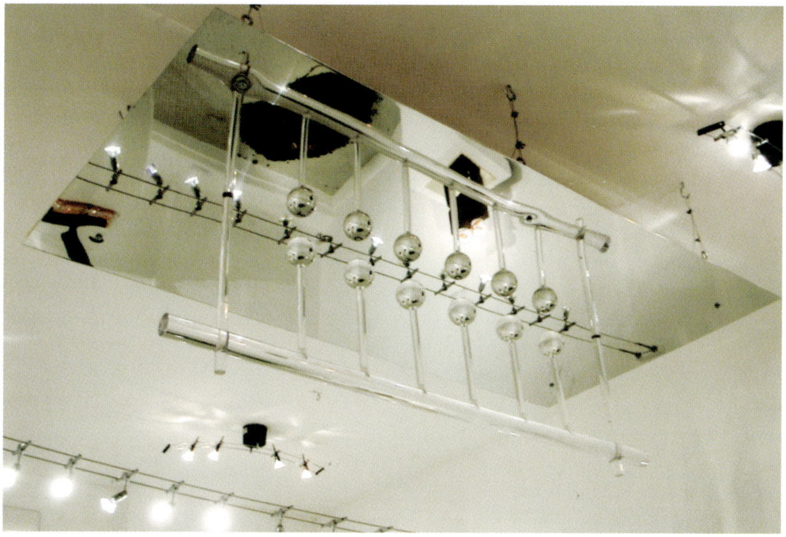



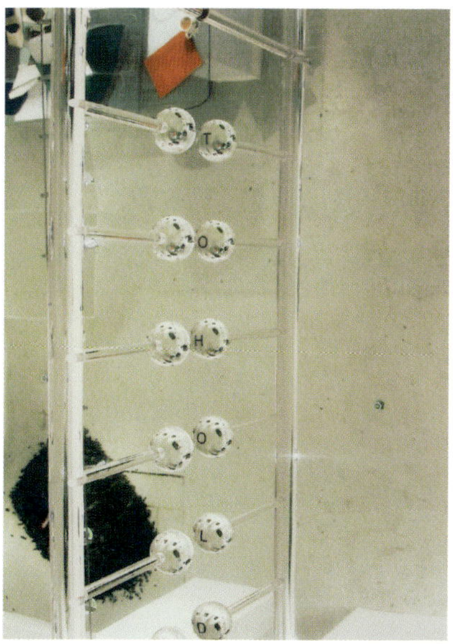

1996-2002

*Understanding your handle*

Stainless steel, letters, glass, acrylic rod

420 x 240 x 128 cm

Ceiling piece

1996-2002

*Understanding your handle* (detail)

Stainless steel, letters, glass, acrylic rod

420 x 240 x 128 cm

Ceiling piece

The largest glass sculpture in the Zest Gallery's exhibition offered a more challenging response to this theme of holding onto infinity, of getting a grip on the universe, of bridging the gap between the self and everything else. An overhead installation, *Understanding your Handle*, consists of a stainless-steel canopy eight feet long and four feet wide, that serves as a metal mirror. From it are suspended six glass ball handles on acrylic rods, set just too high to hold, yet each one is etched with a letter in its bulbous end, spelling the message TO HOLD in the reflection. On reading but realising you cannot reach up and hold the handle the viewer, in a split-second, activates different cells of the mind; the automatic physical response is overruled by a more self-conscious, contemplative, way of thinking. The viewer holds the thought, the idea, rather than the actual handle, and the overhead reflection invites reflection on the need to reach up and grip something safe from this moving Earth, something to hold onto in life. The reflection of the handle stretches into infinity, awaiting its holder from above. The idea of the 'handle' also carries associations in American slang of personal identity (hence the title) as when you are asked 'What's your handle?'

Martin had the idea while standing on a London Underground train, swinging from a strap-handle. The black ceramic ball-shaped handles on spring-like metal coils (always a rather endearing feature) were made obsolete around the year 2000 by modern carriages with simple holding rods. So Martin went off to London Underground's maintenance depot to see what he could salvage. Coming away with a box of old handles, he knew they deserved to repay their years' of public service by being made into a great sculpture. The idea evolved into this installation. Many other artists would have exhibited just the cardboard box of handles, as a sad, ugly comment on the loss of the sense of security in our everyday lives post '9/11' and the '7/7' terrorist attacks on the London Underground network. That is the difference, the creative optimism in the pursuit of beauty that makes Martin's art so rewarding.

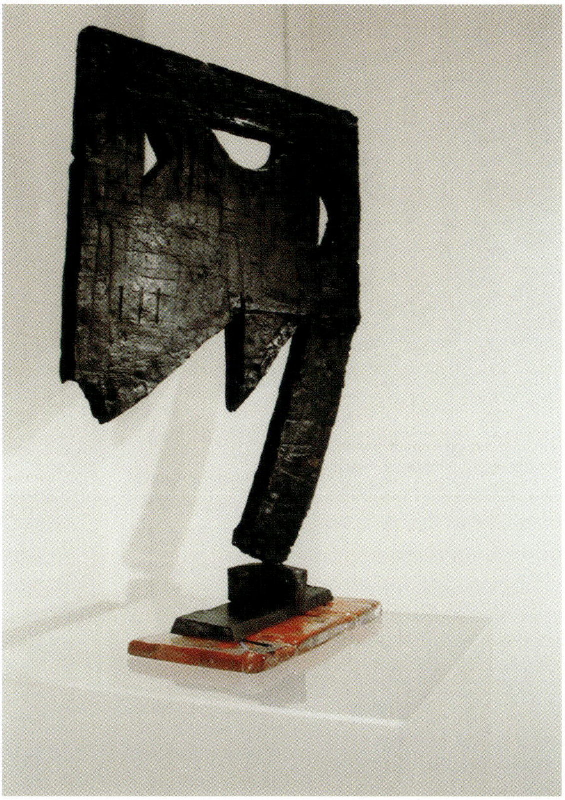

1997-2003

*The Firebird sculpture*

Bronze, glass and brass

46,5 x 37 x 30 cm

2002-3

*The Firebirds Place*

*Glass, Brass and Grass*

Wood chippings

63 x 190 cm

Floor installation at exhibition

Zest Gallery, London

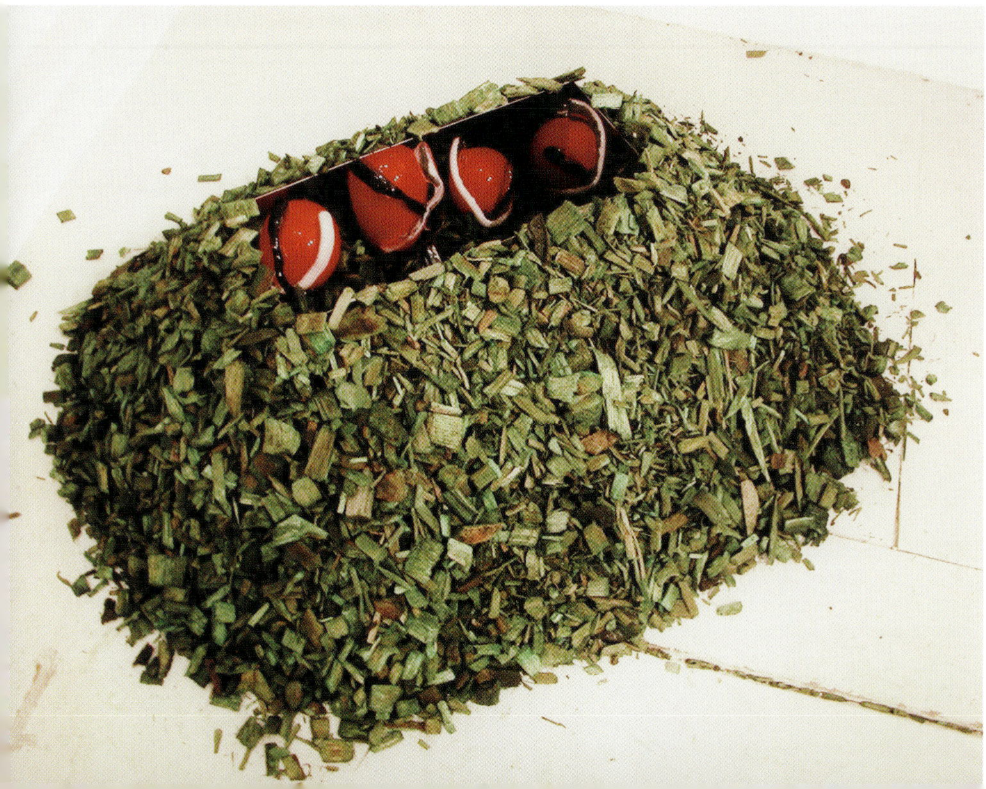

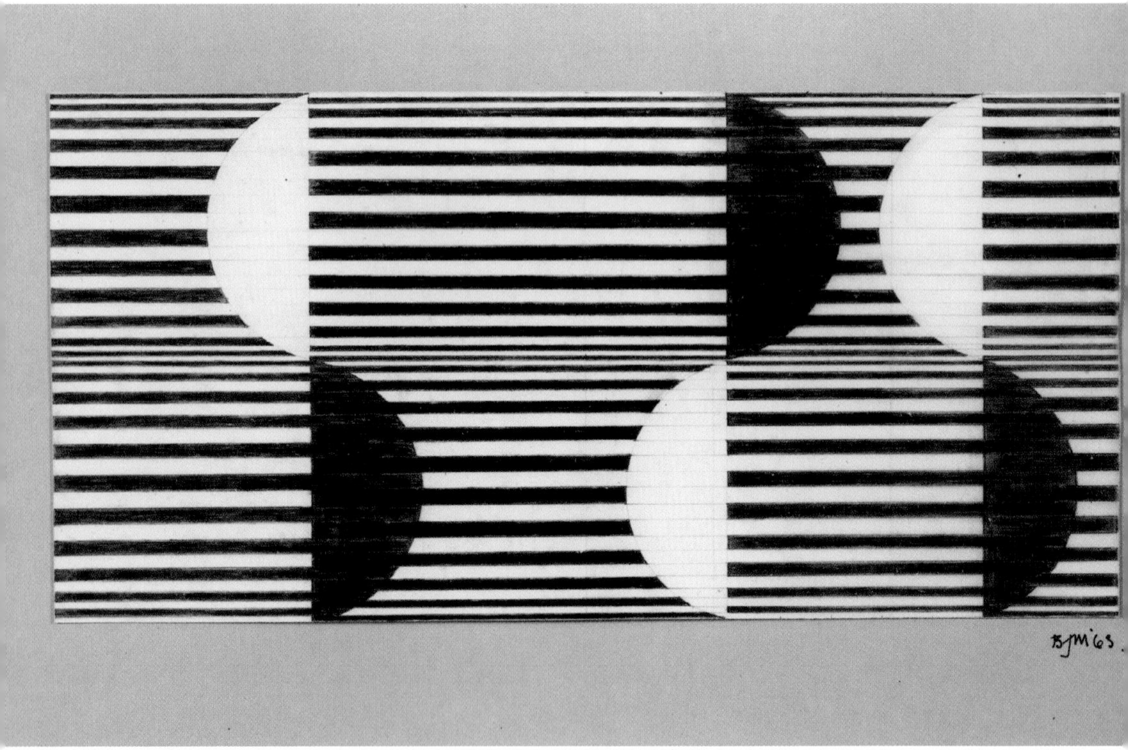

## *Mapping in watercolour*

# 11 The Radian Series



There comes a special moment in many people's lives when you are first in Florence and confront the dome of the Duomo. Suddenly, you are totally alone. Just you, Brunelleschi and the Italian sky, even if you see it first from afar, dominating the city's skyline. The dome is like no other, for it is terracotta red with vertical white ribs that curve up into a stone finial, crowned by a golden orb. There it is, the tip of man's Earth; the point where this Early Renaissance roof touches the sky is the interface between the greatest of human endeavour, nature and the heavens. It all comes together in that golden orb.

1963

*Causal Rhythm*

Graphite on card

10 x 25,5 cm

Arts Council England

(Private Collection)

So it was for Barry Martin when he visited Florence for the first time in 1978 with his wife, a few months after their marriage. What made this once-in-a-lifetime moment of encounter even more special was something he noticed, or felt. Around the edges of the dome the Tuscan sun shimmered as it should against the azure sky, as the bells from Giotto's campanile of Santa Maria del Fiore tolled out across the landscape, into the rolling overlapping hills. But there was also this irradiation, like a heat haze, a spectral colour changing its frequency, and those bone-like ribs of the dome seemed almost to swell and absorb it, as if the dome were a breathing membrane. Everything, everything, seemed to be coming together. It was almost as if the Florentine architect's structure had hit on the very design system of the entire universe, like tuning in an old radio and suddenly hearing the Music of the Spheres.





That moment haunted him. Back in London, in the gardens of Chiswick House, he felt some faint echo of the same sensation, stirred by the dome of Lord Burlington's Palladian villa. There, the architecture of the well-ordered universe is encapsulated in a wider, shallower, dome, one indebted to the ancient Pantheon in Rome and to its 16th-century offspring, by the architects Palladio, Peruzzi, Vignola and Scamozzi. While researching the Masonic symbolism of the design and decoration of Chiswick House (as discussed in Chapter 5) Martin read of the connection, established in the Renaissance, between harmonic proportions in architecture and Platonic theories of a mathematical universe. As Rudolf Wittkower explained in *Palladio and English Palladianism* (London, 1974):

> If the laws of harmonic numbers pervade everything from the celestial spheres to the most humble life on Earth, then our very souls must conform to this harmony. It is, according to Alberti an inborn sense that makes us aware of harmony. The visible form of applied mathematics was immediately and intuitively perceptible. For the men of the Renaissance this architecture, with its strict geometry, the equipoise of its harmonic order, its formal serenity and, above all, with the sphere of the dome, echoed and at the same time revealed the perfection, omnipotence, truth and goodness of God. And they were convinced that universal harmony could not reveal itself entirely unless it was realised in space through architecture conceived in the service of religion'.

Chiswick's dome also brought to Martin's mind a modern equivalent to the domes of Renaissance cathedrals: the vast dish of the Jodrell Bank

Observatory where the Lovell Radio Astronomy Telescope scan the skies for the remotest cosmic waves, for messages from across the universe, and even lets scientists hear the hiss left by the expiratory energy of the Big Bang. A regular reader of the monthly magazine *Astronomy Now* and viewer of television's *Sky at Night*, Martin keeps up to date with the sight-seers of space and the ongoing debates over the technical relationship between Space and Time. By the 21st century, theoretical issues that inspired his art forty years before are now facts. NASA's Hubble Space Telescope, orbiting the Earth since 1990, regularly sends back astounding images that confirm that our universe is expanding, that document how light is bent by the magnetic attraction of stars that make the existence of Black Holes incontrovertible.

**_The Radian Series_ is a personal celebration of a relationship that Martin no longer worries about, but instead enjoys, to the point of exhilaration**





Ideas and issues that were the stuff of abstruse dense texts, diagrams and wacky Science Fiction illustrations just a generation ago you can now hold in your hand in photographs. Glossy colour magazines present the outer limits of the known universe as if they were just perfectly-composed sunset watercolours by Turner or Colour Field paintings by Olitski. The celestial sky is now not only visible, but can be subject to aesthetic contemplation, as a spectacle of pure, clear colour, captured in photographs. This transfer of the cosmic into the particular is further facilitated by the arrival of personal computers. Thanks to Google Earth, while sitting at home we can now see Earth from Outer Space, and then zoom in, right into our own back gardens. Forty years on from when Barry Martin confronted it all, the awareness of the physical relationship between the sense of oneself and everything else, it is all there; you can see it, at the click of a mouse. So where does that leave you, as an artist?

*The Radian Series* is a personal celebration of a relationship that Martin no longer worries about, but instead enjoys, to the point of exhilaration. The creative drive comes not from personal exploration but rather from a need to share his sense of arrival. The title of the series describes the angle at the centre of a circle that produces an arc whose length is equal to that of the circle's radius. The radian is a metaphor for a relationship of geometrical perfection.

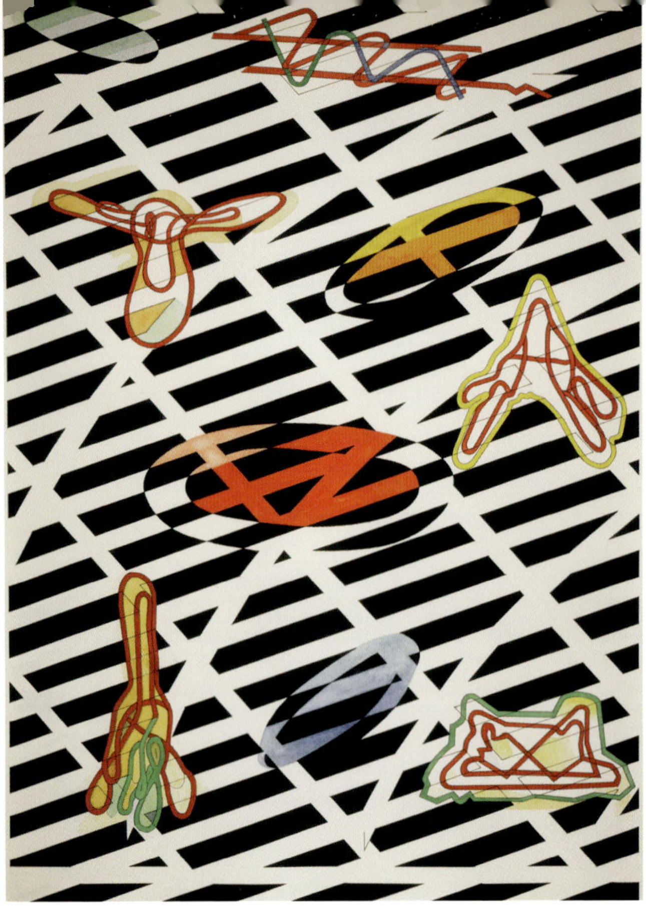

2006
*Radian Interceptor*
Pure watercolours on heavy watercolour paper
145 x 120 cm
(Private Collection)





Martin returned to a theme that he had explored before, in the days of Op Art: the way parallel lines can seem to move and resonate, as in *Causal Rhythm* (1963, Arts Council England). This play of black and white, dark and light, he took one step further with his abstract paintings that appear to be superimposed in strips, as two fields of painted colour sliding in and out of each other, as in *Whole with Machine intrusions* (1974). Martin had also explored earlier the idea of combining a geometrical structure with floating symbols, as in the series of charcoal drawings on the theme of the ladder (*Gates and Ladders No. 2*, 1995). But he felt the need for a new, cleaner, visual language, one that would 'nail it down more', that would match the clarity and explicitness of recognition that he now felt, and the sheer excitement he feels 'at having lived to see all this'.

Each work begins with the largest single sheet of paper that is commercially available (other than as continuous rolls). Measuring 6 by 4 feet, the 'double elephant' size of watercolour paper is thick, heavy and highly absorbent. He chose watercolour for the series, in preference to oil or acrylic, for the purity it demands and gives, for the medium affords no hiding place for the faint-hearted and for corrections. As with his kinetic sculptures made only of light, his goal is purity of colour. Watercolour forces Martin to paint with precision which, on this scale, requires him to work slowly, flat on the floor. His sharp, high-tech aesthetic might seem more appropriate for a Computer Aided Design system, and lend itself to limited edition prints, but he wishes to retain the sense of personal communication between the artist and viewer 'like a monk working on an illuminated manuscript, anonymous yet intimate'. As an aside, he confesses to his satisfaction at finding how watercolour can be used on this large 'macho' scale, taking a medium traditionally reserved for the sensitive, subtlest effects of landscape painting and wielding it to address some of the biggest issues.

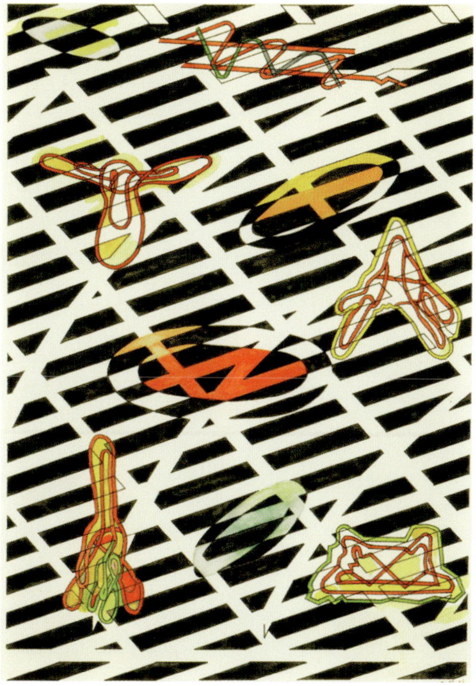

2006
*Radian Interceptor*
Pure watercolours on heavy watercolour paper
30 x 15 cm
(Private Collection)



Martin first draws out his field in steep perspective, like some futuristic game board or a map of the cross-currents of the universe, the vortices that hold everything together across Space and Time. The actual source of his inspiration was the black and white marble floors that appear in 17th century Dutch interiors, as painted by Vermeer, De Hooch and Van Hoogstraten. At the key points of intersection he positions motifs, 'units of importance', like the furniture in the Dutch paintings or like sculptural bosses in the vaulting of a Gothic building. They range from the triple-domed façade of St Mark's in Venice via endless Cats Cradle knots to the electro-magnetic field around a Black Hole. The *Radian Series* presents Martin's universe as an infinite game of Snakes and Ladders, tied up with String Theory and linked by Worm Holes, one in which 'you can only go up'.

So far removed from the light sculptures and abstract paintings of his youth, the *Radian Series* also provides Martin with a language with which to address more local issues. For example, in 2006 he felt that someone of his generation, someone who was there, should mark the fiftieth anniversary of Pop Art, a movement for which Martin has little time. Taking the two figures from the celebrated collage by Richard Hamilton, *Just what is it that makes Today's Home so Different, So Appealing*? (1956, Tubingen, Kunsthalle) he presented in graphic form his view that the movement had failed to consummate, and should be re-named 'Flop Art'. The explicit, in-your-face vulgarity of the quoted image of 'Mrs Pop' was designed to affront the English sense of politeness. The sense of fun and mischief-making would have been appreciated by Burlington's neighbour at Chiswick, William Hogarth.

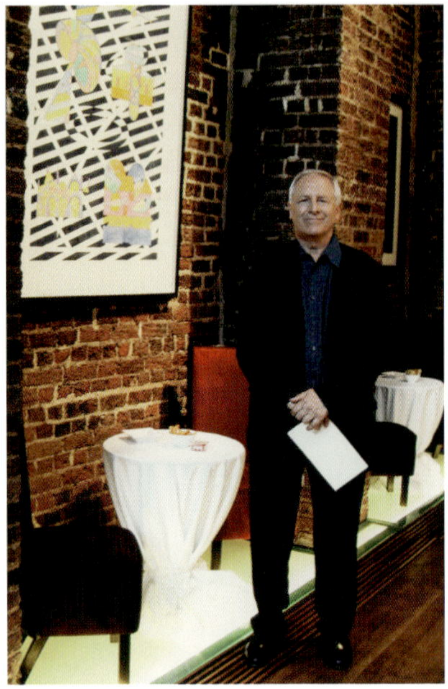

2006-7
*Radians with Chiswick House*
Pure watercolours on heavy watercolour paper
164 x 120 cm
Accompanied by the artist at Mol's Place
(Private Collection)





**the domes of the V&A, can stand for both the absorption and emission of creative energy**

The subject evolved into *Domestic Kinetic: Spring Cleaning with Style in the early 21st Century*. Here the ubiquitous new-build suburban home is sliced by spinning kinetic discs that are throwing out all the unnecessary detritus of modern life, including Mr and Mrs Pop themselves. Martin's attack on vacuous consumerism sits on the Space-Time grid of the *Radian Series* and shares its pure watercolour palette, enriched with visual quotations from Klee, Kandinsky and Malevitch that follow in the paths of the discs, as if promising redemption through art.

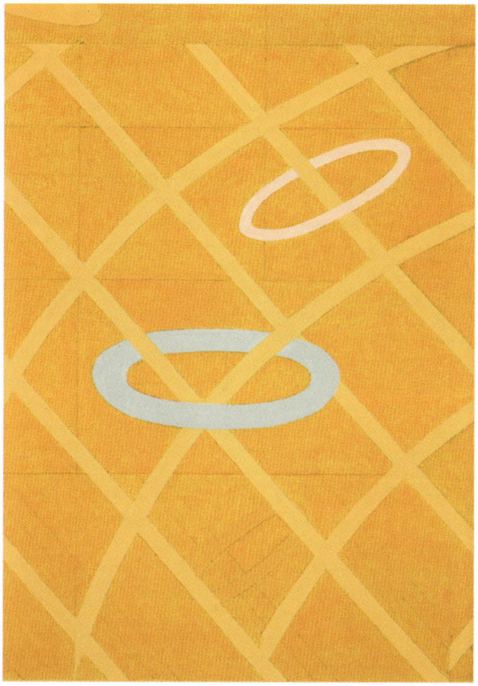

2004-5

*Radians and Domes No. 4*

Oil on board

35 x 22 cm

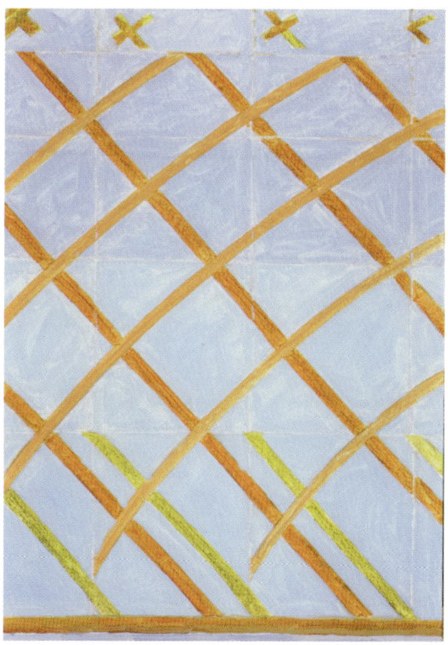

2004-5

*Radians and Domes No. 1*

Oil on board

28 x 14 cm

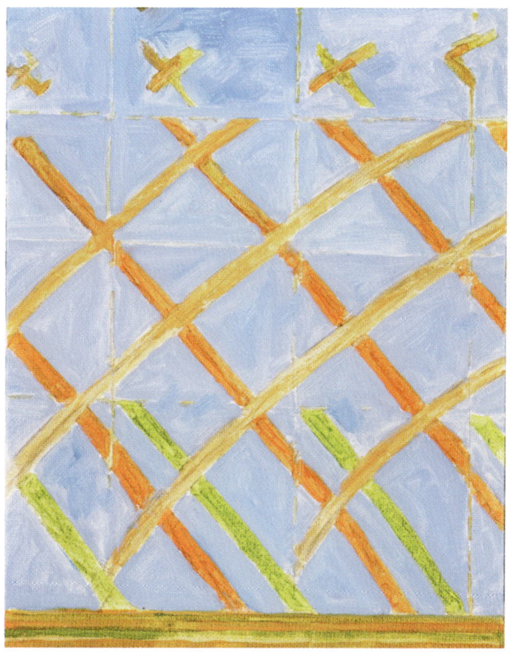

2004-5

*Radians and Domes No. 2*

Oil on board

40 x 20 cm

For the 150th anniversary of the opening of the Victoria & Albert Museum at South Kensington, in 2007, Martin was one of 150 artists, designers and architects invited to contribute a page to a commemorative album. His image of the V&A floating in the universe amid emblems of its collections drew on his memories of Florence. The serried domes of the national museum of art and design can have a similar effect, as points of contact. Rather like the lids of pressure cookers or inverted radar dishes, the domes of the V&A, he feels, can stand for both the absorption and emission of creative energy. Beneath their protection, the finest examples of human endeavour over centuries, from East and West, are assembled. Like the symbols with which he punctuated the watercolours, the museum's treasures are keys into the dynamic network that the *Radian Series* maps. Just as they did when Martin came to the V&A as a teenager in search of the wider world, so the same objects still radiate the energy of inspiration across the centuries and continents.





2004-5

*Radians and Domes No. 3*

Oil on board

40 x 20 cm

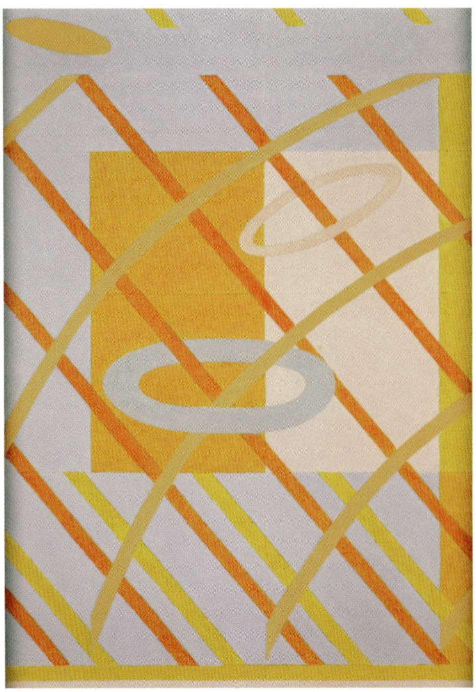

2005-6

*Monument to the Space of the New Millenium*

Aluminium, acrylic sheet, wood, electric light, printed mate

40 x 30 x 30 cm (model for monument)

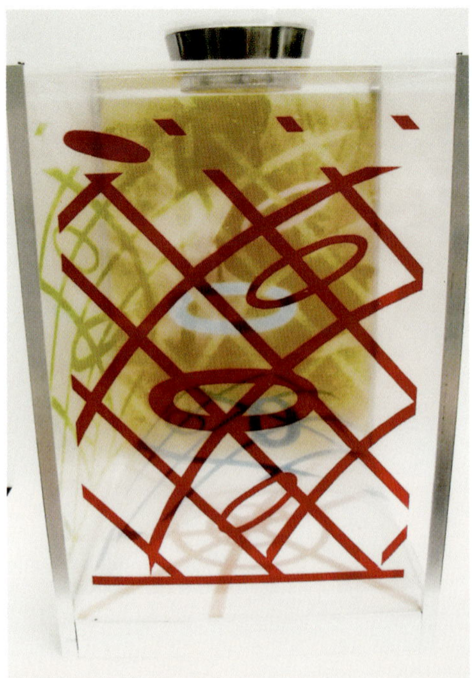

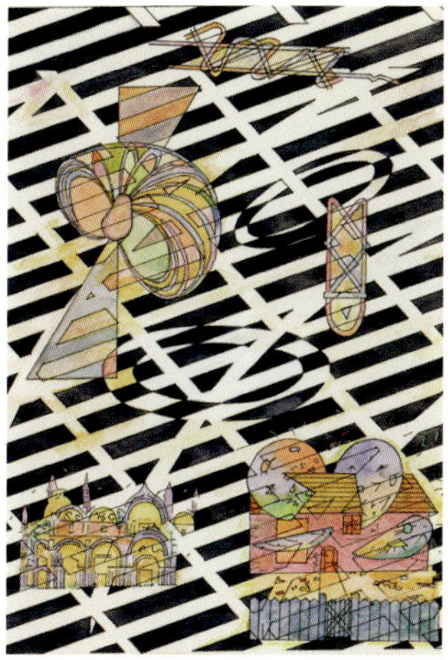

2007

*Domestic Kinetic*

Pure watercolours on heavy watercolour paper

135 x 90 cm

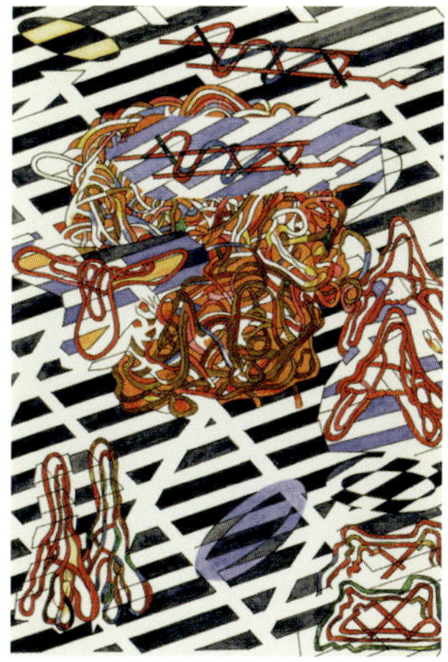

2005-6

*Infinity - Identity*

Pure watercolours on heavy watercolour paper

150 x 110 cm

(Private Collection)





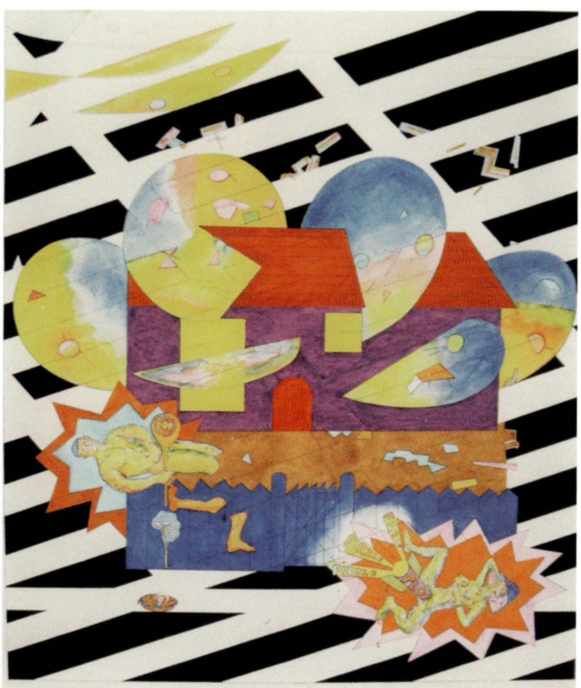

2006-7

*Spring cleaning in the 21st century style*

Pure watercolour on heavy watercolour paper

135 x 100 cm

With their black and white grid structure, clearly drawn motifs and rainbow palette the watercolours that make up the *Radian Series* could almost serve as designs for stained glass windows in some 'New Age' cathedral dedicated to the glorious celebration of the era of Space-Time. The series is, at the time of writing, but a work in progress. Martin's favourite phrase, 'the tomorrow of my yesterday', signals his reluctance to look back unless he is looking forward, for what matters to him as an artist, with his characteristic sense of urgency, is the work in hand. The art of Barry Martin still has a long way to go.

If in the 21st century art has an avant-garde one must conclude by asking why the theme of cosmic speculation, of confronting intellectual agoraphobia before the third and fourth dimensions, is not the driving force that it was when Kinetic Art offered a path to the future in London around 1970. Long after Martin's machines have ground to a halt, and many British artists of that generation have reached the end of their careers, the fundamental challenges of Space-Time that gave Kinetic Art its cutting edge, cannot all have been explained away. They remain a source of inspiration and energy to anyone who may be prepared take on the wider role of the artist in society, a responsibility that Martin keeps alive.

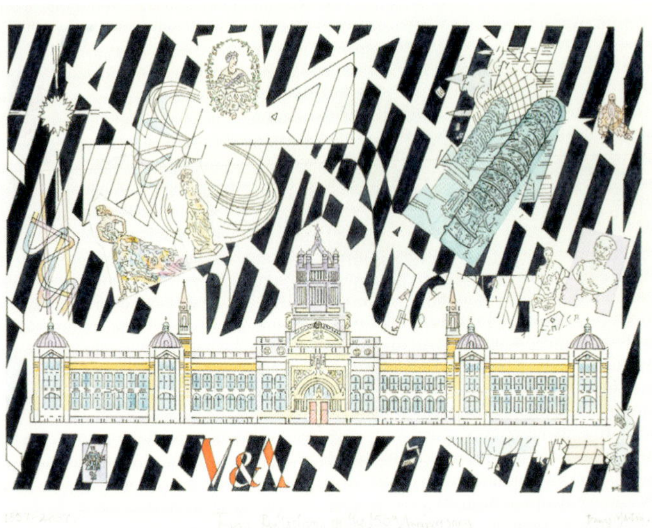


2007

*Victoria & Albert Museum 150th anniversary commission*

watercolour and ink on paper

26 x 38 cm

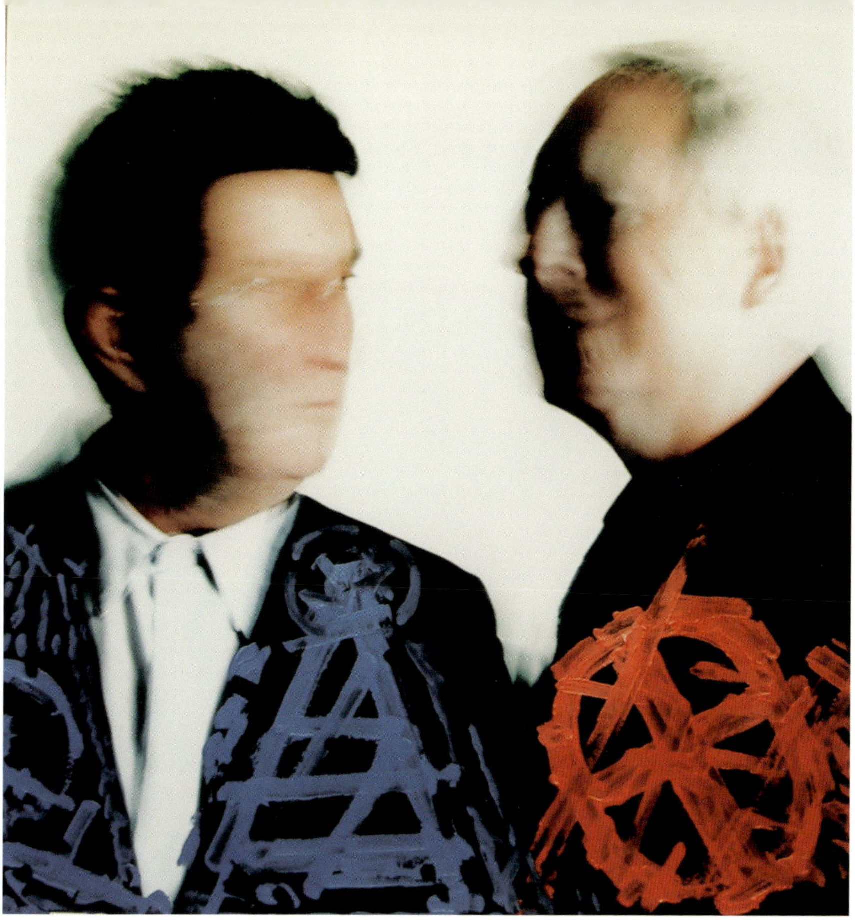

2007

*Movement Image of McLean* (left)
*and the artist with Painted*
*Additions by the Latter*
Photograph by Bob Miller
56 x 56 cm

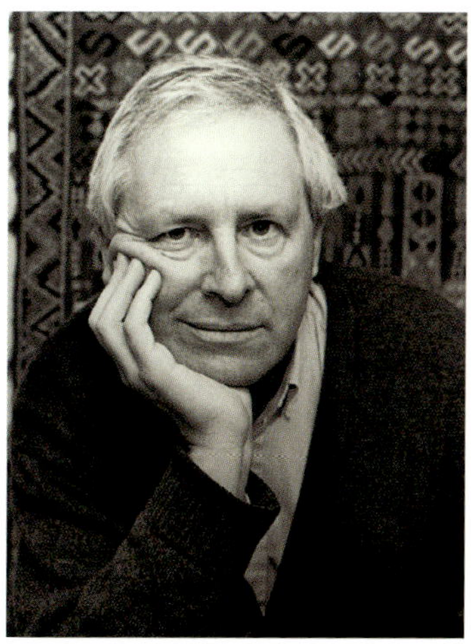

2007

Portrait of the Artist

# Biography

Barry Martin was born in 1943 in Amersham, Buckinghamshire.
He studied at Goldsmiths' College of Art, University of London 1961-66and at the St Martin's School of Art 1966-67. He taught in many art colleges including: The Royal College of Art, London; The Slade School; The Royal Academy Schools; Goldsmiths' Collage; St. Martins School of Art; Kingston University; Croydon College; ect.

*Has work in many public, corporate and private collections.*
Public and Corporate Collections include: The Tate Gallery; Museum of Modern Art, Paris; Science Museum; British Museum; Arts Council of England; Northern Arts Association; National Portrait Gallery; London Borough of Bromley; De Beers Diamonds; ICI; London Hospital Arts Trust; Zaragoza Museum of Fine Art, Spain; The Fuba Collection, South Africa; Hasting Museum; The Savoy Group, London; University of London, Goldsmiths' College; The City University; The Government Art Collection; Victora & Albert Museum; Deutsch Bank: National Trust: English Heritage; Orensanz Museum, Pyrenees, Spain; Triangle Collection, New York; Unilever, London; Department of the Environment; Air/Space; Harrodian School, Barnes, London; Erno Goldfinger for Willow Road, Hampstead, London.



# Exhibitions



## Group shows

2000

Tate Gallery, London *Recent Acquisitions* exhibition to accompany the inaugural opening of Tate Britain.

Museum of Modern Art, Paris *Viola* main summer exhibition,

Royal Society of British Sculptors *Summer Exhibition* inuagural show,

1999

291 Gallery, London *Porcupines*

1997

Festival Hall, London *Mind sports Olympiad*, review *The Times*

1996

Entwistle Gallery, Cork St, London *36 Hour Non-Stop Homage to Marcel Duchamp* created by the artist this was the first time a gallery was opened throughout the night

1995

Hasting Museum of Art, *Bad Bishops and Red Rooks,* exhibited 18 drawings and other work on paper, Gave lecture on work

Chiswich House, London, *New View* exhibit 14 large drawings under the auspices of English Heritage, Hamilton Forbes Gallery, Chelsea Harbour, London, *British Sculpture Since 1945*

1994

The Slade School of Art and The Architectural Sssociation, London 2 day symposium entitled

*Action* debate my work along with Bruce MCLean, Professor John Aitken, Peter Struyken, Gordon Pask, Christian Zwaniken

1993

Exhibit work on channel 4 Television interviewed by Carol Vordeman

Exhibition of work to accompany world Chess Match between Nigel Short and Gary Kasparov as the official artist, sponsored by *The Times*, newspaper

1992

Beaux Art Gallery, Brussels, *Echec et Mat,* exhibited work along with those of Duchamp, Ernst, Man-Ray, Brooodthaers, Richard Hamilton

1984

*International Exhibition of Paintings an Drawings*, Naples, Italy

1983

City University, *12 collages*, London

*Small Works Celebration for Briget Bardot*, Milan. Italy

1982

*London Group*, Camden Art Centre

*International Exhibition of Drawings*, Bilbao, Spain

*12 British Painters* Touring Exhibition, Japan

Newcastle Poly. Gal. Small Drawing Also '81, '79

*Studio Exhibition*, Space Studios, Berry Street, London.

1981

*London Group*, South London Art Gal.

1980

*Drawing Show*, Morley Gal.

1979

Contemporary Arts Society. Mall Gallery

1978

*Artist's Market*, London Warehouse.

*British Art Show*, Art Council '79 '80

1977

*South Bank Sculpture Exhibition,* 100 Years of St. Martin's Art School

*Artist's Market*, Warehouse Gallery

*British Painting 1952-1977*, Royal Academy

*12 British Painters*, Arts Council and British Council Exhibition for Iceland, Also wrote introduction for the *Queen's Silver Jubilee* catalogue of British Sculpture exhibited in Battersea Park, London

1975

*Group Show*, Air

*Group Show*, Hoya

1974

*London Group*, Whitechapel

1973

*Group Show*, Grabowski, London

Harlow, Essex, *Movements*

1972

Arts Council, *Spectrum*, Alexandra Palace

1971

*London Group*, R.A.

I.C.A *Electric Theatre*

1970

*London Group* R.A.

*Manufactured Art*, Camden Arts Centre, London

Arts Council of G.B. Hayward Gallery, *Kinetics*

Onnasch Gallery Berlin (Air)

1969

Gelsen Kirchen Museum, Berlin (Air)

1968

Documentary film made for BBC 2 Shown Canada, Australia

*Manifestation of Light-Light Artist's*, Bromsgrove Fesival, Birmingham (Air Exhibition)

*London Group*, R.A. Elected Member

*Poet's Choice*, A.I.A Gallery

1967

*London Group*, R.I. Gallery London

1966

*London Group*, R.I. Gallery London

*Young Contemporaries*, Whitworth Art Gallery, Manchester, *Sculpture* A.I.A London.

## One man

2004

Inaugural Exhibition The Drawing Gallery, London

The Firebird Series: Votive Movements in bronze, glass, grass and brass. Zest Gallery, London.

Going Forward to Drawing – a Retrospective. The Drawing Gallery, London.

2003

The Art of Chess. The Gilbert Collection, Somerset House, London. Martin's work accompanied art by Damien Hirst, Jake and Dinos Chapman, Yoko Ono and others. Catalogue by Timothy Stevens.

Galerija Riga, Novigrad-Cittanova, Croatia

Retrospective, Art of Chess, Gilbert (collection) Somerset House. London

2000

LED. COM. Drawings, prints, Kinetic word sculpture and performance Saturday 4th November 2000 at the World Chess Tournament between Gary Kasparov and Vladimir Kramnik, London.

Riverside Studios, London, official artist for the world championship shess match between Kasparov, Kramnik

1999

Olympia London, *Reflections on Structions on Structure and Meaning.*

1991. Chess Images. Sandra Higgins Fine Arts, Bourdon Street, London, W1. Selection of drawings and paintings.

1982

Mashomac, NY. USA

1981

Gwynn Hoges Gallery, Oxford

*Studio Show*, Space, Berry Street, London

1980

Goya Gallery, Zarogosa, Spain

1978

Patrick Seale Gallery, London

Taranman Gallery, London

1977

Newcastle upon Tyne Polytechnic Art Gallery, Newcasle upon Tyne,

Studio International Gallery, London (Formerly Art Net)

1975

Hoya Galley, London

1973

Frere Jacques, Kensington

1971

Richard Demarco Gallery

1970

Arts Council - Serpentine Gallery

1968

*Pavilions in the Parks*

## Two Man

1975

Hoya Gallery, London

1965

Compass Gallery, Glasgow

## Recent Events

2007

V&A 150th Anniversary Album, Victoria and Albert Museum, London.

2007

Mixed Exhibition. The Drawing Gallery, London.

2006

Pairs – 5 artists. The Drawing Gallery, London.

2006

Art Fair. Islington, London.

2005

S.O.F.A. Chicago International Art Show.

2005

40-40. The Drawing Gallery, London.

2004

Mixed Exhibition. The Drawing Gallery, London.

2001

Drawing *Causal Rhythm*, 1963 purchased by Arts Council of England. Also acquire working drawing for series *Revelation Tret* 1965-66 (a kinetic sculpture already in their collection purchased 1968)

2001

Invited by The University of London, The Slade School, to create a print under their auspices. Create *Rim or Imager*, printed by Coriander Press, London

1999

Elected member of the Royal Society of British Sculptors,
Invited by English Heritage to unveil the Blue Plaque in London to commemorate the great English and world chess champion Howard Staunton
Organise painting and drawing summer school in Marche region, Italy

1998

5 works cast by The Royal College of Art, London. Serveral works purchased by German colectors.
Bronze relief sculptures, relief bronze purchased by Harrodian School, London.
Organsie painting and drawing summer school at the Medici hunting fortress, Trebbio, Florence, Italy

1997

Organise painting and drawing summer school with architect Jasper Jacob, at St. Jory, France.

1996

Martin writes *The Times* obituary for Alexina (Teeny) Duchamp
Invited to spend two weeks in Jordan by Prince Mohammed bin Talal, (the late King Husssein's youger brother). View the country from top to bottom impressed by Petra.
Design the Howard Stauton memorial grave in Kensal Green Cemetry. Unveiled the summer, 1995. Chess and Art: Hastings Chess Congress Centenary Exhibition. Hastings Museum and Art Gallery, England. Eighteen chess-related works.

1991; 1993

Co-organise, *Art and Chess* symposia, Tate Gallery, London along with John Cage, Teeny Duchamp (the late Marcel Duchamp's wife), Raymond Keene, Richard Humphreys, Tate Senior Curator (the first of these symposia was in 1991 to wich the above came),

1989

Move into newly completed studie in Chiswick House grounds, West London,

1988

Awarded inaugural Picker Lectureship, Kingston University, Kingston, London

## Reviews

2007

'The Fifth Howard Staunton Memorial Chess Tournament' by Jonathan Speelman. *The Guardian* on Saturday, 11th August 2007. Description of the Artist's opening Performance to draw lots and paintings. Players include: Michael Adams; Ivan Sokolov; Jan Timman.

'A Masonic Temple in West London?' by Matthew Scanlon. *Freemasonry Today*, Refers to Martin's discoveries of symbols and proportions at Chiswick House and grounds.

'Chess' by Raymond Keene. *The Times*, August 25th 2007.

Drawing of lots for the fifth Staunton Memorial held at Simpson's-in-the-Stand London. Martin used radio controlled racing cars to determine the pairings and colours.

2004

Chess by Raymond Keene. *The Times*, June 12th 2004. On the relationship of Barry Martin's chess, film, performance to Duchamp and other recent film makers using chess as their subject.

2003

'Artist willing to Challenge the Status Quo', *The Times*, September 3rd 2003.

2000

'Paintings by Numbers'. *The Times*. Review of the artist's work as official artist of the 2003 World 'Chess' Championship at the Riverside Studios.

1999

'Plaque for home of chess supremo' by Rachel Double. *Kensington and Chelsea Times*, October 8th 1999

Story of the artist unveiling blue plaque for Howard Staunton.

'Peace Piece'. *The Times*. Diary Commentary on theft of 'War-Mal' sculpture made by the artist from a contemporary exhibition in London.

1997

'Winning Move No.10'. *The Sunday Times* Diagram of chess game the artist played against William Hartson at the Royal Automobile Club, London.

1994

'Men of Staunton – Or are they?' *Chess Monthly*, October 1994. The artist wrote about the origins of the Staunton Chess men and the association with Freemasonry.

1993

'The Times World Chess Championship'. *The Times*, 17th June 1993. Includes a game played by the artist against the British Champion, Julian Hodgson G M.

1993.

'Draw gives Kasparov victory and £1M' by Daniel Johnson. *The Times*, October 22nd 1993.

1991

'Art and chess: The French Defence' by Don T. Buckle. *Art Monthly*, February 1991.

1984

*Art Monthly*, Interview 'Caro, Martin, Gibbons, Morris'. Feb.

1983

Unpublished article, 'Triangle Workshop, Art Procces as an Art Work', Aurelio Orensanz

Catalogue and Statement, 'Triangle Artists'

1982

*Pine Plane Express*, Triangle Artists

*New York Times* 'Mashomac Artists July 18th'

*Art & Antiques* Nicolas Usherwood '6 Artists'

*1981-2*

*Art Monthly* John Thompson. 'Barry Martin's Recent Paintings' Dec/Jan

1981

*Arts Review*, 'Barry Martin's Work'. Mary Rose Beaumont, Gwynn Hodges Gallery

1980

Radio Interview with Marino Jambrina, Entrevista R.N.E 14.1.80 'Barry Martin'

*Herald* 'Barry Martin' Aragon, N. Spain. 13th Jan.

1979

Book. WALLIA '200 British Artist', Publisher-Bergstrom

1978

*Artsscribe*, 'Barry Martin at the Taraman gallery', Ben Jones May/June

*Arts Review*, 'Barry Martin'. Oswell Blakeston, April

*Art International*, 'London Exhibitions', Malcolm Quantrill, Dec.

*Art Monthly* 'The Work of Barry Martin', Bryan Robertson Nov.

*Art Monthly* 'Making More of the Little One's Got', Peter Townsend, Nov.

1975

*Arts International*, 'London Shows' Fenella Crichton. Dec

*Arts Review*, 'Barry Martin'. Fenella Crichton. Dec

*Arts Review*, 'Barry Martin'. Catriona Turk. 14th Nov.

*Studio International*, 'Barry Martin'. Fenella Chrichton. Jan/Feb.

*The Spectator*, 'Art'. John McEwen. Nov. 15th

*Studio International*, 'Antonio Sena & Barry Martin'. Fenella Chrichton May/June

*Arts Review*, 'Antonio Sena & Barry Martin'. Denis Bowen

1974

*Studio International*, 'The London Group' Fenella Chrichton

*Arts review*, 'The London Group'

1972

Joe Melia 'Full House' BBC T.V.

1971

*William Tucker*, 'Ian Stephenson and Barry Martin' (20 min)

*Ink*, Sept.' Alexandra Palace' P.9 Arts Council group

*Arts Review*, 'Mixed Show Buckingham Gallery' Barbara Wright

*The Express*, 'Aside Lines'. Jan. 2nd.

*The Guardian*, 'Six English Artists' Cordellia Oliver Oct. 5th

*The Daily Mirror*, 'Art broken' July 14th

1970

30 mins. interview Spanish national Radio, 'The work of Barry Martin broadcast'. Jan.

*The Aragon Herlad*. 'Colour in Barry Martin's Work'

C.O.I. 4 min film 1970 Arts Council. 'The Serpentine Exhibition'

David Bellan, Radio interview BBC3, 'Light in the work of 3 atrists'

20 mins. interview Northern Spanish Radio Network. 'Barry Martin's Paintings'. Jan.

Alexander Walker, Interview Radio, 'The First Serpentine Exhibition' BBC3

*Arts Review*, 10th Oct. Guy Burn

*Art & Artists* 'the London Group' 1914-1970 Max Wykes-Joyce

*Studio International*, May 2oyh Bernard Denvir London Column

*Financial Times* 'Artists at the Serpentine' Marina Vaizey Aug. 8th

*The Sunday Times* Feuilleton Hayward Show Reproduction 29th Mar. Reproduction of recent works

*International Herald Tribune*, Oct. 7th 'Art in London' Max Wykes-Jones

*Queen Magazine*, June Elizabeth Glazebrook

1969

*The Times*, 'Modern Art in Scotland' Edward Lucie-Smith July 7th

*The Guardian*, '2 man Show' Compass Gallery Cordelia Oliver 10.06.69

Scotsman, 'Barry Martin Paintings' Emilio Coca 03.06.69

Glasgow Herald, 'William Crozier & Barry Martin' Martin Baillie 07.06.69 Edward Lucie-Smith Book English Art 1968/9

1968

*The Times*, 'Pleasure Domes of Art'. Aug. 8th. Guy Brett

*Studio International*, 'Pavilions in the Parks' Paul Overy

*The Guardian*, 'Poet's Choice' Norbert Lynton

*Arts Review*, 'The London Group' Marina Vaizey

*Arts Review*, 'Pavilions in the Parks'

*Petticoat Magazine*, Nov. 9th. 'Pavilions in the Parks'

1967

*Arts Review*, 'The London Group'

1966

*The Times*, Nov. 16th. 'Five Picked out from the Young Contemporaries'

*Arts Review*, Dec. 5 'Young Artists' I.C.A.

*Studio International*, Dec. Edward Lucie Smith 'London Commentary'

1965

*Arts Review*, 'Sculpture 65' December

## Interviews on Radio and Television

1970

*The First Serpentine Exhibition,* Interview with Alexander Walker. BBC Radio 3.

1970

Central Office of Information. Film (including the artist's work) about the Arts Council of England's inaugural exhibition at the Serpentine Gallery.

1971

*Light in the work of 3 Artists: William Tucker, Ian Stephenson and Barry Martin*. Interview with David Bellam. BBC Radio 3.

1972

*Full House' by Joe Melia*. BBC1 television presented the artist's moving light structures.

1993

Interview with Carol Vorderman about the artist's recent work as official artist for the World Chess Championship between Garry Kasparov and Nigel Short. Channel 4 television.

1999 The artist interviewed unveiling the Howard Staunton blue plaque in Notting Hill, London. BBC1 television News. Also on World News.

2000

The artist's exhibition at the Riverside Studios, London as the official artist for the World Chess Championship between Gary Kasparov and Vladimir Kramnik. Channel 4 television news.

2003

Interviews on the opening of one-man exhibition at Gallery Rigo, Cittanova, Croatia, Italian National Television News and on Slovenian National Television News.





# Writings by the artist


'The problem of British sculpture'. *Studio International*, vol. 183, no. 944, May 1972, pp. 186-8.

'The artist as individual'. The Artists' Union in Holland. A discussion between Barry Martin and Bob Boneas'. *Studio International*, vol. 186, no. 957, July/August 1973, pp.2-3.

'New Work by Philip King'. *Studio International*, vol. 186, no. 957, July/August 1973, p.40.

'British Sculpture'. *One*, no. 1, October 1973, pp.17-20.

'William Turnbull at the Tate'. *One*, no. 2, January 1974, pp.23-25.

'Philip King'. *Studio International*, vol. 187, no. 967, June 1974, pp. 277-280.

'John Hoyland'. *Studio International*, vol. 189, no. 975, May – June 1975, pp.177.

'On the occasion of Anthony Caro's retrospective exhibition'. *Studio International*, vol. 189, no. 975, May - June 1975, pp.233-5.

'Jeremy Moon Retrospective, Serpentine Gallery'. *Studio International*, vol. 191, May -June 1976, p.300.

'Developments in the Sixties and Seventies' in A Silver Jubilee Exhibition of Contemporary British Sculpture, GLC Battersea Park, 1977, unpaginated.

'Composition with Red by Piet Mondrian'. *A Perceptual Study*. Hilstone Press, London, 1984

# The tomorrow of my yesterday

## The complete works of Barry Martin

Text(s): Julius Bryant, with essays by Adrian Glew, Richard Humphreys and Raymond Keene

Design: Ronald Meekel.nl

Production: Veenman Publishers/Sebastiaan Hanekroot

Lithography: Pictura Imaginis, Heiloo

Printing: Veenman Drukkers, Rotterdam

Publisher: Veenman Publishers/ Gijs Stork

Sevillaweg 140
3047 AL Rotterdam- NL
phone +31 10 245 3333
fax +31 10 245 3344
HYPERLINK "mailto:info@veenmanpublishers.com"
info@veenmanpublishers.com
HYPERLINK "http://www.veenmanpublishers.com"
www.veenmanpublishers.com

ISBN 9789086901159
Distribution

D.A.P.
155, Sixth Avenue, 2nd floor
New York, NY 10013, USA
phone +1 212 627 1999
HYPERLINK "mailto:dap@dapinc.com"
dap@dapinc.com

Idea Books
Nieuwe Herengracht 11
1011 RK Amsterdam, NL
phone +31 20 622 6154
HYPERLINK "mailto:idea@ideabooks.nl"
idea@ideabooks.nl

Art Data12, Bell Industrial Estate
50 Cunnington Street
W4 5HB London, UK
phone +44 20 8747 1061
HYPERLINK "mailto:info@artdata.co.uk"
info@artdata.co.uk

Vice Versa Vertrieb
Immanuelkirchstr. 12
D-10405 Berlin, Ger
phone + 49 (30) 61609236
fax +49 (30) 61609238
email info(at)vice-versa-vertrieb.de.
Internet www.vice-versa-vertrieb.de

Special thanks to: Jan Mol, Susie Clark, Anne Marie Nuss